Myth and Deity in Japan

The Interplay of Kami and Buddhas

Miwayama mountain in June (Sakurai-shi, Nara)

Standing Eleven-faced Kannon Bodhisattva,
Kōgenji Temple (Shiga)

JAPAN LIBRARY

Myth and Deity in Japan

The Interplay of Kami and Buddhas

Kamata Tōji

Translated by Gaynor Sekimori

Japan Publishing Industry Foundation for Culture

Notes on the Translation
This book follows the Hepburn system of romanization. Except for place names found on international maps, long vowels are indicated by macrons.

Myth and Deity in Japan: The Interplay of Kami and Buddhas
by Kamata Tōji. Translated by Gaynor Sekimori.

First published 2017
by Japan Publishing Industry Foundation for Culture (JPIC)
3-12-3 Kanda-Jinbocho, Chiyoda-ku, Tokyo 101-0051, Japan

Paperback edition: December 2018

© 2009 by Tōji Kamata
English translation © 2017 by Japan Publishing Industry Foundation for Culture

All rights reserved

This book is a translation of *Kami to hotoke no deau kuni*
(KADOKAWA CORPORATION, 2009).

English publishing rights arranged with KADOKAWA CORPORATION.

Jacket and cover design by Seno Hiroya
Front and cover photo: Standing Wooden statue of Zaō Gongen (Zaō-dō, Kinpusenji Temple).
Photograph by Kuwahara Hidefumi
Frontispiece photograph by Yano Tatehiko

Printed in Japan
ISBN 978-4-86658-052-4
http://www.jpic.or.jp/japanlibrary/

JAPAN LIBRARY

Contents

Foreword   vii

Author's Preface   ix

CHAPTER ONE

The Mechanism of Combination   1

The Merging of Cultures 5
The Meeting of Kami and Buddhas... 8
The Kami of the Kasuga Taisha and Onmatsuri 11
Shinto and the Buddhist Dharma 16
Kojiki, *Nihon Shoki*, and *Fudoki* 21

CHAPTER TWO

The Encounter of Shinto and Buddhism in the Early Japanese State   29

The Formation of the Early Japanese State 30
What Is Shinto? 32
Buddhism... 37
Mythology and the *Ritsuryō* State... 44
The Coming of Buddhism to Japan 53

CHAPTER THREE

The New Buddhism of the Heian Period   67

Heian-kyō, Capital of State Spiritual Protection 78
Confucianism and Daoism in Japanese Religious Culture 86
Spirit and Faith 91

CHAPTER FOUR

Kami and Buddhas in the Medieval Period   95

The Birth of a New Spirituality 97
Medieval Myth 101
Ise Shinto 102
Yoshida Shinto 105
Japan as the Land of the Gods 110

CHAPTER FIVE

Nativist Studies and a New View of Kami-Buddha Combination   113

Shinto and Buddhism under the Tokugawa Shogunate 113
The Intellectual Environment of the Edo Period 117
Kami and Buddhas in the Modern Period 123
The "New Nativism" of Yanagita Kunio
    and Orikuchi Shinobu 135

CHAPTER SIX

Epilogue: Toward a New Kami-Buddha Combination   149

The Five Myths and Their Modern Meaning 150
Making War and Making Peace 160
The Postwar Myth: Spirituality and the New Nativism
   of Yanagita Kunio and Orikuchi Shinobu 166
Japanese Spirituality Today 179

Notes   183

Bibliography   197

Index   209

Plates follow half title page.

Foreword

Around twenty years ago when I gave a lecture about Shinto in Munich, I received a great laugh when I said that the deities of Japan were referred to as the "eight million gods and goddesses." I realized then how difficult it was to explain about Japan's kami to people living in countries and cultures with a tradition of monotheism.

Shinto is often described as the "indigenous" religion of Japan. However, upon careful study, we find that its "eight million gods and goddesses" originate not only in Japan but also India, China, Korea, and the Middle East. Large numbers of deities from other countries and cultures thus are included among Japan's kami.

Japan is not the only country where this situation prevails. In other countries of Asia, too, local deities have come into contact with the gods, buddhas, and bodhisattvas that originated in India and elsewhere. Each country has its own special circumstances, just as does Japan.

The "special circumstances" in Japan may be described as a religious culture centering on kami and Shinto. When the buddhas and bodhisattvas came to Japan, the deities that they encountered were largely formless and not institutionalized; it was only later that they gradually assumed form (as with images) and institutions (like the Jingikan). This is clear from how they appear in the eighth century historical records, the *Kojiki* and the *Nihon shoki*. The *Kojiki* makes no reference at all to the Buddha or Buddhism. The *Nihon shoki*, on the other hand, gives detailed and vivid descriptions of the encounters and tensions between Buddhism and the kami.

The idea of kami-buddha combination (*shinbutsu shūgō*) is at the core of Japanese culture. In this work I trace the encounter and interplay between kami and buddhas over Japan's long history, beginning with the different portrayals of their relationship in the *Kojiki* and the *Nihon shoki* and proceeding from an era when trees and grasses were thought to have the power of speech (*kusaki koto tou*), through the time when all was pacified through the action of the word (*kotomuke yawasu*), to the age of the *Kokinshū*, where "all living things have their song," the realm where poetry is itself a mantra (in the hands of poet-monks like Saigyō and Shinkei), and to the realm of noh plays.

Even before the encounter of kami and buddhas, the kami themselves were already combining with other kami (*shinjin shūgō*), resulting in the "eight million gods and goddesses" of Shinto. Through an examination of the dynamics of this process, we can better understand the distinctive features of Japanese religion and the role it plays in contemporary society.

The present book is based on a series of four lectures I gave at the temple Shōkokuji in Kyoto in 2003 and 2004, expanded from the lecture notes published by the temple in 2005 under the title of *Kami to hotoke no seishinshi saikō* (A Reconsideration of the Spiritual History of Kami and Buddhas) and edited extensively for this English edition. I would like to take this opportunity to express my gratitude to the Rev. Saburi Shōjun and the Rev. Arima Raitei of Shōkokuji for their great help.

Kamata Tōji
January 31, 2017
Kami hate no / umi yama meguru / hotoke kana
(In step with the kami / traversing seas and mountains / the myriad buddhas.)

Author's Preface

In the early summer of 2000, I visited Niutsuhime Shrine at the foot of Mt. Kōya and the temple of Kongōbuji on its summit with Ozaki Yasuhiro, the head priest of Hirano Shrine, an ancient shrine in Kyoto, and Yamaguchi Takuya, a priest at the Seimei Shrine that venerates the renowned yin-yang diviner (*onmyōji*) Abe no Seimei. Niutsuhime Shrine, also known as Amano Taisha, is a truly awe-inspiring place, and it is easy to understand why Kūkai, who founded his Shingon monastery on that mountain, thought so highly of it.

The shrine's forest was imbued with spiritual power. We were shown around the premises by its head priest, Niu Kōichi, who told us about its history and other items of interest. After performing on a stone flute, a transverse flute, and a *horagai* (conch) as an offering to the shrine, we set off for Mt. Kōya. There we visited Kongōbuji, the main temple of the Kōyasan Shingon sect and paid our respects to the splendid Niutsuhime Shrine (Miyashiro) located west of the Kondō (main hall) and the pagoda. The help Kūkai received from the kami Niutsuhime and Kariba Myōjin (the kami considered her child) enabled him to found the Mt. Kōya monastery. This pattern of a coactive relationship between kami and buddhas is very important as the basic model for kami-buddha combination.

Professor emeritus Matsunaga Yūkei, former president of Kōyasan University, head of the Mt. Kōya subtemple Hōjuji, and president of Senshū University (and now also head of the Kōyasan Shingon sect and Kongōbuji) understands the two sides of Kūkai's character as "the coexistence of a universal outlook and a practical orientation." He sees this "universal and social" aspect as embodying Indian cosmology (Kōyasan, Kongōbuji) and Chinese practicality (at the Tōji Temple in Kyoto).

It would not have been that difficult for Kūkai to subsume Indian and Chinese deities, buddhas and bodhisattvas, and Japanese kami, since he encompassed the whole universe through the Diamond and Womb Realm mandalas. Mt. Kōya was founded through the acquiescence and help of the local deities, and Tōji by that of the deity Hachiman—very much a state tutelary deity—and of Inari, venerated by the Hata clan, which was closely concerned with the establishment of the new capital at Kyoto. This typifies the strong pattern of coworking between kami and buddhas.

Kūkai's polarization between Tōji and Mt. Kōya is indivisible from the dual Shinto and Buddhist structure in Japanese religious culture. And it is not Shinto and Buddhism alone—Daoism and yin-yang ideas are also part of the mixture. At any rate, for me, Kūkai is one the key persons in the present book. Living during a time when the capital was successively moved from Nara to Nagaoka and then to Kyoto, he may be regarded, for good or worse, as a central figure in the creation of Japanese Buddhism and of the basic structure of kami and buddha interplay in his response to Heian-kyō as a spiritually defended capital through a system of Buddhist state protection. During my visit to Niutsuhime Shrine and Mt. Kōya, I could not help reflecting upon Kūkai's greatness and the great power of his basic design.

Three years later, in the summer of 2009, I organized a pilgrimage to Kongōbuji and Niutsuhime Shrine starting from Tenkawa Daibenzaiten Shrine, at the foot of the Ōmine Mountains, as a summer activity of Tōkyō Jiyū University, running from August 26 to 30. It was a walk along a road where buddhas and kami are in close proximity, very much according to the theme of this book.

It is said that Kūkai had performed the *goma* fire ritual at Tenkawa, during which an image in the form of Benzaiten rose up out of the flames. Images of Benzaiten appeared all over the country, and one can be seen in the museum at Enoshima Shrine in Kanagawa prefecture.

In the three years previously I had become involved, at the urging of the scholar Yamaori Tetsuo and others, in the setting up of a kami-buddha pilgrimage route consisting of 150 shrines and temples between the Ise Shrines and Enryakuji on Mt. Hiei. This Shinbutsu Reijo (holy sites of Shinto and Buddhism) initiative marks the birth of a new kami-buddha combinatory culture, a milepost for the working together of Shinto and Buddhism in the future.

Soon after my visit to Niutsuhime Shrine and Mt. Kōya in 2006, I moved to Kyoto, living in the Ichijōji area at the foot of Mt. Hiei. While walking on Mt. Hiei and through the hills of Higashiyama, I set out to devise a practice I called Higashiyama Shugendō that typified the form kami-buddha combination may take in the modern age.

This volume treads in the footsteps of my previous works concerning Japanese spirituality and expands their subject matter to include a discussion of the idea of a Japanese "One." I hope to refine this further in the future.

CHAPTER ONE

The Mechanism of Combination

Let's start with the conch shell, a sacred instrument and a fascinating one from the viewpoint of cultural history. The shell itself is found in the seas of southwestern areas of Japan as far north as the Kii peninsula, as well as in the tropical areas of the Pacific and Indian Oceans and the Caribbean Sea. It is used during traditional religious rituals not only in Japan but also in India, Thailand, Tibet, Indonesia, Hawai'i, Samoa, Honduras, and Costa Rica, among others. In India, the birthplace of Buddhism, it is called the *shankha* and is the emblem of Vishnu, the god who preserves the universe.

In the *Lotus Sutra*, the most important of the Mahāyāna Buddhist scriptures in Japan, the conch shell is mentioned six times in the context of "blowing the conch of the great teaching" of the Sutra so that it resonates throughout the world. For example, in the introductory chapter we read, "The Buddha, the World-honored One, is now intending to preach the great Law, to pour the rain of the great Law, to blow the conch of the great Law, to beat the drum of the great Law, and to expound the meaning of the great Law." A similar passage occurs in verse form in the "Parable of the Magic City":

> Be pleased, honored of gods and men,
> To roll the supreme Law-wheel,
> To beat the drum of the great Law.

To blow the conch of the great Law,
Universally to pour the rain of the great Law,
And save innumerable creatures!

It appears again at the end of "The Story of the Bodhisattva Medicine King": "This man ere long will accept the bundle of grass and take his seat on the wisdom plot; he will break the Māra host, and blowing the conch of the Law and beating the drum of the great Law, he will deliver all living beings from the sea of old age, disease, and death." Again, the chapter "Encouragement of the Bodhisattva Universal Virtue" says: "This man will ere long go to the wisdom-floor, destroy the host of Māra, attain Perfect Enlightenment, and rolling onward the Law-wheel, beating the Law-drum, blowing the Law-conch, and pouring the rain of the Law, shall sit on the lion throne of the Law."[1] The Law-conch and the Law-drum are thus instruments essential to spreading the truth of Buddhism, and the person who blows the conch can be considered the foremost of those who announce and spread the teachings of the Lotus. Thus Nichiren, the great Lotus practitioner, was known as someone who blew the conch of the great Law.

The *Muryōjukyō* (Sutra on Contemplation of the Buddha of Infinite Life), the central sutra of the Pure Land tradition, likewise refers to the conch. "The Buddha beats the Dharma drum, blows the Dharma conch, brandishes the Dharma sword, hoists the Dharma banner, rolls the Dharma thunder, hurls the Dharma lightning, brings the Dharma rain, and bestows the Dharma gift."[2] The *Shugen sanjūsan tsūki* (An Account of Shugendō in Thirty-Three Sections), a text of esoteric mountain asceticism, expands further on the merits of the conch:

> The conch is the inner realization of the meaning of sound, word and reality[3] and the Dharma gate to the Diamond Realm. It thus transmits the meaning of the Dharma formlessly and outside the teachings. . . . The sound when I blow the conch of the great Law resonates throughout the

trichiliocosm. It penetrates the ears and lightens heavy sin, enabling all everywhere to enter the gate of the letter A (阿). The discourse of the Tathāgata is like the lion's roar. This is because the lion is the king of beasts. Hearing his roar, all beasts perish at once. In the same way, when living beings hear the discourse of the Tathāgata, their defilements are destroyed at once. Therefore practitioners of Shugen should immediately manifest the discourse of the essential body of a buddha, identical with the essence of all existences, containing the great conch in this very body. The verse says "The sound of the conch of samādhi and the teaching of the subtle law of the One Vehicle pass through the ears and do away with all the defilements so that one immediately enters the gate of the letter A."[4]

The "voice" (sound) of the conch of the great Law penetrates all the worlds of the cosmos (the trichiliocosm, literally, the three thousand, great thousand worlds) and destroys the defilements of all living beings and enables them to enter the gate of the letter A, which is the realm of enlightenment. Attaining enlightenment with this very body (*sokushin jōbutsu*) here means blowing the conch in one's present physical form.

Native Hawai'ians use the conch when praying or singing. In March 1998, I visited Maui and held an outdoor fire festival with ceramic artist Kondō Takahiro and the Hawai'ian shaman Kupuna Nahi'ena'ena. I conducted the lighting of the fire as a priest combining the traditions of both Buddhism and Shinto, reciting ritual prayers called *norito*, playing both a transverse flute and a stone flute, and blowing the conch. As I did so I seemed to hear an echo from somewhere. It was the sound of a conch being played by Nahi'ena'ena in rhythm with me. It was an unanticipated "jam session" played on the conches of Japan and Hawai'i. The ritual continued, moving to chanting by Nahi'ena'ena. Throughout the evening we prayed, danced, and played music before the altar on the slopes of Mt. Haleakala overlooking the sea, and talked with other participants. I learned from this experience about rites and rituals using the conch in Polynesian culture.

Figure 1.1. Conch shells in the author's collection from Japan (top left), Tibet (bottom left), Hawai'i (top right), and Bhutan (bottom right). Photographs by Ōishi Takanori

Similar rituals can be found around the Caribbean, and the conch is also used in many types of folk music. Enormous spiral shells are found in tropical and subtropical regions, and they are used in various local cultures and in religious ceremonies.

Of great interest has been the discovery of conches made of clay at Jōmon period sites in Japan. One was excavated from the Kamiyama site in Niigata prefecture, which suggests that people of that time ate these shellfish, valued the shells, and perhaps had the practice of blowing them, but of course there is no clear evidence that they were used for ceremonies. Some scholars maintain that conch blowing was transmitted to Japan by Buddhism from India or that it only took root after the emergence of Shugendō (esoteric mountain asceticism), but such discoveries make those arguments difficult to maintain.

In other words, the conch is found in many places and quite likely was present prior to the introduction of Buddhism. In Japan, where it was part of indigenous culture, its role and uses merged after it was brought in from India via China and the Korean peninsula with Buddhism. Shugendō did later employ the conch independently within its own system of practice, but it was not the first to use it. The conch thus represents the merging of forms and traditions from various places over many centuries.

The Merging of Cultures

For more than thirty years I have made the case that a religious view based on "kami-buddha combination" (*shinbutsu shūgō*) forms the mainstream of Japanese culture and that "kami-kami combination" underlies it.[5] Combinatory notions can be found at the very root of the spiritual culture that developed in the Japanese archipelago over the millennia from the Paleolithic period (ca. 40,000 B.C.E.–14,000 B.C.E.) to the Jōmon period (ca. 14,000 B.C.E.–ca. 300 B.C.E.), whose sites, with distinctive cord-marked pottery from various periods, have been discovered in localities scattered over a wide area of the archipelago. Buddhism was transplanted to this fertile soil around the sixth century C.E. and for the next 1,400 years took shape by merging, combining and coexisting with the native kami. A similar situation occurred in India and China.

Geological and geographical conditions underpin both kami-kami combination and kami-buddha combination. This combinatory religious culture grew out of the natural features and local conditions of the Japanese archipelago, and indeed, religion itself can never be independent of the context in which it emerges and evolves. The variety of Japan's landscape and climate derives from the narrow, elongated nature of the archipelago with its many island groups. This complex and varied natural landscape existing in a comparatively small area became consummately linked over time with aspects of other cultures, in the form, for example, of kami-buddha combination. That landscape was the soil that provided the connections and the interface for a varied and multifaceted combinatory culture.

The archipelago came into being at the end of the Ice Age, about twelve thousand years ago, with a distinctive vegetation, ecosystem, and climate. According to a publication by the National Museum of Nature and Science in Tokyo concerning the natural history of the Japanese archipelago,[6] rich flora and fauna inhabit this archipelago of 6,800 large and small islands that runs more than 3,000 kilometers from the subarctic north to the subtropical south. Two warm currents, the Kuroshio and its branch the Tsushima, flow from the south, and two cold currents, the Oyashio and Liman, from the north, colliding off the shores of Japan.

The geological basis of the combinatory culture that emerged in the archipelago is plate tectonics. Japan is located on the junction of four major tectonic plates, which makes it one of the most seismologically volatile places in the world. These plates are the Eurasian continental plate in the west, the North American continental plate in the north, the Pacific oceanic plate in the east and the Philippine Sea oceanic plate in the south. This junction is marked by the rift line of the Fossa Magna ("great trench"), running north to south, and the Median Tectonic Line, running east to west. Japan is the only country in the world sitting atop four overlapping plates.

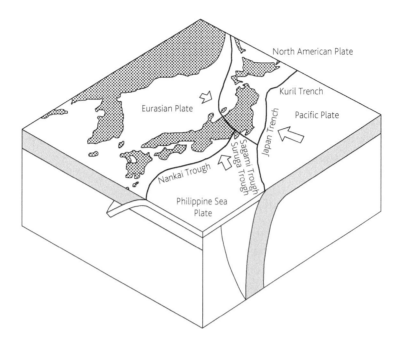

Figure 1.2. Continental and Oceanic Plate Boundaries, Japan.
Source: Hagiwara Yukio, *Saigai no jiten* [Encyclopedia of Natural Disasters], (Asakura Shoten, 1992)

Overlying this geological and oceanographic complexity is a historical-geographical diversity born of the inflow of peninsular (Korean) elements from the north, continental (Chinese) elements from the west and oceanic elements (Pacific Islands) from the south. The hybrid, combinatory culture born in Japan from this flow of cultures and people is reflected directly and indirectly in religion also, giving rise to a diverse, multilayered, pluralistic, and combinatory structure: kami-kami combination, kami-buddha combination, and kami-Confucianism-buddha combination.

Combinatory religion is not simply a mishmash or a shared house. It has its own distinct theories (for example, that kami are emanations of Buddhist divinities, or that Buddhist divinities are emanations of kami),[7] its own aesthetic forms and its own sophistication, where beauty, the sacred, and spirituality are closely linked through words, the plastic arts, and physical performance, as for example in temple architecture, festivals, gardens, noh, the tea ceremony, and flower arrangement.

My purpose in writing this book is to inquire into what I might call the "combinatory magnetic field" that is the Japanese view of kami and buddhas and look at how that view has changed in the course of history. I will also consider the future direction and possibilities of such a view.

The Meeting of Kami and Buddhas

The religious ethos that has developed in the Japanese archipelago is essentially an outgrowth of the meeting of kami and buddhas, a meeting that has fostered and activated imagination and creativity from deep within Japanese culture.

This meeting could be described as having had a "deep impact," since even today it can be considered the basic model for the framework and structure of the way Japanese understand the world. As a result of the interactive relationship brought into play by that meeting, kami became buddhas and buddhas became kami, following the paradigms of *honji suijaku* (kami as emanations of buddhas) and "inverse *honji suijaku*" (buddhas as emanations of kami). This was a complex and fascinating phenomenon.

What is kami?

In order to look more deeply into this meeting, I would first like to consider the meaning of "kami" from the word itself. "Kami" is written with the Chinese character *shen* (神), pronounced *shin* in Japanese.[8] It appears in compounds like *seishin* (mind, spirit), *shinsui* (essence, heart, soul), *shinsei* (sacred), *shinmei* (deity, divinity) and Shinto. It expresses that which is most subtle, essential, and profound. However, as a single-character word, it is only pronounced "kami."

What then is "kami"? It refers, in short, to anything held in the highest esteem, as expressed by the honorific suffix *-sama*. Thus Amaterasu-sama refers to the great sun goddess Amaterasu ōmikami.

The "kami" in Ame no minakanushi no kami, a deity appearing in the first chapter of the First Book of the *Kojiki*,[9] has a similar honorific sense, as it does in the kami of the two deities who appear next in the text, Takamimusubi no kami and Kamumusubi no kami.

Kudakajima, an island to the southeast of the Okinawa mainland, is regarded as the island of the kami (*kami no shima*). It is the standard form in Okinawan to use the suffix -*ganashi* for -*sama*, as in Upunushi-ganashi ("great lord"), when referring to a deity. Deities with such designations have the same semantic content and function as those kami appearing in the registers of deities on the Japanese mainland. Thus, both "kami" and "ganashi" may be seen as honorific forms of address.

That which is "superb"

So far we have discussed "kami" as a term expressing the greatest reverence for a deity. If we were to create a catalog of Japanese culture, kami would be a category of sacred entities manifesting divinity, divine power, godliness, spirituality, spiritual power, and spiritual level.

In the *Kojikiden* commentary on the *Kojiki*, the Nativist scholar Motoori Norinaga (1730–1801) defined "kami" as "anything whatsoever that is outside the ordinary, that has superior and extraordinary power, provoking awe."[10] According to Motoori, anything that is superior can be a kami. In other words, anything at all that is venerated with awe and respect is a kami.

Since everything thought to be "superb," by Motoori's definition, is capable of being a kami, kami are everywhere. Whatever makes us exclaim "Superb!" or "Wonderful!" or "Outstanding!" can be a "kami," and so kami proliferate like bamboo shoots after rainfall. This is why they are aptly referred to as the "eight million deities" (*yaoyorozu*)—that is, "countless." These "eight million deities" incorporate forms and dimensions of existence that are flexible and diverse, having wondrous powers imbued with a sacred energy. "Kami" is associated with all the reverence and knowledge about the sacred, its powers and phenomena, held by the people living in the Japanese archipelago. The individual items in the category of "kami" includes spirits, spiritual powers, ghosts, the uncanny, and miracles.

There are, in addition, many suffixes/prefixes that express divine power, divinity, and spirituality in more concrete terms, and so we can make separate subcategories for *chi* (spirits, particularly of nature), *mi* (spirits that preside over a wide area), *hi* (spirits associated with abstract functions), *mono* (powerful outside influences), *nushi* (lord of a place), *tama* (life-giving spirit of an ancestor or dead person, force), *oni* (malevolent spirits), *mikoto* (honorific title of a kami), and so on. The categories can be outlined as follows:

One-syllable suffixes
(1) Compounds with *chi*: Ikazuchi (thunder deity), Kaguzuchi (fire deity), Mizuchi (water/snake deity), Orochi (giant snake), Nozuchi (earth deity).
(2) Compounds with *mi*: Yamatsumi (mountain deity), Wadatsumi (sea deity).
(3) Compounds with *hi*: Musuhi (spirit of creation), Naohi (spirit that rectifies wrong), Magatsuhi (spirit of disorder).

Two-syllable terms:
(4) Compounds with *mono* (物): Ōmononushi, *monozane* (essence from which kami are generated).
(5) Compounds with *nushi* (主): Ōkuninushi, Kotoshironushi, Hitokotonushi.
(6) Compounds with *tama* (魂): Ōkunitama
(7) Oni (鬼) (demons)

Three syllable suffixes:
(8) Compounds with *mikoto* (命, 尊):
    Izanagi no mikoto, Izanami no mikoto, etc.

All of these terms, expressing various levels and situations related to divine power, divinity, spiritual power, spirits, and spirituality, are in the "kami" category, and it was through them that a kami-centered culture was fostered in Japan.

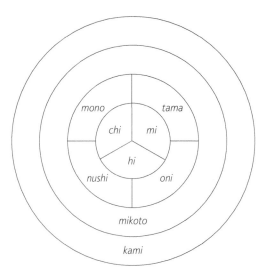

Figure 1.3. Categories of Kami

The Kami of the Kasuga Taisha Onmatsuri

Let us turn now to a specific example of how the kami manifest themselves, by looking at the Onmatsuri Festival of Kasuga Taisha, a shrine founded in Nara in the middle of the eighth century. The festival is held at the Wakamiya Shrine, built in 1135 on the grounds of Kasuga Taisha, for four days every year from December 15 to 18, with the main events being held on December 17.

I had seen the festival twice before and went again in 2007. Late at night on December 16, a group of about one hundred Shinto priests, wearing white robes and carrying *sakaki* (*Cleyera japonica*) branches, moved the Wakamiya kami out of the shrine. Their loud calls, invoking the deity and urging spectators to be respectful, reverberated around the precincts. I heard that one hundred students from Kōgakkan University at Ise had volunteered to act as watchmen during the ritual. It was apt that the kami of Wakamiya—the "young shrine"—should be served with the strength of these young people.[11] All lights had been extinguished, and in the depths of the darkness of the old Heijō capital the procession wound away, like a small fleet, through the Kasuga woods. The kami had to return to the shrine within twenty-four hours, and that journey was made later on the 17th.

Moonlight filtered down on the scene. This journey of the kami was a time of mystery and wonder, and also had a sense of nostalgia to it. The spectators followed the procession, moving quietly and solemnly. Something about it had a beauty that brought tears to people's eyes, and yet it was wild and untamed. The presence and manifestation of the deity there was no doubt very similar to the feeling of being deeply blessed that the poet Saigyō (1118–90) experienced when he wrote about his own visit to the Inner Shrine at Ise.

What divine being
Graces this place,
I know not, and yet
Feeling so deeply blessed,
My tears well forth.[12]

Though Saigyō did not know what unseen deity was there in that place, he unmistakeably felt its presence in the here and now. Where does such a feeling come from? How does it rise so spontaneously?

The Kasuga Onmatsuri was filled with tension, sublimity, and a touch of the wild. The night cries of the deer, messengers of the Kasuga kami, echoed all around, plaintive and solemn. The pathos emanating from the transience of things was palpable.

The Onmatsuri, which has been designated an Important Intangible Folk-Cultural Property by the Japanese government, is said to have begun in 1136, instituted by the regent, Fujiwara no Tadamichi (1097–1164), to bring relief to the people at a time when they were suffering from famine and disease as a result of heavy rain and flooding. The festival invited the Wakamiya, the divine spirit of Ame no oshikumone no mikoto—who is regarded as the son of Ame no koyane no mikoto and Himegami, who are enshrined respectively in the third and fourth shrines of Kasuga Taisha—to enjoy offerings of *gagaku* music and *kagura* dance. As a result of the lavish festival put on by the Fujiwara clan, sparing no expense, the crisis was averted; the rain and flooding were brought under control and good weather prevailed. The festival, held without interruption ever since, has taken root as a rite of prayer for a bountiful harvest and the welfare of the people. The richness of the music and dance offered to the deity brought prestige to the Fujiwara clan. What interests me most in the repertoire of dance offerings at the Onmatsuri is the *seinō* dance, a marvelously mysterious sequence that has an almost avant-garde feel. It is thought to have greatly influenced the noh style of dance developed by Kan'ami (1333–84) and his son Zeami (ca. 1363–ca. 1443), since Zeami mentions it in *Fūshikaden* (*Book of the Transmission of the Flower*), his treatise on noh.

The seinō *dance and* sarugaku

Both the the *seinō* dance itself and its music are formless and disordered to the extent they could be called discordant and unskilled. As the dance repeats itself seemingly without any artistry, a sense of unearthliness builds until finally it reaches the sphere of the sublime — much like the extremes of avant garde. The *seinō* dance is probably more avant garde and anarchic than any contemporary dance or music. Its appeal strikes me as akin to that of punk music.

This dance is performed by six male dancers wearing white cloths over their faces. It is said they cover their faces in this way because the dance is closely associated with the Isora deity, ancestor of the Azumi clan, who performed it to calm the sea to allow Jingū to cross to wage war in the Korean penisula. He is said to have hidden his face because he was ashamed of the oyster shells covering it. This does not explain the strangeness and other-worldliness, though. The uncanniness of the *seinō* dance in fact suggests a dance of the dead. It is the first dance performed in the repertoire of dance offerings to the deity.

The *sarugaku* guilds of actors — including Kan'ami and Zeami — in the Yamato region centered on Nara grew out of this Kasuga Taisha festival. According to Zeami, noh developed from *kagura*. In his *Book of the Transmission of the Flower*, he states that the orthography of *sarugaku* (申楽) derives from that of shrine dances (*kagura* 神楽) through the removal of the left-hand radical of the character for divine (神).

In the opening section of the fourth chapter of this work, "Matters Concerning the Kami," Zeami wrote: "*Sarugaku* is said to have begun during the Age of the Gods. When Amaterasu ōmikami shut herself up in the heavenly rock cave, the world was plunged into perpetual darkness. The myriad deities gathered on a "heavenly" hill called Amanokaguyama and performed *kagura* and comic dances to lure her out. Ame no Uzume no mikoto came forward and, holding a branch of the *sakaki* tree with a folded-paper offering attached, raised her voice, lit lanterns, and stamped her feet. She became possessed and performed both song and dance. Quietly listening to the voices of the kami, Amaterasu opened the cave door a little, and light again returned to the land, and the faces of the kami shone white with the brightness. It is said that *sarugaku* had its beginnings in the amusements of that occasion." Zeami continues: "Prince Shōtoku handed down *kagura* for the sake of later generations. He removed the left-hand radical from the character for divine (神), leaving just the right-hand side of the character (申), which means 'to speak' and is pronounced *saru* in Japanese. Combining this with the character for 'entertainment' (楽) gives the name *sarugaku*. It means 'to speak' (申) of 'pleasure' (楽) and in this way is distinguished from *kagura* (神楽)."[13]

This is a most ingenious origin story.

Fundamental differences

I have developed the following formula to illustrate the fundamental differences between kami and buddhas.

(1) Kami simply are, but buddhas become.
(2) Kami appear, but buddhas depart.
(3) Kami stand, whereas buddhas sit.

First, "kami" is a general term based on the various powers under the category of "sacred." A kami simply is, the sacred energy of the natural and spiritual worlds, whereas a buddha is a human being who attains the state of buddhahood upon achieving enlightenment through ascetic training. The basic difference between them is that a kami represents the power of existence while a buddha is a human being who has gained wisdom.

Second, a kami is a spiritual and sacred entity that responds to people's prayers and offerings of thanks and praise (*matsuri*) and appears where such offerings are given. On the other hand, a buddha departs from this shore of delusion and suffering that is our secular world and crosses to the other shore of enlightenment. There is a contrast here between coming and departing. During the Onmatsuri festival at Kasuga Taisha, the kami is perceived as coming when it is called into the sacred ritual space by an act of invitation (*wazaogi*). A buddha, on the other hand, seeks to leave this defiled secular realm and reach the undefiled realm of Nirvana and the Pure Land of Sukhāvatī. From a Buddhist point of view, kami appear within the defiled realm of human beings temporarily and partially resolve problems related to the defilements, while a buddha liberates people from the defilements fundamentally and eternally.

Third, kami stand while buddhas sit. Perhaps it is mere coincidence, but kami are counted in Japanese using the suffix for "pillar" (*hashira*) and buddhas using the suffix for "seat" (*za*). Perhaps this is because, while kami are divine spirits thought to appear standing erect like pillars, buddhas are imagined as sitting in the meditation posture to attain enlightenment. Examples of kami as "pillars" are found in a number of shrines, for instance, at the Onbashira festival of Suwa Taisha Shrine, where sixteen trees are prepared as pillars to symbolize shrine renewal every six years; the "heart pillar" (*shin no mihashira*) of the Ise Shrines; and the "purified pillar" (*imibashira*) of Izumo Taisha Shrine.[14] Reclining statues of the Gautama Buddha, seen commonly in Southeast Asia, and seated statues like the Great Buddha of Nara and Kamakura show a clear contrast between the vigorous energy of the kami and the unmoving spirit of a buddha, sitting quietly in the tranquility of Nirvana. In later times, under Buddhist influence, kami, too, started to be counted using the suffix *za*. The Register of Shrines in the tenth century *Engishiki* (Procedures of the Engi Era) states that the total number of kami in the country was 3,132 *za*. There were also village groups called *miyaza* that were responsible for shrine festivities.

	(1) Mode	(2) Directionality	(3) Form
kami	Is	Appears	Standing
buddhas	Becomes	Departs	Sitting

Figure 1.4. Fundamental Differences between Kami and Buddhas

This analysis suggests the existence of fundamental differences between kami and buddhas. Yet despite their clear difference, in Japan they have intersected and merged in what is called kami-buddha combination (*shinbutsu shūgō*). This is what I refer to as the meeting of kami and buddhas, and I would like in the course of this book to look at its origin, its formation, its process of development, and its characteristic features.

Shinto and the Buddhist Dharma

The first appearance of the word "Shinto" was in the *Nihon shoki*, a history of Japan dating from 720. It appears in three places. The first is in the Prologue on Yōmei Tennō (r. 585–87), which says, "The Sovereign [Yōmei] had faith in the Buddhist Dharma (*buppō*) and revered Shinto." It is noticeable that here "Shinto" appears in contraposition to "Buddhist Dharma." The meaning of the passage seems to be that Yōmei believed in the Buddhist teachings as a personal faith but also respected traditional "Shinto" rites. In this period, belief in the newly arrived Buddhism was a matter of personal faith and devotion. So, whereas the question of personal belief was key in Buddhism, "Shinto," not having any "teachings" in the Buddhist sense, could only be the object of respect or disrespect. This means that "Shinto" was part of everyday life as the traditional religio-cultural support of the community and the state.

Kannagara no michi

The Chinese form of the word 神道, *shendao*, can be found in the *Yijing* (The Book of Changes) and in the official history, the *Jinshu* (Book of Jin, compiled 648), where it is used to refer to occult practices, not to the myriad kami as in Japan. In the Japanese context, "Shinto"—referring to traditional kami beliefs in contraposition to the imported religion of Buddhism—thus had a meaning quite different from the contemporaneous use of *shendao* in China.

The second example of the use of "Shinto" in the *Nihon shoki* is in the Prologue on Kōtoku Tennō (r. 645–54): "The Sovereign [Kōtoku] revered the Buddhist Dharma but scorned Shinto." The example cited as demonstrating his scorn is that he ordered sacred trees on the grounds of Ikukunitama Shrine in Settsu province to be cut down. In other words, he did not revere the divine spirits resident in the trees. We should note how strong awe and reverence for sacred trees were in society of the time, the subtext here being that even someone of high rank like a sovereign should not rashly cut down trees in a shrine. In such accounts, we find expressed a deep-rooted cultural attitude of awe and reverence toward life.

The third example also comes from the chronicle of Kōtoku in an item from the third year of his reign, which reads, "Kamunagara" (惟神, "as a kami would") means to "conform to Shinto." It also means to "possess oneself of Shinto" (Taika 3.4.26). This is a notation added to the text explaining 惟神 as it was used in the imperial decree issued that day. The passage is difficult to understand and has led to a number of interpretations. It defines *kamunagara* (the ancient reading of 惟神, now usually read *kannagara*) as acting in accordance with "Shinto," and here "Shinto" exists of its own accord. There are two instances of the word "Shinto" here, and the question is, do they both have the same pronunciation and the same meaning, or are they different? One interpretation is that the first instance should be read as "kami" and the second as "the way of the kami." The passage can then be understood as indicating a situation where the Great Way, the way of the kami (Shinto), continues to extend broadly and deeply in accordance with the kami (Shinto). This interpretation makes sense in terms of sentence structure, context, and meaning, and this is the reading that I endorse.[15]

These instances of "Shinto" in the *Nihon shoki* are significant because they explain "Shinto" as *kamunagara/kannagara no michi* (the way in accord with the kami), a tradition belonging to Japan from ancient times different from the newly imported "Buddhist Dharma." From early on, this suggests, there was a consciousness that the kami and "Shinto" were very different from the buddhas and the "Buddhist Dharma." The imported religion in fact gave "Shinto" an awareness of itself.

The ferment of geography and culture

Let us look at another example of *kannagara*. Kakimoto no Hitomaro, a late seventh-century poet whose works appear prominently in the *Man'yōshū* (Collection of Ten Thousand Leaves), an anthology of poetry dating from around 760, wrote that Japan was a divine (*kannagara*) land where people need not invoke the deities (*kotoage*).[16]

> The rice-abounding Land of Reed Plains
> Is a divine [*kannagara*] land
> And people need not offer invocations,
> Yet [today] I do so:
> Praying for your safe travel and good fortune,
> Without hindrance from evil.
> So that you will find good fortune,
> I offer my prayers over and over,
> Like the waves spilling on the rocky shore,
> A hundredfold, a thousandfold.

(Appended verse [*hanka*])
Yamato, the land called Shikishima,
Is a land protected by
The power of the word [*kotodama*];
Fare you well.[17]

Hitomaro wrote this poem for an envoy departing for China. While describing the distinctive quality of Yamato (Japan) as a land that is already divine so people need not invoke the deities, he takes it upon himself to venture to make such an invocation so that "you" may undertake the long journey safely, in the hope that "we" meet again on "your" return. As the appended *hanka* illustrates, "not offering prayers" (*kotoage senu*) is the inverse of *kotodama*, the belief in the power of words, that whatever is uttered will become a reality. This suggests that there existed in Yamato a strong conviction that it was a land "protected by *kotodama*." To put it another way, it was an expression of a self-awareness that Japan was not a land of reason like China but a land of poetry.

"Not making an invocation" implies not using words to present an argument. This means that for Japanese, there was no need for traditional culture or for "Shinto" to be explained in words, since the "Way" transmitted itself naturally into people's minds (this was later connected with the phrase *ishin denshin*, transmission of the teaching from mind to mind without depending on words).

Thus "Shinto," as expressed by *kannagara*, refers to the manners and modes concerning both the beliefs and the life of the Japanese nurtured naturally within the "wind and earth" of the Japanese archipelago and were formalized and refined over the course of history. Traditions handed down concerning prayer and services (*matsuri*) for the kami that were based on feelings of reverence and awe for these sacred presences were systematized within both beliefs and everyday living.

Japanese sensed the greatness and majesty of this world and of all the phenomenal universe. "Shinto" is a systematization of the lore of their humble response. It encapsulates the ways of thinking of the Japanese about the sacredness of the universe, and within it are interwoven ways of praying to and revering all things in the universe. Shinto grew on a bedrock of ancient Eurasian/Pacific Basin ritual culture, but the forms, modes, and content that made up "Shinto" took shape within the history, and the natural and cultural landscape, of Japan. In this sense, Shinto and Japan are inseparable.

Kannagara no michi, as an expression describing "Shinto," means something like "a way of living according to the actions of kami who have come about of their own accord," or "the way where the will and actions of the kami exist just as they are." In other words, it is "the way that is in accord with the will of the kami." It has three vectors: "the way *from* the kami," whereby blessings in the form of creation and development are bestowed by the kami to its descendants;" "the way *to* the kami," where prayer and services are offered by people to the kami as expressions of faith and gratitude;" and "the way *with* the kami," that is, kami and people working harmoniously together. It is at the point where all three intersect that Shinto, as the *kannagara no michi*, thrives.

To summarize, Shinto, as the way of the kami, is a three-dimensional crossroads: the way *from* the kami, *to* the kami, and *with* the kami.

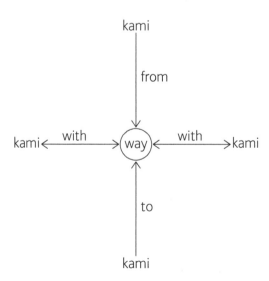

Figure 1.5. Three Aspects of Shinto

Kojiki, *Nihon Shoki*, and *Fudoki*

Unlike Buddhism, "Shinto," as the "way of the kami," did not have a systematized dogma, a theory of proselytization, or a praxis, but this does not mean it was never coordinated as a systematized religious culture from ancient times down to the present. Its myths and history appear in two works compiled at the beginning of the eighth century, the *Kojiki* (Record of Ancient Matters, 712), Japan's oldest literary work, and the *Nihon shoki* (Chronicles of Japan, 720), the earliest of the official histories.

The myths and legends recorded in these two works are often referred to generically as the "Kiki" myths. However, there is a surprisingly great difference between the myths in the two books: though both record myths and history, they are quite dissimilar in their content.

This difference is already apparent in their titles. The *Kojiki*, the record of ancient matters, gives particular attention to myths and hero legends. It was based on earlier records, no longer extant, called *Kyūji* (Ancient Accounts), which recorded legends, and *Teiki* (Imperial Records), handed down by various clans, that were memorized by a court attendant called Hieda no Are and compiled by the courtier and chronicler Ō no Yasumaro. It is basically a collection of old tales, which have a strong uniformity in both how they were narrated and the form in which they were written down. Consisting of three books, the *Kojiki* concludes with a brief account of the reign of Suiko Tennō. It is symbolic that it should finish with a female sovereign whose title means "considering the past." The *Kojiki* seems more like a private, confidential document than a work compiled at the command of the ruler.

The *Nihon shoki*, by contrast, is an official history, Japan's first, which was written with the situation in East Asia, particularly that in China and the Korean peninsula, very much in mind. It thus has a strong sense of "Japan" in terms of a national identity. This is clear, for example, from the orthography used to write the name of the legendary hero, Yamatotakeru no mikoto. In the *Kojiki*, his name is written 倭建命, and in the *Nihon shoki* 日本武尊. In the first instance, the Yamato element is written with the character 倭 that was conventionally used to write "Yamoto;" this was used originally in China to refer to Wa, the name given to the people living in the archipelago. In the second, the characters for Nihon/Japan (日本) are used.

The focus of the *Nihon shoki* is on the origins of Japan and its development down to the time of writing. It is divided into thirty chapters. The first and second deal with the age of the kami (*kamiyo*) and the last with Jitō Tennō, also a female sovereign, whose posthumous name, too, is symbolic in that it means "maintenance," focusing on the continuation of the royal line down to that time.[18]

A decisive difference between the *Kojiki* and the *Nihon shoki* is in the kami of creation that appear in the opening chapters of each. According to the *Kojiki*, the first deity to come into existence was Ame no minakanushi no kami, whereas in the *Nihon shoki* it is Kuni no tokotachi no mikoto. The first accentuates the "heavenly" element (*ama/ame*), while the later accentuates the earthly (*kuni*). They therefore reveal a different notion of deity. Another difference is in the large number of alternative records included in the *Nihon shoki*, a practice not found anywhere in the *Kojiki*.

Motoori Norinaga considered the *Kojiki* to be the book that best expressed the spirit of ancient times, the Japanese spirit (*Yamato-gokoro*), Yamato being the location of many of the ancient capitals. However, generally speaking, it is the *Nihon shoki* that is by far the more distinctively Japanese. In the *Kojiki* there is a clear political theology that makes Takamanohara (Plain of High Heaven) the sacred axis; in other words, the *Kojiki* expounds a "Takamanohara theology," with its theological elements centered on Takamanohara and Amaterasu.

Since, however, the *Nihon shoki* is a compilation made up of main text and alternative records, it lacks consistency, and it is not easy to grasp the overall flow. Why was such a complex and confusing work written, incorporating as it does so many different narratives? It confuses the reader from the very first chapter. If the authorities were aiming at a unified and centralized system of government, choosing such a pluralistic structure for the document would seem in fact to weaken state authority.

Seen from another angle, though, the *Nihon shoki* is trying to select and record as much as possible the individuality and the numerous voices of the myriad kami. It might be called an expression of innumerable lines of thought, at the opposite pole from unification, as it strives to gather up and combine various ideas and traditions. While the *Kojiki* has a consistency as narrated lore, the *Nihon shoki* is a polyphony of voices.

We can say, therefore, that the official histories[19] of the Japanese state began with a kind of mixed voice choir. As a volume of myth and history, the *Nihon shoki* is not at all typical, and it is this atypical work that is held up as one of Japan's first books. It has a singular form of mythical and historical expression not seen in China or the Korean peninsula.

The kami of the ancient records

The kami that appear in the opening chapters of the *Kojiki* and *Nihon shoki* are considerably different. In the *Kojiki*, at "the beginning of heaven and earth," there were three kami who "came into existence as single deities, and their forms were not visible": Ame no minakanushi no kami, Takamimusubi no kami and Kamimusubi no kami.[20] Book 1 of the *Nihon shoki* says that "when heaven and earth were not yet separated and yin and yang had not yet divided," three "divine beings" were produced: Kunitokotachi no mikoto, Kuninosatsuchi no mikoto and Toyokumunu no mikoto.[21] We should note the fact that the first kami to appear in the *Kojiki* has the suffix *nushi*, whereas in the *Nihon shoki* the suffix is *tachi*.

The *Nihon shoki* has six variant versions following the main one. The kami appearing here are:

Variant 1
    Kunitokotachi no mikoto (also called Kunisokotachi no mikoto);
    Kuninosatsuchi no mikoto (also called Kunisatsutachi no mikoto),
    Toyokuninushi no mikoto (also called Toyokumino no

mikoto, Toyokabuno no mikoto, Ukabunonotoyokau no mikoto, Toyokunino no mikoto, Toyokabuno no mikoto, Hakokunino no mikoto, Mino no mikoto).

Variant 2
    Umashiashikabihikoji no mikoto,
    Kunitokotachi no mikoto,
    Kunisatsuchi no mikoto.

Variant 3
    Umashiashikabihikoji no mikoto,
    Kunisokotachi no mikoto.

Variant 4
    Kunitokotachi no mikoto,
    Kunisatsuchi no mikoto.
    Also, Ama no minakanushi no mikoto, Takakamimusubi no mikoto, Kamimimusubi no mikoto.

Variant 5
    Kunitokotachi no mikoto.

Variant 6
    Amatokotachi no mikoto,
    Umashiashikabihikoji no mikoto.
    Also, Kunitokotachi no mikoto.

The name Kunitokotachi no mikoto appears in five of the variants. If we consider that an alternate name for this kami was Kunisokotachi no mikoto, as given in Variant 1, then Kunitokotachi appears in Variant 3 as well, meaning all six have one form or the other of his name. There is a "Kunitokotachi theology" here in contrast to the *Kojiki* "Takamanohara/Amaterasu theology." In fact, the word "Takamanohara" is used only twice in the "Age of the Kami" chapters of the *Nihon shoki*, emphasizing differences from the *Kojiki* in the narrative regarding Amaterasu—the ruler of Takamanohara.

Kami in the fudoki

The *fudoki* (Records of Wind and Earth) are regional gazetteers, the records of local customs, myths and legends, natural conditions, scenery, place names, products, and history for each province, compiled at the order of Genmei Tennō in 713 in the context of the establishment in Japan of a unified state based on Chinese-style law codes (*ritsuryō*) introduced in the seventh and eighth centuries. Five remain substantially intact: those from Hitachi, Harima, Izumo, Hizen, and Bungo. There are as well fragmentary quotations in various books, called *fudoki itsubun*, for other provinces.[22]

The five extant *fudoki* contain numerous independent accounts of local lore and traditions, different from what appear in the *Kojiki* and the *Nihon shoki*, and this makes them an incomparable source for ancient history. Of particular interest, a large number of myths differing from those two works are recorded in the *fudoki* of Izumo province, whose power in the ancient period rivaled that of the Yamato court. This shows that there was a rich tradition of myths in the archipelago, quite apart from those of Yamato.

One example of this is the "land-pulling" (*kunibiki*) myth, which differs from the creation myth featuring Izanami and Izanagi found in the *Kojiki* and *Nihon shoki*. The *Izumo fudoki* states that the deity Yatsukamizu omitsunu no mikoto, calling "Come on, land! Come on, land!" drew land from the Korean peninsula to create more land for the province of Izumo. As well, the text records many variants where Ōkuninushi is called by other names: Ame no shita tsukurashishi ōkami and Ōanamochi no mikoto. It also contains the birth myth of Sata ōkami, who is thought to be the same deity as Sarutahiko. A comparative study of the myths and legends recorded in the *fudoki*, the *Kogoshūi* (Gleanings from Ancient Stories, 807) and the *Kujiki* (Record of Old Matters, ninth-tenth century) with those in the *Kojiki* and *Nihon shoki* brings such differences into stark relief and the reasons behind the compilation of these texts appear.

Let us now sort out the terms kami (神), spirit (霊, *rei*), miracle (霊異, *reii*) and spiritual power (霊威, *reii*). At some point Japanese came to call anything "kami" that imparted a sense of the sacred. The kami can be broadly categorized in three ways.

(1) Nature deities: Natural phenomena and natural objects like thunder, rocks, sea, mountains, earthquakes, etc.
(2) Animal and vegetation deities: Animals like snakes, boars, and deer; trees like cryptomeria, camphor, and katsura.
(3) Cultural deities: Deified human beings who have achieved great deeds, like Empress Jingū, Yamato Takeru, Sugawara no Michizane, and Tokugawa Ieyasu.

Motoori Norinaga defined "kami" in the *Kojikiden* as "anything whatsoever that is outside the ordinary, that has superior and extraordinary power, provoking awe." This means that anything that is both great and out of the ordinary can potentially become a kami, as can anything that receives prayer. The myriad kami have a flexible and diverse dimension as well as an existing shape. Kami can thus be regarded as a category of various modes and forms of sacred energy.

As discussed above, this is a category of reverence and knowledge about the sacred, its powers and phenomena held by the Japanese. It covers such items as spirits, spiritual powers, ghosts, the uncanny, and wonders. There are "eight million kami," which can be subcategorized according to words—such as *chi*, *mi*, *hi*, *mono*, *nushi*, *tama*, *oni*, and *mikoto*—in their names that express their divine power, divinity, and spirituality.

In the *Man'yōshū* the word *chihayaburu* (mighty, powerful) is used as a pillow word, or epithet, for kami. This *chi* is the same element that we found in words such as Ikazuchi, meaning spirit or spiritual power. The condition where its sacred energy vibrates and moves at furious speed is well named "kami." Another pillow word we find in the *Man'yōshū* is *tamakiharu*, which is prefixed to *inochi* (life). Its etymology is "spirit (*tama*) + reach the extreme (*kiharu*)" or "spirit (*tama*) + come (*ki*) + pass (*heru*)/expand (*fukureru*)." "Life" has the connotation that the *tama* (soul, spirit), which gives life, enters the body, attains growth, and eventually reaches its end. The *chi* in *inochi* is also the same *chi* found in *chihayaburu*.

In this way, a culture that called the maelstrom of sacred energy "kami" was fostered in the Japanese archipelago. These kami are described collectively as the "myriads" of kami (Jp. *yaoyorozu*, literally eight million, or *yasorozu*, literally eighty million). These terms are stereotyped expressions signifying the existence of countless numbers of kami.

The word "God" as it is used in Judaism, Christianity, and Islam denotes a deity who is one, absolute, transcendent, omniscient, omnipotent, and good, and who is the creator of all things in the natural world. The Japanese concept of "kami" is very different, to the extent of being bewilderingly so. "God" (Yahweh, Jehovah, Allah) is conceptually completely different from what the Japanese call "kami."

The kami of Japan are diverse, complicated, mysterious, and ever-changing entities. Nature and natural phenomena like the sun, moon, stars, wind, water, stones, fire, and thunder are considered to be their manifestations and workings. For example, the sun deity is called Amaterasu (literally, "illuminating the heavens" and the moon deity is called Tsukiyomi (literally "reading [the phases of] the moon"), and all the various natural phenomena have their own individual deities. These kami are actually enshrined: for example, Amaterasu is enshrined at Ise Jingū and Tsukiyomi in a shrine on the summit of Gassan (the "mountain of the moon") in Yamagata prefecture. Shrines are sacred spaces. Among the myriad kami are animals like bears, boars, deer, snakes, monkeys, rabbits, and frogs. Kami are considered to dwell within natural phenomena, which display their workings. Japan's polytheistic belief, which has been called animism and pantheism within the fields of religious studies, cultural anthropology, and philosophy, strongly preserves the animism, shamanism, and totemism of many primitive religions.

In Japan, Buddhism (which arrived in the year 538) developed the doctrine that "grasses, trees, the land itself, all will attain buddhahood."[23] This incorporated "Shinto" (as *kannagara no michi*) ideas about divinity, nature, and life. It is in this idea that everything —mountains and rivers, grasses and trees, down to the land itself— will become buddhas that we find the beginnings of a combinatory kami-buddha view that all are kami and all are buddhas.

CHAPTER TWO

The Encounter of Shinto and Buddhism in the Early Japanese State

The previous chapter discussed the basic differences between kami and buddhas, Shinto and Buddhism, and, more broadly, how "deity" is understood in Japan. The relationship between kami and buddhas, construed in terms of their combination (*shinbutsu shūgō*), is an undercurrent in Japanese culture, and this relationship informs the framework of Japan's religious institutions and their ties with the state, its thought and ideology, its literature and the customs of the people. Nowhere is the encounter between kami (and what became known as Shinto) and buddhas (Buddhism, the Buddha-Dharma) drawn more starkly than in the accounts concerning the introduction of Buddhism to the Japanese court, sometime in the sixth century.

This chapter looks at the deities and mythologies that underpinned the early Japanese state and examines the role played in its development by a combination of indigenous and imported elements. A brief sketch of Buddhism as it developed in India forms the backdrop for a description of how it was first received at the Japanese court. Two examples show how indigenous and imported elements played out in the lives of two important religious figures: Prince Shōtoku, the so-called father of Japanese Buddhism, and En no Gyōja, the semi-legendary founder of Shugendō.

The Formation of the Early Japanese State

The myth that supported the early state, which emerged around the middle of the seventh century, was formed from existing animistic beliefs allied with a political theology that set out the type of leader needed for a centralized agrarian society. As I have described, what is called Shinto developed out of beliefs that had existed from before the Japanese archipelago was formed, beliefs with a Eurasian, pan-Pacific scope. In the prehistoric period, seafarers rode the ocean currents to travel between Japan and the islands of the South Seas, and there were land links to the Eurasian continent. Beliefs at this time are thought to have been animistic and totemistic, centered on nature and spirits, and this basic belief pattern probably did not fundamentally change even when the hunter-gatherer way of life gave way to agriculture during the Yayoi period (ca. 300 B.C.E.–300 C.E.). What changed was the form of subsistence and social organization. Unlike a hunter-gatherer society, an agricultural one is sedentary, and this necessitates a different type of leadership and organization.

In a hunter-gatherer society, people are directly linked to their natural surroundings. Hunters must be able to take their game without danger to themselves, which means their leaders are chosen for their hunting skill, knowledge, and judgment. A settled farming community, on the other hand, has to deal with issues related to the distribution and use of produce, and this must be done in a way that minimizes complaints and dissatisfaction. Its leader must therefore be someone good at human relations, a skilled communicator able to coordinate and negotiate. Group and communal order in an agricultural society is of far greater importance than in a hunter-gatherer one, since people have to share a social design and agree to mutual arrangements to determine, for example, how water and foodstuffs are distributed and how relations between people are managed. The larger groups engaged in agriculture grew and the more surplus rice that was produced, the greater the need for a system of social control.

In Japan, such a system took shape between the seventh and eighth centuries in the form of the *ritsuryō* state, an umbrella term given to the centralized administrative system headed by the *tennō* ("heavenly sovereign"), derived from Sui and Tang period Chinese law. Essentially, the *ritsuryō* system was based on the state ownership of land: private ownership was not permitted, and the government administered land allocation. These political changes are known as the Taika ("Great Change") reforms that were launched in 645 when Prince Naka no Ōe (who later became Tenji Tennō) and his close aide Nakatomi no Kamatari (614–69) defeated the dominant Soga clan. Tenji (r. 668–71) made his capital at Ōmi, on the southern shore of Lake Biwa where the city of Ōtsu now stands; it was here that he ordered the compilation of an administrative code (known as the Ōmi code but not extant) to put the *ritsuryō* system into practice. After Tenji died in 671, a violent succession dispute ensued, leading to the outbreak of what is known as the Jinshin disturbance. Tenji's brother Tenmu emerged the victor in 672 and became ruler. He consolidated the *ritsuryō* reforms, issuing the Asuka-Kiyomihara code in 689. He also built up the Ise Shrines and began the compilation of an official history. It is thought that the title of *tennō* came into use at this time to refer to the sovereign of the Yamato state.

The Taihō code was enacted in 701 during the reign of Monmu (r. 697–707), grandson of Tenmu. The code further reinforced the centralized administration system. A capital called Heijō-kyō was built on the site of present-day Nara in 710, and an administrative and land tenure structure was put in place based on the public (that is, state) ownership of land (*ōdo ōmin*), by means of a household registration (*koseki*) system, a state land allocation (*handen*) system, and a taxation system based on grain tax (*so*), a tax in kind (*chō*) and a labor tax (*yō*). The armed forces protecting the capital were also reorganized. The country's first literary works—*Kojiki*, *Nihon shoki*, local gazetteers called *fudoki*, the *Man'yōshū*, etc.—were compiled in this period, defining the understanding of history that informed the *ritsuryō* state.

Before discussing the relationship between the new centralized state and religion, let us look more closely at the two main protagonists, Shinto and Buddhism.

What Is Shinto?

Shinto emerged naturally out of the climate and culture of the Japanese archipelago and was shaped by ideas and cultures from abroad. It is the system of prayer and ritual (*matsuri*) based on feelings of awe and reverence held by the inhabitants of Japan toward sacred entities that came to be called kami, refined in the customs and conventions of daily life.

Insight into how kami were understood can be found in Endō Shūsaku's novel *Fukai kawa* (Deep River). Ōtsu, who is studying in a Catholic seminary, says, "I don't think God is someone to be looked up to as a being separate from man, the way you regard him. I think he is within man, and that he is a great life force that envelops man, envelops the trees, envelops the flowers and grasses."[1] We see here a way of thinking reminiscent of the Tendai Buddhist idea of original enlightenment, that "grasses, trees, the land itself, all will attain buddhahood." Ōtsu's understanding of God is almost certainly Endō's own. Though the European superiors at the seminary criticized what he described as a pantheistic view, calling it heresy, Ōtsu could not change it. It was the reality of God that shone out from the deepest part of his sensibilities.

For Endō, there was not all that much difference between the kami of Shinto, the buddhas of Buddhism and the God of Christianity. All were the life of the universe, the "great life force."

Further hints for understanding kami can be found in the word *chihayaburu*, mentioned in Chapter 1 as an epithet for kami. The element *chi*, which contains a wide variety of meanings—spirit, wind, blood, mother's milk, road, etc.—expresses extremely rapid and powerful motion. In this sense it penetrates everything from divinity and spirit to physicality and materiality, rooted in a driving force and life itself. Originally "life" (*inochi*) meant "the living *chi*, the breathing *chi*."

The word "kami" thus refers to a variety of aspects: kami causes all things in the universe to be, is the source of the power that blows breath into them, and is the origin of the life force and creativity. The creation myth in the first chapter of the *Kojiki* speaks of two kami with the element *musubi* in their names, the second to come into existence, Takamimusubi no kami, and the third, Kamimusubi no kami. *Musubi* (lit., tie or bind) is the generative force and the natural vitality of all things. Feelings of awe and reverence for, and beliefs about, this vitality and the creative power of the universe and nature became myths that were passed down as beliefs about the *musubi* kami. The word "musubi" has the connotations of "natural vitality" and "union"—celebrating fecundity and fertility—and the *matsuri* of Shinto express thankfulness for, and rejoicing in, this natural vitality and are a mutual communication between kami and human beings. Shinto *matsuri* were held seasonally to pray and give thanks for the bounty of nature and were directly connected to people's daily lives. The kami of Shinto are thus the origins of life, the basis of existence, and the power that causes all things to be, as well as their expression.

Kami beliefs, or Shinto, are not a "religion" with teachings like Buddhism and not a philosophy but rather the oral culture of prayer to and *matsuri* for the kami, as they took root in the Japanese archipelago. That culture was underpinned by the habits of supplication integrated into the mythology and into the rituals and the practices of daily life. They are the way of prayer transmitted from the ancestors.

A Westerner's sense of the kami

Lafcadio Hearn (1850–1904), who arrived in Japan in 1890, was the first European to visit the Izumo Taisha Shrine in Shimane prefecture. He wrote about his feelings about the Shinto kami, of discovering kami within phenomena, in the chapter on "Kitzuki" in his *Glimpses of Unfamiliar Japan*. "There seems to be a sense of divine magic in the very atmosphere, through all the luminous day, brooding over the vapory land, over the ghostly blue of the flood—a sense of Shintō."[2] He also wrote:

> Buddhism, changing form or slowly decaying through the centuries, might seem doomed to pass away at last from this

Japan to which it came only as an alien faith; but Shintō, unchanging and vitally unchanged, still remains all dominant in the land of its birth, and only seems to gain in power and dignity with time. Buddhism has a voluminous theology, a profound philosophy, a literature as vast as the sea. Shintō has no philosophy, no code of ethics, no metaphysics; and yet, by its very immateriality, it can resist the invasion of Occidental religious thought as no other Orient faith can.... But the reality of Shintō lives not in books, nor in rites, nor in commandments, but in the national heart, of which it is the highest emotional religious expression, immortal and ever young. Far underlying all the surface crop of quaint superstitions and artless myths and fantastic magic there thrills a mighty spiritual force, the whole soul of a race with all its impulses and powers and intuitions. He who would know what Shintō is must learn to know that mysterious soul in which the sense of beauty and the power of art and the fire of heroism and magnetism of loyalty and the emotion of faith have become inherent, immanent, unconscious, instinctive.[3]

Hearn understood that Shinto would continue to preserve its own culture because, having no founder, no theology, no sacred texts, and no voluminous philosophy or literature as does Buddhism, it can resist the invasion of Western thought. Both Christianity and Buddhism produced a vast theology, philosophy, and literature, but there is nothing of the sort in Shinto. This very "immateriality" embraces all, acting like a womb or catalyst to nurture and transform. Unlike Buddhism, Christianity, and other "universal" world religions, Shinto is an ethnic religion that grew up within the history and culture of the Japanese people. As described above, it is a way of prayer and ritual, venerating that which engenders awe and respect as kami. By contrast, Buddhism is a system of beliefs and practices associated with realizing enlightenment and attaining buddhahood.

Is Shinto a religion?

Generally, as Buddhism is called a religion of "enlightenment and compassion" and Christianity one of "love and forgiveness," Shinto may be described as a religion of "awe, *matsuri*, and beauty."

"Buddha" means "an enlightened person." Seeking the liberation of all living beings is a manifestation of the compassion that comes of spiritual awakening. In Christianity, the Messiah (Savior) is the will and love of God made incarnate in a man, and the words of Jesus Christ, the crystallization of the love of God, are the Gospels, which teach the forgiveness of sins for all humankind.

A "religion" is frequently defined in terms of its founder, doctrine, scriptures, and organization. In Buddhism, the founder, Gautama Siddhartha (also known as Shakyamuni or the Buddha), and his followers down the generations taught doctrines such as nonself (Sk. *anātman*), impermanence (Sk. *anitya*), dependent origination (Sk. *pratīya-samutpāda*), and emptiness (Sk. *śūnya*), compiled texts including the *Sutta-nipata* (Collection of Suttas), the *Dhammapada* (Path of Dhamma), the Lotus Sutra and the Heart Sutra, and formed religious sects and schools out of their founders' experiences and judgments—including the Tendai, Shingon, and Pure Land schools in Japan. In Christianity, Jesus and his disciples and later followers formulated doctrines and creeds concerning love, salvation, and the coming of the kingdom of God. The New Testament became its main scripture, and activities were organized according to sect and denomination, such as Roman Catholicism, Protestantism, and the Greek Orthodox Church. Islam, too, had Mohammed as founder, a doctrine based on the six articles of faith and the five pillars, a scripture in the Quran and sects like Sunni, Shia, and Sufism.

This is the image most modern people have of religion. If we look at Shinto in the same terms, there is, as Lafcadio Hearn astutely pointed out, no founder, no doctrine, no scriptures, and no religious organization. Of course, there are the myths recorded in the *Kojiki*, the *Nihon shoki*, and the various *fudoki*, and there are rites as carried out even today in shrines. However, these are not things created by a founder, or doctrine taught by a founder, or scriptures that are the foundation of the teachings, or the activities of a unified organization. Does this mean Shinto is not a religion?

There are said to be two types of religion: traditional and didactic. Shinto is a classic example of the first. Whereas world religions like Buddhism, Christianity, and Islam have founders, Shinto, whose origins are unclear, does not. Rather, it was passed down through the oral traditions of tribes and peoples as myths and rites, supported by the spirit of community.

Words and language are the basis for these communal "oral traditions." The compound *chihayaburu kami*, for example, is a "primary word" (*kongengo*)[4] that most deeply underpins this communal lore. In the same way, *matsuri* is a "primary word" of Shinto whose etymology has been traced variously to (1) *matsu* (wait) (2) *tatematsuru* (offer up service), and (3) *matsurou* (attend to, or submit to the will of, the kami). The *matsuri* is the point where the Shinto worldview coalesces: they are events where people wait for the kami to manifest and then present them with food offerings and dance performances; these rites/festivals are conducted to bring about the harmony and balancing of existence according to the will of the kami.[5]

The *matsuri* is the concrete manifestation of the Shinto view of the world. Since the *matsuri* is at the basis of everything to do with living and its institutions, both "rites/festivals" (*matsuri*) and "government" (*matsurigoto*) were called *matsuri*. The basis of government was the performance of rites. The ancient *hime-hiko* (female-male) system and the *onari-ukeri* system of Okinawa[6]—like the complementary balance between Himiko and her brother, described in the Chinese history *Wei zhi* (Chronicles of Wei, ca. 297), where the queen of Wa (what later became "Japan") performed rites while her younger brother took care of administration—demonstrate the importance of the cooperation and complementarity of rites and government.

Shinto, lacking scriptures and other trappings of religion, is a traditional oral culture handed down through the generations concerning the ways of performing *matsuri*. Thus the word for Shinto, which is written with the character for "way" 道 , is in contrast to the words for Buddhism 仏教 and Christianity キリスト教, which use the character for "teaching" 教. The old term for Shinto, in fact, is *kannagara no michi*: the "way according to the kami."

The *Kojiki* and the *Nihon shoki* are not the scriptures of Shinto but rather prized repositories of ancestral lore transmitting ancient customs. Of course, the people who compiled these myths and tales did so for their own reasons, including political ones, as the two works clearly show. It is significant, though, that the *Nihon shoki*, the first of Japan's official histories, recorded multiple versions of certain accounts, with both a main text and variants, thus revealing a respect for the communities from which sprang the various traditions, rather than simply imposing a regime based on monistic power and authority.

It is certainly possible that there is a difference in importance between the main text and the variants in the *Nihon shoki*. But as is clear from the fact that the opening creation myth of the *Kojiki* is presented in the *Nihon shoki* as the fourth of six variants, being introduced with the phrase "it is further stated," the text clearly tried to respect to the greatest extent possible the traditional oral culture of various regions and clans. Are there any other examples in the world of myths written down in this way? Does it represent the impartiality of that era of Japanese history? At its basis is the importance given to "ancient customs" and so was an expression of the highest respect for traditional culture and wisdom.

Buddhism

There is no essential connection between this mythical tradition and Buddhism. Buddhism is the path revealed by the Buddha, the teachings of truth expounded by an enlightened person, as well as the way to buddhahood through religious training. Gautama Siddhartha, its founder, was a revolutionary who implemented religious reform and disavowed the ancient traditions of Indian myth and magic and folk beliefs. He was not someone born out of myth but an actual person who became awakened to the Truth (the Dharma), attained enlightenment, and was known as the Buddha.

The Buddha as revolutionary

The Buddha denied mythical thinking, going beyond it to practice the way of enlightenment and liberation and open the way of the true human being by discerning the phenomena of the world exactly as they are. Buddhism's criticism of and aloofness from traditional culture is fundamentally different from Shinto. The Buddha decisively rejected ideas about the occult and its use to attain worldly benefits (*genze riyaku*). He resolutely negated magic and divination, and his view that the Vedic magic of the ancient sacred tradition had no place in the pursuit of the true way is found in the *Suttanipāta*.

> Neither meat nor fish, nor fasting,
> Nor nakedness, nor a shaven head, matted hair nor dirt,
> Nor donning rough garments of animal skin, nor tending the sacred fire,
> Nor even the many penances done in the world for eternal life,
> Nor (Vedic) mantras and offerings, nor sacrifices and seasonal feasts,
> Will purify a person who has not crossed beyond spiritual doubt.[7] [249]

> In him whom belief in the efficacy of omens like shooting stars, dreams and signs is destroyed,
> That monk who has avoided the resulting consequences would properly lead a homeless life.[8] [360]

> He should not practice charms,
> Interpret physical marks, dreams, the stars, animal cries,
> Should not be devoted to practicing medicine or inducing fertility.[9] [927]

This is a clear disavowal of the Vedic practices of Brahmanism. In particular it denies Athuravedic magical formulas, the kinds of magical practices mentioned in Verse 927, and so at the same time the Athuravedic worldview and its magical practices.[10] Japanese folk beliefs and Shinto closely resemble that Vedic religious culture.

Gautama Buddha clearly discerned what the use of magic and fortune-telling did to people and society by becoming channels for desire. Thoughts breed desire, and the flow of desire produces thoughts in an ever-intensifying vicious circle, which the Buddha formulated as links in the cycle of death and rebirth. He wanted to demythicize and disempower thoughts and desires by going beyond the magical practices and religious possession practices of the ritualist and the shaman.

The Buddha sought to reach out beyond both this world and the next, beyond the knowledge and authority and system of Brahmanism. For Buddhism, knowledge was the wisdom that could penetrate the farthest places, beyond magic and religion, beyond animism and shamanism. Having a thorough knowledge of traditional Brahmanical magic and religion, the Buddha's insistence on demagification was conscience-driven.

The Buddha also rejected traditional ideas about caste that ordained that to be born a Brahmin was to be a Brahmin, insisting rather that of whatever birth, a person could become a Brahmin through his actions and behavior. In speaking of the *brahmana*, one who had rid himself of sinful action, as the "true" Brahmin, he points the way to going beyond the Brahmanical view of what a "Brahmin" is.

For example, the "Discourse on Outcastes" (*Vasala Sutta*) lists the conditions that make an "outcaste" and teaches that one becomes a "true Brahmin" through deeds.

> Whoever is quick to anger, harbors hatred, discredits the good in others, holds mistaken views, and is deceitful, he is an outcaste.
> Whoever kills living things in this world, whoever has no sympathy for living things, he is an outcaste.
> Whoever destroys and conquers villages and towns and is an oppressor, he is an outcaste.

Whoever steals what belongs to others and takes what has not been given, in village, town or city, or in the forest, he is an outcaste.

Whoever runs away without paying when he has incurred a debt, saying "I have not borrowed anything from you," he is an outcaste.

Whoever covets even the smallest thing, kills a person traveling along the road and takes whatever he has, he is an outcaste.

Whoever tells lies when questioned as a witness, either for his own sake or for others, or for the sake of wealth, he is an outcaste.

Whoever associates with the wives of relatives or friends, either by force or with consent, he is an outcaste.

Whoever does not support his mother or father, grown old, though he is wealthy, he is an outcaste.

Whoever strikes his father, mother, brothers, sisters, or mother-in-law, or angers his relatives with harsh words, he is an outcaste.

Whoever says what is detrimental when questioned about what is good and speaks ambiguously to be evasive, he is an outcaste.

Whoever commits an evil deed and wishes that others might not know about it, and hides his actions, he is an outcaste.

Whoever goes to the house of another and eats choice food there but does not repay the courtesy when the host visits his house, he is an outcaste.

Whoever deceives by lying, whether he is a *brahmana*, an ascetic, or any other mendicant, he is an outcaste.

Whoever speaks harshly to a *brahmana* or a mendicant who visits his house at mealtime and does not offer food, he is an outcaste.

Whoever in this world, shrouded by ignorance, speaks what is not true in order to gain something, he is an outcaste.

Whoever, debased by pride, exalts himself and belittles others, he is an outcaste.

Whoever is given to anger, is miserly, has base desires, and is selfish, deceitful, knows no shame himself and is shameless toward others, he is an outcaste.

Whoever reviles the Enlightened One, or his disciple, or a recluse, or a householder, he is an outcaste.

Whoever, not being an Arahant [one worthy of offerings] pretends to be so, is a thief of the universe, the lowest of outcastes.[11]

In Brahmanism, the outcaste was originally regarded as the lowest of all the classes and castes. The Buddha flatly rejected this understanding and turned it around, interrogating its essential meaning. He did not regard a person an "outcaste" because of birth or class but rather because of his deeds. A "true Brahmin" was someone who did not give way to anger, who did not bear grudges, who did not steal, who did not lie, who knew shame and was polite, in other words, one who could control his mind and his actions. In the items in the list, the Buddha stressed that the point that an outcaste is not one by birth but by deeds. This was a revolutionary idea that attacked the Brahmanical class system from within. The way taught by the Buddha was thoroughly anti-Brahamanical and anti-Vedic: in other words, nontraditional.

Transposing this to Japan, ancient Indian folk beliefs, Brahmanism, and Hinduism had much in common with Shinto, in that they were traditional, magical, derived from myth and ritual, and centered on ritual performance. The five lay precepts of Buddhism (not to kill, not to steal, not to commit adultery, not to tell lies, and not to drink intoxicants) also had an anti-Brahmanical aspect. "Not to kill" was a criticism of the Brahmanical practice of animal sacrifice, while "not to drink intoxicants" denied the Brahmanical ritual behavior of offering *soma* (wine) to Agni and drinking it, becoming intoxicated and falling into a trance. In this sense, Buddhism lay far from the shamanistic and magical spiritual worldview.

The Buddha's teachings are clear and simple. It is deeds rather than birth that are important. A person who is "tamed by the Truth, endowed with self-restraint," who has "let go of sensuality," and who is without pride, covetousness, and attachment is called "a Brahmin who has removed the impurity of grief," and is a Tathāgata, "cleansed of pollutions [and] bearer of the last body."[12]

Development of Buddhism

The Three Treasures refer to the Buddha (the Enlightened One), his teachings (the Dharma), and his community (the Sangha). The Sangha originally meant the group of *bhikkhus* (monks) who had renounced their worldly lives to undertake religious training, seek the Buddhist Truth, and attain enlightenment. Whereas Shinto's *kannushi*, ritualists serving the kami, were at one time "wives of the kami," closely connected with shamanistic ecstasy and sexual fertility rites, *bhikkhus*, and later Buddhist priests, took an attitude of self-denial towards sex, standing aloof from it in the attempt to remove attachment and defilements like desire. Later thirty-two physical characteristics of a great man were ascribed to the Buddha. Among them was a retractable penis, called the "horse-penis mark." The Buddha's penis was held inside the body, like a horse's, so that it could not be seen. This expresses the overcoming of sexual desire.

The Buddha rejected shamanism and magic because he well knew that they compounded people's desires and mental suffering. Human suffering, he realized, could not be relieved in any fundamental way through shamanism.

The content of the Buddha's enlightenment can be summarized in terms of nonself (Sk. *anātman*), impermanence (Sk. *anitya*), dependent origination (Sk. *pratiyya-samutpāda*), lack of a self-nature (Sk. *asvabhāva*), and emptiness (Sk. *śūnyata*). People generally believe that things are real and substantial and so cling to them, becoming trapped by desire and karma. Thus they are unable to escape the wheel of death and rebirth. By attaining the "right view" about the root of desire, a person realizes that the material world has no substance at all. This is of fundamental importance. In Buddhism the "nonself," or "emptiness," is not a simple negative.

Rather, these are concepts that express relativity, interdependence, and provisionality.

The Buddha's religious reformation developed in diverse forms, with the growth of sects and schools and the compilation of a broad range of texts. Later, Buddhism absorbed elements of ancient Indian folk beliefs, Brahmanism and Hinduism, and out of that process eventually emerged Mahāyāna and esoteric Buddhism. It was these evolved forms of Buddhism that entered Japan from the Korean peninsula and China. This Buddhism, compared with the original teachings of the Buddha, was a combinatory form that contained elements of Indian folk beliefs and that had become sinified through Chinese translations of the Indic texts. These features were particularly strong in the esoteric Buddhism the Japanese priest Kūkai brought back to Japan from China in the early ninth century.

Despite their fundamental differences, in Japan kami and buddhas, Shinto and Buddhism, mixed and merged in a phenomenon scholarship calls "kami-buddha combination" (*shinbutsu shūgō*). This was made possible because of the understanding Shinto and Buddhism shared about nature and existence: kami-nature, spirit, and buddha-nature alike existed within nature and all phenomena. Both Shinto and Buddhism recognized the reality and power of something that allowed existence, and they shared the common understanding and sense that this had many forms and shapes.

Pictorial representations of this kami-buddha combinatory universe are known as Shinto mandalas (mandara). Famous examples include the Nachi Sankei Mandara that venerates the Nachi Falls, the highest in Japan, as a *shintai* (receptacle in which a kami resides), and the Tenkawa Mandara, which portrays the water deity (Benzaiten) as a dragon. The combination of kami and buddhas, Shinto and Buddhism, came about in the context of the landscape, culture, and natural environment of Japan.

Japanese Buddhism and Shinto had a mutual influence on each other, coexisting and partially blending. Shugendō, a form of religion specific to Japan, emerged out of this combination. It represents a typical East Asian combinatory religion, a mix of ancient mountain beliefs and practices, Shinto and Buddhism, and was also influenced by the practices and rites of the *hwarang* of Silla.[13]

Mythology and the *Ritsuryō* State

The mythology underpinning the *ritsuryō* state is contained in the two chronicles compiled by order of the court, the *Kojiki* (712) and the *Nihon shoki* (720),[14] which recorded the origins of the state according to myth and lore. Though they contain many old oral traditions that predate the founding of the state, as the historian Tsuda Sōkichi (1873–1961) pointed out, they show a clear political agenda and concern. At root, they were constructed, in terms of both narrative and form, to establish the legitimacy and inevitability of *tennō* rule in the "central land of the reed plains" (that is, Japan), placing the lineage and authority of the royal house within myth and history. In this sense they represent a particular political theology, the ethos of mediation and shared rule. Their compilers did not record the myths and lore of the various clans without change. Rather, they organized and structured them, selecting one version as the base and joining it with others to create the narrative. In this way, for example, ancient clans like the Nakatomi, Inbe, and Mononobe were positioned according to their support of the royal house.

The founding myths

At the core of these ancient accounts is the story of the establishment of rule in the land. It describes how descendants of the "heavenly deities" (*amatsukami*), the kami residing in the High Plain of Heaven (Takamanohara), were sent to the "central land of the reed plains" (Ashihara no nakatsukuni), also known as the "land of the plentiful reed plains and of the fresh rice-ears" (Toyoashihara no mizuho no kuni), that is, Japan, with the mission to pacify it. This they achieved after many difficulties, defeating warring tribes and concluding ties with them. These are state myths explaining the establishment of the Yamato court that amount to an official theology; they are quite different from the oral traditions passed down by the individual tribes and clans.

The *Kojiki* and the *Nihon shoki* contain a number of myth cycles concerning this "land": how it was formed, apportioned, expanded, transferred, and ruled. The opening chapters of both works tell how the land was engendered (*kuniumi*) and how the kami came into being. The islands of the Japanese archipelago (Ōyashima, the "eight great islands") were born when the male kami Izanagi and the female kami Izanami called to each other and had sexual contact (*mito no maguwahi*). The islands were the children of Izanami's womb. The first island (child) to be born was Hiruko, meaning "leech child," and the second was Apa. These were not regarded as being successful and were floated away in a reed boat and so are not counted among the "eight great islands." This happened, it was explained, because Izanami addressed her partner first when they met after circling a pillar in opposite directions. This explanation is considered to have been added in accordance with imported Confucian ideas about male supremacy; in Japan, notions of the divine female had flourished in the Japanese archipelago since the ancient past. Izanagi and Izanami went around the pillar again and this time Izanagi spoke first. The third island (child) born was Awaji, perhaps meaning, "island on the route to Awa."[15] The two kami went on to create more islands and also kami. Finally, Izanami gave birth to the fire deity, Kagutsuchi, in the course of which her genitals were burned. She sickened, and as she was dying, she vomited, and from this vomit were born a pair of kami, Kanayama-hiko and Kanayama-hime, associated with metals (Kanayama means "metal mountain"). Another pair, Haniyasu-hiko and Haniyasu-hime, earth and clay deities, were born from her feces, and Mizuhanome, a female water deity, was born from her urine. The fact that Izanami's feces, urine, and vomit transformed into earth, water, and metal means they are not just soiled products but the conversion of the kami's vital energy. They possess various nutrients within themselves that become the raw material maintaining life and living. As Masuda Katsumi suggests, the narrative of the birth of these kami from Izanami's feces, urine, and vomit can also be considered to represent the formation of mountains through volcanic eruptions.[16]

Izanagi, grieving his wife's death, in a rage slashed Kagutsuchi to death. More kami were born from the blood that splashed from his sword. In death, Izanami passed to the land of Yomi. To this point she had been a kami of production, bestowing her vital force to give birth to large numbers of islands and various kami. When next she is seen in Yomi, she has become a deity of rage and destruction and portrayed as a fearful deity. When Izanagi, who had followed her to bring her back, saw the dreadful condition of her corpse, he fled. Izanami pursued him as far as the pass leading out of Yomi, where she cursed him, threatening to kill one thousand people every day in his land. She has made a complete switch: from being a kami of life, she has become a kami of death; from bestowing life, she strips it away. Her name was then changed to Yomitsu ōkami (the great kami of Yomi) or alternatively Chishiki no ōkami (etymology unclear). In this way Izanami became a central presence in the netherworld (the land of Yomi), with the power to govern both life and death. Her fearsome destructive power is evidenced in her curse to kill one thousand people every day.

Izanagi, having fled in fear of what he had witnessed, decided to cleanse himself of the pollution of Yomi and went to the Plain of Ahagi in Odo, at Tachibana in Hyūga, Tsukushi (Kyushu). As he let the water of the river flow over him, a kami called Amaterasu no ōmikami was born when he washed his left eye, a kami called Tsukiyomi no mikoto was born when he washed his right eye, and a kami called Susanoo no mikoto was born when he washed his nose. These are called the "three noble children" (*mihashira no uzu no miko/sankishi*). Izanagi charged Amaterasu to rule the High Plain of Heaven, Tsukiyomi to rule the realms of the night, and Susanoo to rule the oceans.

Susanoo, however, wept and howled, grieving for Izanami, and his weeping "caused the verdant mountains to wither and all the rivers and seas to dry up." Izanagi then expelled Susanoo to the land of Nenokatasu (Yomi). Susanoo visited the High Plain of Heaven to take leave of his sister Amaterasu. Declaring he had won a contest between them, he "raged with victory, breaking down the ridges between the rice paddies" and "defecated and strewed the feces about in the Hall of the First Fruits." His violent behavior did not stop there, and finally he skinned a pony "with a backward skinning" and flung the blood-soaked skin into the room where a heavenly weaving maiden was weaving the divine garments. She was startled and struck herself against the shuttle and died. Afraid of Susanoo's violence, Amaterasu went and shut herself up in the heavenly rock cave, sending the world into complete darkness. In their wisdom, the other kami decided to perform a *matsuri* to break the deadlock. They made mirrors and strings of *magatama* beads and set up a sacred space (*himorogi*) demarcated with *sakaki* branches. Ame no Koyane intoned a solemn liturgy, and Ame no Uzume, her sleeves and hair bound up with a vine and holding bundles of bamboo leaves in her hands, performed a sacred dance (*kagura*) in front of the rock cave, stamping her feet, exposing her breasts and genitals, and becoming possessed. She succeeded in luring Amaterasu out of the cave, and once again the heavenly realm was filled with light. In other words, Uzume had resurrected the sun deity, whose seclusion in the rock cave (a space also symbolizing the womb) implies symbolic death.

This is the basic story of the creation of the land that became Japan, how it was divided between the three children of Izanagi, and how Amaterasu was lured out of seclusion in the rock cave.

The beginning of ritual and the performing arts

We will note that Uzume's possession (*kamigakari*) represents a shamanic type of behavior, while her performance, called *wazaogi* in the texts, is that of a priest or ritualist. *Wazaogi*—which also means "actor"—pertained originally to dramatic ritual action to summon a kami. It was much later that it came to mean comic singing and dancing, or more broadly the performing arts, losing its shamanistic resonance. Uzume was both an actress and a dancer.

What is interesting about the Uzume myth is that when Uzume became possessed, all the kami who were there began to join in her dance. A tradition recorded in the early ninth-century *Kogoshūi*, containing the myths and history passed down to the Inbe clan, is that when Amaterasu appeared and illumined the surroundings, they cried out loudly with joy:

> *Ahare, ahare* (the sky is illuminated)
> *Ana omoshiro* (Ah, how delightful)
> *Ana tanoshi* (Ah, what joy)
> *Ana sayoke* (Ah, how refreshing is the sound of the breeze in the bamboo grass)
> *Oke* (The grasses and trees sway gently)[17]

The Uzume performance and the episode in which the sun deity was brought out of the cave is said to have been the beginning of *kagura* and to be the origin of both Japanese kami ritual and the performing arts. Interestingly, in the *Nihon shoki*, *kamigakari* (divine possession) is transcribed both as *wazaogi* (俳優) and *kamigakari* (顕神明之憑談), evidence that the acting profession, too, may trace its origins to divine possession.

Another myth cycle, which also involved Uzume, concerns the descent of Amaterasu's grandson Ninigi to rule the terrestrial realm (*tenson kōrin*). Uzume was one of the kami who accompanied Ninigi. At that time an indigenous deity called Sarutahiko ōkami stood at Amenoyachimata (the "eight crossroads of heaven"), the boundary between the heavenly and earthly realms, waiting to welcome and guide the heavenly kami. He was tall and long-nosed, his eyes glowed red, and he was very strong.

Ninigi and his retinue, seeing the fearsome-looking Sarutahiko blocking their way, sent Uzume, known as a deity who could face and overwhelm others, to inquire who he was. Like Sarutahiko, Uzume had an unusual feature, a malevolent glare, and so was not intimidated by his piercing gaze. Just as she had done at the rock cave, she bared her genitals and forced Sarutahiko to submit.

During the historical period that preceded the writing of the myths, baring the genitals was part of an essential ritual action called *tamafuri*, reinvigorating the spirit of the sun deity by shaking a ritual object or the ritualist's own body. Uzume's divine possession and genital-baring before the rock door of heaven may well be the mythological expression of the winter-solstice festival, celebrating the sun's rebirth.

Uzume's action can also be thought of as a ritual summoning another ancient sun deity. If so, it was her action that brought about the substitution of the old indigenous sun deity Sarutahiko with the new one, Amaterasu. This meeting could therefore symbolize the subjugation of one deity and the summoning of a new one.

Legend says that Uzume married Sarutahiko. Her descendants took Sarutahiko's name and were known as Sarume. They were a hereditary priestly clan responsible for dances and kami rituals.

Figure 2.1. Ame no Uzume. Takachiho Shrine, Miyazaki prefecture.

Figure 2.2. Sarutahiko. Takachiho Shrine, Miyazaki prefecture.

It is significant that in all the *Kojiki* and *Nihon shoki* accounts, it is only Sarutahiko who is described in any great detail. The *Nihon shoki*, for example, says, "He is over seven feet tall, his nose is seven hands long... and his eyes resemble eight-hand mirrors, shining brilliantly like red *hōzuki* [Chinese lantern plant]."[18] His mouth and posterior were bright red. There is no other instance in the official histories of a kami being described so specifically.

Particularly interesting is the appearance of the eyes. Two similes are used. The first is that they resemble red *hōzuki*. Exactly the same simile is used in the description of the eyes of Yamata no orochi, the great serpent with eight heads and eight tails killed by Susanoo. The second is that they shine like the "eight hand mirror" (*yata no kagami*) that symbolizes the spiritual power of Amaterasu. This mirror is the first of the three treasures, known as the three regalia of the ruling house. Such a description suggests that Sarutahiko possesses an awesome spiritual power similar to Yamata no orochi's and Amaterasu's, intimating that his nature is both monstrous and supremely divine.

Susanoo, Ōkuninushi, and Izumo

Another myth cycle ("land transfer," *kuniyuzuri*) concerns Susanoo, Ōkuninushi, and the province of Izumo. After Amaterasu reemerged from the cave, Susanoo was expelled from the High Plain of Heaven and went to Izumo. There he defeated the monstrous serpent Yamata no orochi, described as having bright red eyes, a body on which grew moss, cypress, and cedar, and a length spanning eight valleys; every year it devoured a young girl. It resembled the form of the great snake assumed by the kami of Mt. Ibuki to waylay the legendary hero Yamato Takeru.

Susanoo is a cultural hero. He composed a *tanka* about the palace he built at Suga. This appears in both the *Kojiki* and the *Nihon shoki* and has traditionally been regarded as the oldest Japanese poem.

> *Yakumo tatsu*
> *Izumo yaegaki*
> *Tsuma-gomi ni*
> *Yaegaki tsukuru*
> *Sono yaegaki o*

The many-fenced (*yaegaki*) palace of Izumo
Of the many clouds (*yakumo*) rising:

To dwell there with my wife
Do I build a many-fenced palace,
That many-fenced palace.[19]

All the same, Susanoo is probably the most violent and savage of all the kami appearing in Japanese myths. Besides Yamata no orochi, he killed the food deity Ōgetsuhime, angry at the thought she was polluting the food she offered him, which was produced from her mouth, nose, and rectum. Folklorist Orikuchi Shinobu (1887–1953) said that the nature of kami was both "cruel" and "innocent." However, when we consider that *chihayaburu* (powerful) is used as an epithet denoting the special quality of kami, Susanoo, filled with a ferocious energy, is a typical example of *chihayaburu*, even if he is wild and violent.

Susanoo's descendant is Ōkuninushi, enshrined at Izumo Taisha. The region of Izumo flourished during the Kofun (Tumulus) period (ca. 250–ca. 600), as is clear from archaeological discoveries at the Kōjindani site and others. It was the most important locus for the "kami of earth" (*kunitsukami*), in contrast to the "kami of heaven" (*amatsukami*) residing in the High Plain of Heaven or those who descended with Ninigi. The most important of those kami governing the myriad "kami of earth" was Ōkuninushi.

Ōkuninushi ("great-land-master") has numerous alternate names, such as Ōnamuji, Ashihara no shikoo, Yachihoko, and Utsushi kunitama. With the cooperation of the kami Sukunabikona, he worked at "firming the land" (*kunizukuri*), giving it shape. Later he transferred the land to the line of kami who had descended from heaven. This is taken up in the "transfer of the land" (*kuniyuzuri*) cycle of myths that represents a core component of Japanese mythology. Japan came into existence because of Ōkuninushi's transfer of the land, or to put it more broadly, because of the cooperation between the kami of heaven and the kami of earth. In return for his transferring the land, a grand shrine was built for Ōkuninushi in Izumo. This was Kitsuki (Izumo) Taisha.[20]

The size of the shrine is noteworthy. It was of a scale quite unexpected in shrine buildings. According to shrine tradition, the original structure was nearly 100 meters high (32 *jo*). Records from the time of its rebuilding in 1185 say the main shrine building was 48 meters (16 *jo*) in height. The present building, dating from 1744, is half that size, around 24 meters (8 *jo*). It thus kept decreasing in size over its history.

The first piece of physical evidence of the 1185 building to be found was part of the 48-meter pillar excavated on the Izumo shrine grounds in April 2000. It led credence to the legends surrounding the structure of the original shrine building. If lore indeed reflects fact, a vast building more than 100 meters high was built in ancient times. Why, though, was such a large shrine necessary? Perhaps the answer can be found in the same rationale that lay behind the building of the pyramids—that it was the mausoleum of sacred kings. A shrine venerating Ōkuninushi is one that honors the memory of, and extols, the "great kami," Ōkuninushi. The shrine building therefore must have had to be of a size in proportion to the greatness of the enshrined deity.

The final main cycle of myths recounted in the *Kojiki* and *Nihon shoki* concerns the exploits of Ninigi and his descendants in the terrestrial realm, ending with the eastward migration of Jinmu, the legendary first *tennō*. We will finish this section discussing the connection between Jinmu's spouse and the "kami of earth."

Symbolic union of heavenly and earthly kami

The consort of Jinmu is called Hototatara-isusuki hime and also Himetatara-isukeyori hime. She was the daughter of Ōmononushi no kami, identified by the *Nihon shoki* as Ōkuninushi's *sakimitama* (soul of blessing) and *kushimitama* (soul of auspiciousness).

Significant in the legend of Hototatara-isusuki hime is the first element of her name, *hoto*, an ancient word meaning "female genitals." Her mother, a beautiful woman called Seyadatara hime, was relieving herself over a stream one day when Ōmononushi, seeing her for the first time, transformed himself into a red-lacquered arrow, floated down the stream, and struck her genitals. Startled, she took the red arrow home and put it on display, when it suddenly transformed into a handsome man. The child born of their union was Hototatara-isusuki hime. The *hoto* of her name reflects that she was born as a result of the kami turning himself into an arrow and striking her mother in the genitals.

The myth, which is recorded in the *Kojiki*, is a curious one. Ōmononushi was the local deity of Yamato, which later became Japan's capital region. His daughter, who was thus half-human and half-divine, became the consort of the first ruler of Japan. By taking to wife the daughter of a Yamato kami, Jinmu, a descendant of heavenly kami, was able to unite the ancient state, religiously and ritually as well as politically. The marriage between descendants of kami of heaven and earth also signified the unification of heaven and earth, a unification that is symbolized by the element *hoto* in the woman's name. The woman bearing this name was both the child of the local deity and, like Uzume, a kami-worshipping shaman (*miko*).

The Coming of Buddhism to Japan

According to the *Nihon shoki*, Buddhism was officially introduced from the Korean kingdom of Paekche in 552.[21] At this time the capital (which moved with each sovereign) was located in the area around Mt. Miwa and Asuka. Two of the most powerful families in the capital at the time were the Soga and the Mononobe, and the policy over Buddhism set in motion a struggle between them, the Soga being pro-Buddhist and the Mononobe being anti-Buddhist. When Kinmei Tennō received a Buddhist statue from the king of Paekche, he asked his officials, among whom were members of both clans, whether it should be worshipped or not.

> Soga no Iname replied, "The many countries to the west all worship it. Can Japan alone refuse to do so?" But Mononobe no Okoshi and Nakatomi no Kamako together addressed the Sovereign saying, "Those who have ruled as kings over the world, over this our state, have always taken care to worship the 180 deities of heaven and earth in spring, summer, autumn and winter. If we were to change and worship a

foreign deity we fear we may incur the wrath of the deities of our own land." The Sovereign then declared, "It is fitting we give it to Soga no Imame who has expressed his desire. We shall ask him to worship it and see what results."

Later an epidemic afflicted the land. . . . Mononobe no Okoshi and Nakatomi no Kamako together addressed the Sovereign, saying, "This epidemic has occurred because our counsel went unheard. . . . Throw away the statue of the Buddha at once. . . . So the officials took the statue of the Buddha and threw it into the waters of the Naniwa canal. They then set fire to the temple in which it had been enshrined and burned it to the ground.[22]

The following year (553) Buddhism was mentioned again in a passage dated the fifth month.

A report was received. "The sound of Buddhist chants was heard coming from the sea at Chinu, in the district of Izumi in the province of Settsu. They echoed like the sound of thunder and a radiance shone like the brilliance of the sun." The Sovereign wondered at this and sent Unate no Atabe to investigate the matter. . . . [H]e discovered a large log of camphor-wood, shining brightly as it floated on the surface of the sea. He took it and presented it to the Sovereign, who ordered an artist to make two statues of the Buddha. These were installed in Yoshinodera.[23]

These were the first Buddhist images to be made in Japan. It is clear they were made in the context of the belief in mysterious sacred trees (such as camphor). The wondrous light and sound emitted by the floating log were probably thought to be manifestations of the *chihayaburu kami*. A "sacred tree" imbued with the presence of the kami was chosen as the fitting material to carve the first Buddhist statues made in Japan, since it already had spiritual and divine power dwelling within it.

In the second month of 584, the thirteenth year of the reign of Bidatsu (Kinmei's successor), an eleven-year-old girl became the first ordained Buddhist in Japan. She was Shima, the daughter of a retainer to Soga no Umako (Iname's son), who ordered the ordination. She took the religious name of Zenshin-ni, and Soga no Umako erected a temple in his dwelling for her. Why was it that the first person to be ordained was not a mature male or even a young adult but a young girl?

It is thought that this was done in imitation of the long-standing custom for the daughters of the royal and noble families to become *miko* and serve the kami, according to Shinto tradition. For example, a princess of the royal house served Amaterasu ōmikami at Ise as *itsukinomiya* (or *saigū*), and from the early ninth century one also served the kami of the Kamigamo and Shimogamo Shrines, the tutelary deities of Heian-kyō (Kyoto), as *saiin*. Similarly, powerful old shrines, such as Aso Jinja and Kasuga Taisha, selected shamanistic women from their sacerdotal lineages to serve the kami as "wife." Under the supervision of male priests like *negi* or *gūji*, such sacred young girls became the central ritual figures. The choice of a young girl as the first to be ordained as a Buddhist suggests that in those early days the Buddha was venerated with much the same mindset as were the kami.

Another illustration of the way Buddhism was received in Japan is the connection between the veneration of Buddha relics (*busshari* or simply *shari*) and beliefs surrounding rice. *Shari* originally referred to the cremated remains of Gautama Buddha, but in Japan the word also came to mean "rice." Even today, for example, vinegared rice for sushi is called *shari*. Japanese ideas about the grain spirit, the kami within the rice, seem to have merged here with beliefs surrounding relics.

In relation to the sovereigns' attitudes to Shinto and Buddhism, we have already referred (p. 16) to the statements in the *Nihon shoki* that "the Sovereign [Yōmei] had faith in the Buddhist Dharma (*buppō*) and revered Shinto" and "the Sovereign [Kōtoku] revered the Buddhist Dharma but scorned Shinto." Shinto was to be respected or venerated but was not the object of faith that Buddhism was. Kōtoku (r. 645–54) came to the throne sixty years after Yōmei at the time of the Taika reforms, when, in view of the statement in the *Nihon shoki*, Buddhism can be considered to have taken root at court. Buddhism had been steadily gaining ground, and at this point we find for the first time the situation where it was revered while Shinto was scorned.

The fusion of ideas and practices

One person who cannot be overlooked in a discussion of the history of the relations between kami and buddhas is Prince Shōtoku (572–622). He became regent for his aunt, Suiko Tennō (r. 592–628), in 593 and was a key figure in the creation of a centralized state around Buddhism and the sovereign. As regent, he instigated wide-ranging political and religious reforms, at the root of which was Buddhism. At the same time, while preserving the Buddhist spirit, he introduced Confucian ethical concepts, social rules and procedures, and a social system, and, envisioning a religious state incorporating all, he grafted them onto the kami-kami combinatory Shinto structure. According to the *Nihon shoki*, he compiled a number of historical works, such as the (now non-extant) *Kokki* (National Record) and *Tennōki* (Record of the Sovereigns). In 607, he dispatched envoys to China, then newly unified under the Sui dynasty (581–618), with the aim of differentiating Japan's position among the countries of sinocentric East Asia.

The *Nihon shoki* offers an interesting account of Shōtoku's life, although perhaps not everything should be taken at face value. Here he is portrayed as building the foundations of Japanese religious culture. This was because he himself had a good understanding of the shamanistic phenomena that are at the root of Shinto. The *Nihon shoki* records that he had the ability to foresee the future, saying "He knew beforehand what was going to happen."[24]

There was in earlier times a shamanistic woman who had the same ability to foresee the future, according to the *Nihon shoki*.[25] Her name was Yamato-totohimomoso-hime and she was a wife of Ōmononushi no kami. The fact that Shōtoku had the same ability as one of the greatest shamans in the ancient world means that he, too, had those shamanistic abilities that were an important element in supplicating the kami.

The *Nihon shoki* continues, stating that in addition to this intuitive knowledge, Shōtoku studied both the "Inner Doctrine" (Buddhism and Buddhist sutras) and the "Outer Classics" (Confucianism), the foremost knowledge of the day, and it was on the basis of this understanding that he carried out his political and religious reforms.

His basic idea that "harmony is to be cherished and an avoidance of wanton opposition to be honored"[26] is well expressed in the Seventeen Article Code of 604, which is attributed to him. He planned the unification of the country around the concepts of harmony and sovereign (*tennō*) to create a centralized and peaceful state based on the spirit of Buddhism. The code was laid out as the ideology for a state with a high spiritual level and also as the foundation for the political structure of that state. The second injunction was, "Sincerely revere the Three Treasures: the Buddha, the Dharma, and the Sangha." Shōtoku saw Buddhism as an extremely important new framework for national unification. Without it, people's minds would not be composed. He considered that Shinto and Confucianism alone were too weak to give that support. Confucianism wanted to regulate people's conduct through morality, but ethics alone would be insufficient for reforming and deepening people's consciousness, which Buddhism had the power to do. The Code extolled the Three Treasures as "the last resorts of humankind [and] pillars of faith in every realm."[27] With Buddhism as the foundation, true peace ("harmony") could be achieved.

For Shōtoku, who had witnessed the in-fighting among the clans, it was not enough to build peace by regulating society with an underlying ethical code. It was more important to provide a spiritual core, namely, that of Buddhism. This idea remained strong and became the mainstream of Japanese religious culture. The mutual existence of the three teachings of Buddhism, Confucianism, and Shinto, which continues today, was a spiritual infrastructure laid down by Shōtoku.

The cap-rank system in twelve grades was enacted in 603. It was so called because the color and decoration of the caps worn by officials indicated their rank. The ranks were named virtue, humaneness, propriety, sincerity, righteousness, and wisdom (the latter five being the cardinal virtues of Confucianism) and were divided according to greater and lesser grades. Shōtoku hoped that this would encourage the appointment of talented people, with officials being assigned according to ability, mentality, virtue, moral and personal character, disposition, and the content of the work, not according to family standing or faction.

These reforms were too radical, however, and aroused violent resistance from the powerful families, led by the Soga. Shōtoku found himself isolated, and his reforms collapsed. After his death, his family was annihilated, and all his records were burned.

In contrast to Prince Shōtoku's activities in the public sphere, En no Ozuno (634?–706?), the "founder" of Shugendō, attempted to formulate a magico-religious system based on an eclectic approach to religious training. In the course of the Heian period (794–1185), En no Ozuno became known familiarly as En no Gyōja (En the Ascetic) and in 1799, he was given the *shigō* (posthumous title) of Jinben Daibosatsu by Kōkaku Tennō, more than a thousand years after his exile to Izu.

An early biographical account of him is found in Tale 28 in the first volume of the *Nihon ryōiki* (Record of Miraculous Events in Japan, ca. 822), entitled "On Learning the Dharani of the Peacock King and Thereby Gaining Extraordinary Power to Become a Saint and Fly to Heaven in This Life." Here he is referred to as En no Ubasoku.[28]

> E[n] no Ubasoku was of the Kamo no Enokimi family, presently the Takakamo no asomi family. He came from the village of Chihara, in the district of Upper Kazuraki in Yamato province. He was wise by nature, he studied widely, and had attained ultimate knowledge [the One]. He put his faith in the Three Treasures of Buddhism and made this his life work.... [W]hen he was in his forties and growing old, he

> went to live in a cave, wore vines, ate pinecones, bathed in the fresh spring water, and thus washed away the dirt of the world of desire. He practiced the dharani of the Peacock King Sutra and, in this way, gained extraordinary arts and powers. So he was able to command devils and kami and make them do his will. Once he summoned all of them and said, "Build me a bridge between the peaks of Kane no mitake and Kazuraki no mitake in the land of Yamato. They were perplexed by this. In the reign of the Sovereign who resided at the Fujiwara Palace [Monmu, r. 607–700], Hitokotonushi no Ōkami of Kazuraki no mitake was possessed and slandered him, saying, "E[n] no Ubasoku plans to overthrow the Sovereign." The Sovereign gave orders that he be seized, but because of his magical powers this was not easy to do. Therefore they seized his mother instead. To save his mother, he gave himself up. He was exiled to the islands of Izu. . . . In the daytime, he obeyed the Sovereign's orders and remained on the islands, but at night he went to the heights of Mt. Fuji in Suruga to practice his art.[29]

His historicity is confirmed by an account of his exile to the Izu peninsula in 699 in the *Shoku Nihongi* (Chronicles of Japan, Continued; 794,797).

> En no kimi Ozunu was banished to the peninsula of Izu. Originally he had lived in the Katsuragi mountains and had been reputed as an adept in magic. His student Karakuni no muraji Hirotari slandered him . . . and he was banished to a far-away place. It was said . . . that he often commanded spirits to draw water and to gather firewood for him. If they did not obey his orders, he bound them with magic. (Monmu 3.5.24)[30]

There are many mysteries about En no Gyōja. It is said he secluded himself in the Yoshino mountains to undertake religious austerities but that after the incident related above people were forbidden to practice in the mountains, since the state feared that anti-establishment elements could gain both military force and spiritual power in these isolated places and wanted to prevent a second or third En no Gyōja from appearing.

What were the distinctive features of En no Gyōja's religion? This is not easy to ascertain from the ancient texts. However, he was thought to be a member of the Takakamo family of Katsuragi in Yamato, an old family of ritualists that possessed a legend that their ancestor was a great crow (*yatagarasu*). The *Shinsen shōjiroku* (Newly Compiled Records of Kinship Groups, ca. 815) notes in the section on *agatanushi* (district chieftains) of Kamo that when Kamu-yamato Iware-biko no mikoto (another name for Jinmu Tennō, the first ruler of the land) wanted to go to the Middle Land (*nakatsukuni*) he became lost in the precipitous mountains. At that time, Kamo no Taketsunomi, the grandson of the Izumo kami Kamimusubi no mikoto, transformed himself into a huge crow and flew above Jinmu to guide him so that he was able to reach the Middle Land. Jinmu was greatly pleased and in gratitude awarded Kamo no Taketsunomi the title of "Yatagarasu."

This episode also appears in the *Kogoshūi*, which states that "Yatagarasu, ancestor of the lords of Kamo no agata, came in the form of a crow and served to guide [Jinmu on] his progress through the rugged Uda mountains."[31] Guiding the progress (*idemashi*) refers to the conducting of spirits or the monarch. Here Yatagarasu is identified as the distant ancestor of the district chiefs of Kamo, a name that was anciently given the character of "wild duck" (*kamo*), a word that is thought to share an etymology with *kami* (*kamu, kamo*), that is, "deity." Literally, the name "Kamo no Taketsunomi" means "one with the body of a strong wild duck [*kamo*]." Since the "body of a duck" was equally the "body of a kami," it had the power and vigor of a *chihayaburu kami*. Further, *yata* is a word expressing greatness and nobility. Thus *yatagarasu* means a crow with mighty divine power. The *yatagarasu* legend is perhaps a vestige of shamanic journeys in the form of a bird or perhaps of totemism, with a bird serving as the clan's tutelary spirit.

The *yatagarasu* plays an important role in two ritual events at the shrine of Nachi Taisha in Kumano: the secret rite called "welcoming the water" held early in the morning of January 1, and the *ōgihome* rite performed during the fire festival held on July 14. The first welcomes the spirit of the New Year and marks the renewal of life. The deputy chief priest (*gongūji*), wearing a hat shaped like a *yatagarasu*, goes to a sacred spring at three in the morning and draws water from it. At the time of the Nachi fire festival, the chief priest (*gūji*), wearing a *yatagarasu* mask, stands at the base of the great waterfall of Nachi, the receptacle of the kami (*shintai*), and repeatedly strikes the mirrors that decorate twelve large *ōgi mikoshi* (portable shrines) and symbolize the sun. This has the meaning of instilling a new spirit (*tamashii*) into them. The *yatagarasu* performs the role of creator, breathing the spirit of life into water and fire.

As mentioned, *yatagarasu* corresponds to Kamo no Taketsunomi, who was descended both from kami and a human being and had the supernatural power to transform himself into a "huge crow." This portrayal seems to apply equally to En no Gyōja, who could control spirits and kami and fly through the sky. En no Gyōja may thus represent the realignment of a *yatagarasu*-type myth through the introduction of Buddhist and Daoist asceticism. Was he perhaps the descendant of the mountain folk and the *kunitsukami* who had long lived in the Japanese archipelago? His religious practices incorporated new Daoist and Buddhist (especially esoteric) elements on a foundation of the animistic, shamanistic, and totemistic religious culture that had come down from ancient times.

When En no Gyōja prayed for a tutelary deity while undertaking austerities on Sanjōgatake (Mt. Kinpu), Zaō Gongen and Benzaiten appeared before him and were enshrined respectively in the Zaō Hall on the summit of Sanjōgatake, which became the most important site of Ōmine Shugendō, and on Mt. Misen. Zaō Gongen, revered as the main deity of Shugendō, is a distinctive visual representation of the fusion of traditional Japanese ideas about the kami and features of buddhas, bodhisattvas, and other divinities from Buddhism. The statue portrays the deity standing, right leg raised in a dynamic pose suggesting the figure is leaping into the sky or alighting on earth (see cover image). This pose is a good example of a superb fusion of the figure of a kami and the plastic arts of Buddhist images. It has one head, three eyes, and two arms. The right hand, raised to head level, holds a three-pronged *vajra*, an esoteric religious tool; the left hand, held near the hip, forms the sword mudra. The left foot rests on the rock that welled up out of the earth on Sanjōgatake. It is an image that does not appear in any Buddhist scriptural source and is thought therefore to be a distinctively Japanese deity.

Other versions exist of the deities who emerged in answer to En no Gyōja's prayers. The *En no Gyōja emaki* describes how En no Gyōja secluded himself on Sanjōgatake and prayed for a deity to appear who could save all deluded sentient beings. Three divinities appeared: Śākyamuni, the Thousand-Armed Kannon (Avalokiteśvara), and Miroku (Maitreya). En no Gyōja prayed again, wanting a stronger deity to appear to protect a place of severe ascetic training. Thereupon the fierce-aspected Zaō Gongen manifested himself. It is said that En no Gyōja himself carved an image of this deity from a piece of cherry wood. Shrine traditions at Tenkawa Daibenzaiten Shrine, near Yoshino, say that the first to appear was Benzaiten (Sarasvatī),

Figure 2.3. Tenkawa Daibenzaiten Shrine. Photo by Yano Tatehiko.

but the ascetic considered her too gentle to be able to quell demons and protect a site of religious training, and prayed for a stronger one. Next appeared Jizō, a bodhisattva of compassion and salvation, but the deity was considered too mild. Rejected, Jizō flew to a place called Kawakami, where a hall was built for him. En no Gyōja prayed again for a deity fitting to be the protector of this place of severe training, and then with a loud clap of thunder, the figures of a wrathful buddha burst out surrounded by raging flames. This buddha/kami is said to be Zaō Gongen.

The three images of Zaō Gongen enshrined in the Zaō Hall of the temple of Kinpusenji in Yoshino are seven meters tall, some of the largest in Japan, and they exhibit great power. They are "secret buddhas" (*hibutsu*) only shown at certain times. They are a manifestation of the furious energy of the *chihayaburu kami*, the great natural life force, and express both the power to quell demons and the compassion to save living beings. Zaō Gongen represents a unique combination of the gods of antiquity with the newly arrived Buddhism and of mountain beliefs and practices that later led to the amalgam that was Shugendō.

Shinto and Buddhism for protection of the state

The seventh and eighth centuries were a time of great change in Japanese religious culture. The *ritsuryō* administrative system, with the *tennō* and Buddhism at its core, went on to become a very Japanese form of government, different from the political system and structure of authority in China and from ruling systems found on the Korean peninsula. New ideas from abroad were grafted onto a foundation made up of the vestiges of the ancient tribal and village headman (*shuchō*) systems and consolidated to form the ancient *tennō* and *ritsuryō* systems.

In 694 a capital called Fujiwara-kyō was built in Yamato, near present-day Kashihara in Nara prefecture, and in 710, a permanent capital called Heijōkyō was established in what is now Nara. The court culture of the period, known as Tenpyō culture, flourished under the influences from the continent brought back by official envoys sent to Tang China. Buddhism, as the protector of the state, was absorbed into state policy. In 741, Shōmu Tennō (r. 724–49) ordered the establishment of a network of provincial temples called *kokubunji* with the temple Tōdaiji at their center. The construction of the Great Buddha (*daibutsu*) of Tōdaiji, consecrated in 752, was a symbolic event in this national project. A state enterprise, it subscribed to the idea of state protection (*chingo kokka*) by Buddhist divinities.

However, the country continued to be unsettled, as court rivalries brought tensions to the fore. When Shōmu died in 756, his daughter Kōken, who had succeeded him on his retirement in 749, came under increasing pressure and was forced to abdicate in 758. She later regained control and reascended the throne as Shōtoku in 764. In 769, her favorite, the priest Dōkyō (700–72), received an oracle from Usa Hachiman that proclaimed he would become the next sovereign. The court official Wake no Kiyomaro (733–99), sent to investigate, received a second oracle that discredited the first. Stymied, Shōtoku died the following year. Also in 769, two princesses, Oshisaka and Ishida, schemed to place Shikeshimaro, the son of Prince Shioyaki, on the throne. Prince Shioyaki had been executed five years earlier when the rebel Fujiwara no Nakamaro (706–64) had declared him *tennō*, after placing a curse on Shōtoku. According to the *Shoku Nihongi*, they placed a lock of her hair into a skull taken from the Saho River and recited a killing curse over it. In 772, when Kōnin (r. 770–81) had succeeded Shōtoku, his consort, Princess Igami, daughter of Shōmu, was accused of practicing magical arts to have her son declared crown prince and was stripped of her position.

It was during this period that the Fujiwara clan began amassing the great power that saw it dominate Japanese political life down to the twelfth century and even beyond. In 669, just before his death, Nakatomi no Kamatari, who with the later Tenji Tennō had instigated the Taika reforms in 645, was granted the family name of Fujiwara. His son Fuhito (659–720) was a powerful member of the courts of Jitō (r. 686–97) and Monmu (r. 697–707), and his daughter, who later became known as Kōmyō, was the consort of Shōmu

(r. 724–49). As mentioned above, their daughter succeeded Shōmu as Kōken Tennō (r. 749–58) and again as Shōtoku Tennō (r. 765–70). Fuhito's four sons in turn established branch families of the Fujiwara.[32]

The Fujiwara, by providing the sovereign with consorts, held political power as the maternal relatives of the royal clan, and during the Heian period monopolized the position of regent (*sesshō*). Though the *tennō* was the nominal head of this centralized state system, for most of the period between the eighth and twelfth centuries real power was wielded by leading nobles, mostly by one family or another within the Fujiwara clan but also, when Fujiwara influence temporarily waned, by others such as the Tachibana clan or talented individuals like Sugawara no Michizane (845–903). Thus, while as far as appearances were concerned the *tennō* house was the central body of the state, it was the Fujiwara clan behind the scenes that was dominant, not only politically but genetically; it was their blood that ran the thickest in the royal lineage, since after the eighth century it provided generation after generation of daughters or adopted daughters as consorts to the reigning sovereign or royal princes. The royal house and the Fujiwara clan were two sides of the same coin, complementing one another. In essence, this has continued down to the present.

The Fujiwara were thus closely connected with the fundamental makeup of Japanese politics, as is clear, for example, from their involvement with the compilation of the official histories, which reflect the Fujiwara perception of history. Though the *Nihon shoki* was presented to the throne in the name of Prince Toneri, Fujiwara no Fuhito was probably in charge of the actual editing, and all the other official histories were certainly edited by members of the Fujiwara clan: Fujiwara Tsugutada (*Shoku Nihongi*, 797), Fujiwara Otsugu (*Nihon kōki*, 840), Fujiwara Yoshifusa (*Shoku Nihon kōki*, 869), Fujiwara Yoshitsune (*Nihon Montoku Tennō jitsuroku*, 879), and Fujiwara Tokihira (*Nihon sandai jitsuroku*, 901).

Prince Shōtoku's ideas about combining Shinto, Confucianism, and Buddhism were in one sense passed on, through the authority of the Fujiwara clan and others following the Taika Reforms. However, in another sense they were distorted, since the essential part of the reforms was forgotten and only the outer form remained. This outer form was the Shinto of the *ritsuryō* period, whose framework was, from one point of view, an extremely advantageous system for the Nakatomi/Fujiwara clan.

CHAPTER THREE

The New Buddhism of the Heian Period

In 781, Kōnin's son Kanmu (r. 781–806) came to the throne. Three years later he shifted his capital to Nagaoka-kyō and then in 794 to Heian-kyō (now Kyoto). He looked to a new type of Buddhism to protect the state that relied neither on magic nor on the scholasticism of the Nara schools of Buddhism. The new Buddhism was provided by two of the greatest figures both in that turbulent period whose influence extended to later periods of Japanese religious history, Saichō (767–822) and Kūkai (774–835). They were the engineers who constructed the foundations and fashioned the framework of Japan's religious culture.

Saichō, founder of the Tendai school

Saichō was the founder of Tendai Buddhism. Seeking its independence as a separate Buddhist school, he composed the *Sange gakushō shiki* (Regulations for Students of the Mountain School; hereafter *Regulations*) and worked to obtain permission for a Mahāyāna precepts platform to be built at his temple of Enryakuji on Mt. Hiei, northeast of Kyoto.[1] In particular, his early selection of Mt. Hiei as the site of his temple speaks of his awareness of geomantic principles, since the mountain guarded the capital from the inauspicious northeast direction (*kimon*). His Buddhist practice incorporated four teaching sources: the Lotus Sutra of the Chinese Tiantai school, esoteric Buddhism (Taimitsu), Zen and the precepts. In the twelfth and thirteenth centuries Tendai became the seedbed for a number of movements that opened up new horizons in Japanese Buddhism, including the Pure Land school of Shinran, the Zen of Yōsai and Dōgen, and the Lotus (Hokke) school of Nichiren.

In 818, Saichō wrote in his *Regulations*, "What is the treasure of the nation? It is our religious nature (*dōshin*). Thus those who have this religious nature are the treasures of the nation."[2] Here the "religious nature" is itself a "treasure." Saichō made it mandatory that trainee priests devote themselves wholeheartedly to their training by not leaving the mountain for twelve years. Such a method certainly looked to the future. As a result of Saichō's manifesto, Mt. Hiei became one of the main centers of learning in the world. Though the religious community on the mountain later declined, giving itself over to violence with the employment of *sōhei* (monastic warriors) and torn by in-fighting, it had the ability to criticize the situation that rose from within the mountain and the power to change and transcend it. Many such critics left Mt. Hiei and launched new, popular movements for propagating Buddhist teachings.

Saichō and Kūkai both went to China on the same embassy in 804. Saichō went as a short-term scholar (*gengakushō*) to Mt. Tiantai in Zhejiang province; he studied Tiantai doctrine under Daosui (n.d.) and Xingman (n.d.), Chan (Zen) under Shunian (n.d.), and the esoteric teachings under Shunxiao (n.d.). He received bodhisattva ordination with the Mahāyāna precepts from Daosui before returning to Japan the following year. In 806 his Tendai (Japanese form of Tiantai) school was formally recognized by the government, and he was allowed two "yearly ordinands" (*nenbun dosha*), one to study the meditation course (Shikangō) and one to study the tantric course (Shanagō).

Saichō became involved in a doctrinal dispute with the Hossō priest Tokuitsu (780?–842?) over the provisionality or ultimate truth of the One and Three Vehicles. This concerned the universality, or not, of the buddha-nature. Tokuitsu had authored a work called *Busshōshō* (Tract on the Buddha-nature), which discussed the Hossō doctrine that asserted that there were five different types of sentient beings: those predestined to become bodhisattvas, those predestined to become pratyekabuddhas, those predestined to become arhats, an indeterminate group, and those inherently unable to attain buddhahood (*icchantika*). Tokuitsu therefore asserted that the Three Vehicles (bodhisattva, pratyekabuddha, and arhat) were "real" (able to carry living beings to salvation), criticizing Saichō's claim that the One Vehicle of the Lotus Sutra allowed all to attain buddhahood. Saichō refuted this in a number of works, including the *Shōgon jikkyō* (Mirror Illuminating the Provisional and the True, 817), the *Hokke kowaku* (Vanquishing Misunderstandings about the Lotus, 818), the *Shugo kokkaishō* (Essays on Protecting the Nation, 818), the *Ketsugon jitsuron* (Determining the Provisional and the True, 820), and the *Hokke shūku* (Elegant Words Concerning the Lotus Sutra, 821). Here he upheld the salvific power of the One Vehicle on the basis of the view that all beings, without exception, are endowed with the buddha-nature. What buddha-nature is and how to attain buddhahood are closely connected and are the fundamental questions that have resonated through the history of Japanese Buddhism. Are only some able to become buddhas, or, as held by the Tendai theory of Original Enlightenment (*hongaku*), are all living beings able to do so because they inherently possess the buddha-nature? Or is buddhahood attained in this very body (*sokushin jōbutsu*) through the practice of the three mysteries (*sanmitsu kaji*), the union of the practitioner's body, speech, and mind with those of the deity, as taught in Kūkai's esoteric Buddhism?

Saichō was also the author of the *Kenkairon* (Treatise on the Precepts, 819) and the *Naishō buppō sōjō kechimyakufu* (Transmission Lineage of the Dharma of Inner Realization). Tokuitsu, who asserted that there were three different kinds of attainment, also sought out Kūkai's opinions, but Kūkai did not respond. The debate between Tokuitsu and Saichō was not resolved in their lifetimes; it was brought to an end by his students after Saichō's death, who declared victory. Nevertheless, questions remained, and these contributed to the later development of Tendai doctrine and were a driving force in the production of ideas about Original Enlightenment and of the so-called new Buddhism of the Kamakura period.

Kūkai and the Shingon school

Whereas Saichō laid out his *Regulations* and worked to establish an independent Mahāyāna precepts platform on Mt. Hiei, Kūkai engaged in wide-ranging religious and cultural activities from his bases at Kongōbuji on Mt. Kōya and at Tōji in Kyoto. In 828, he founded an academy called the Shugei Shuchiin (literally, academy for the study of the various forms of scholarship and knowledge) within the residence of Fujiwara no Mimori in Kyoto for the education of ordinary people, saying in its regulations, "The prosperity and decline of things depend on the people concerned, and the rise and fall of people depend on the Way [they follow]." This was in the winter of his fifty-fourth year.

Kūkai had entered the state academy, the Daigakuryō, in the capital Heijō-kyō, when he was eighteen, but soon left, disliking the aristocratic bias of the students there. He was something of an outsider, and became a self-ordained mendicant practicing the Ākāśgarbha ritual for gaining perfect recall (*Kokūzō gumonjihō*). He knew better than anyone the problems with the advanced education of the time. The Daigakuryō was the official educational institution for training

Figure 3.1. Kongōbuji Temple. Photo by Yano Tatehiko.

students from the higher ranks of the aristocracy for the upper echelons of government service. Provincial institutions also existed to educate the sons of local officials, so these, too, were rank based. The curriculum in all these schools was devoted to the Confucian classics. Kūkai burned with the idea of a broader education without regard to social rank, and the curriculum of his Shugei Shuchiin, therefore, included not just Confucianism but also Buddhism and Daoism, as well as training in technical subjects. Lacking adequate backing, however, the school closed ten years after Kūkai died. His dream of a center of learning that would last hundreds of years was unfortunately not realized.

Mt. Kōya continues today as the center of the Shingon school. We can get a sense of how different it was from Mt. Hiei by considering the eminent figures who emerged from the two Buddhist centers. Comparing Kūkai and Saichō individually, Kūkai would probably seem the greater in terms of the breadth and intensity of his activities. Nevertheless, looking at the twelve hundred years since their deaths, Saichō would likely loom larger than Kūkai in terms of the people who have emerged from their respective legacies. Saichō had a clear vision of the future, as seen from the statement in his *Regulations for Students of the Mountain School* that "those who have this religious nature are the treasures of the nation," leading to the emergence of such religious luminaries as Hōnen, Shinran, Dōgen, Yōsai, and Nichiren from Mt. Hiei.

Like En no Gyōja, Kūkai had an intense interest in magico-religious practices, and he developed these during his ascetic training as a young man in the mountains and valleys of Shikoku and other places. Born the son of a provincial official named Saeki in Sanuki province, Kūkai was known as Mao during his childhood. Normally, the son of a low-ranking provincial official was unable to enter the Daigakuryō, but a maternal uncle, Ato no Ōtari, was a Confucian scholar who was a tutor at court. This connection allowed Kūkai to enter the academy, albeit three years later than normal (usually students entered the academy at the age of fifteen). There he studied the Chinese classics. He was surrounded by sons of high-ranking members of the nobility who were younger than he was. Even if they did not study, they would be assigned high official positions after graduation and advance through life with little effort on their part. But what did Kūkai's future look like? Unable to bear studying with the young aristocrats, he dropped out after a year. At nineteen he went into the Yoshino mountains and then went from place to place in Shikoku practicing the *Kokūzō gumonjihō*, an esoteric ritual whose purpose is, on completion, to be able to memorize all the sutras. It involves repeating the mantra of the bodhisattva Ākāśagarbha (Kokūzō) — "Nōbō Akashakyaraba on arikyara mari bori sowaka" — one million times. Kūkai later wrote that he practiced at Mt. Tairyū in Awa, at Cape Muroto in Tosa, Mt. Kinpu in Yoshino, and Mt. Ishizuchi in Shikoku, among others. The practice had much in common with the asceticism of En no Gyōja. It is thought that during his time in the mountains, Kūkai increased his contacts with local mountain people and with networks of metal workers mining veins of mercury. His selection to join the 804 embassy to China was possibly due to the support of the immigrant Hata clan, the Fujiwara clan, and technical experts in various fields.

Saichō, by contrast, went to China for one year as a government-supported, short-term scholar (*gengakushō*). He had been officially ordained in 780 and received full ordination on the precepts platform at Tōdaiji in 785. He was thus a full-fledged member of official Nara Buddhism and could look forward to a promising future as a religious reformer. As a leading light among Buddhists of the new era, he came to the attention of Kanmu Tennō, who consulted him about the situation of Buddhism in Japan. Kūkai's career was quite different: he was a hard-working student who had dropped out of the state academy after a year to become a self-ordained ascetic, felt more at home in the mountains and along the sea, and was officially ordained only a few months before his departure for China. The time of Kūkai and Saichō was quite a dramatic interlude in the history of Japanese religion.

Kūkai lived most of his life in the shadows, in a sense, working behind the scenes and relying on unofficial networks. His involvement with esoteric Buddhism increased the mystique that surrounded him. The lack of clarity around his entry to the academy, the eleven years following his leaving it, the reasons behind his visit to China, and the nature of his death (*nyūjō*)[3] all lent strength to the mystery. A certain amount of money must have been required to enter the school, and political influence must also have played a part. Yet Kūkai appeared out of nowhere into the backstage of history. Who pushed Kūkai forward in this way? Was it Kūkai himself? Was there someone behind him?

Kūkai was self-ordained,[4] unlike Saichō, who was an official priest, and again unlike Saichō, who went to China as a government-funded student, Kūkai went as a *ryūgakushō* (long-term student) with the expectation that he would stay twenty years to study Buddhism. However, he returned just fifteen months later, having received the final stage of esoteric transmission (*denpō kanjō*) from Huiguo (746–805), the tantric master, in Chang'an. He was not permitted to return at once to Heian-kyō (Kyoto), which had become the capital in 794, instead spending the next three years in Dazaifu (Kyushu) in confined circumstances.

On his eventual return to Kyoto in 809, Kūkai settled at Takao-sanji, northwest of the capital. Gradually the importance of the sutras, texts, commentaries, and other items he had brought back from China, as well as the teachings of the tantric tradition (later to be termed Shingon) that he had succeeded to, became known. He wrote in his *Shōrai mokuroku* (Inventory of Imported Items, 806), "Going with nothing, I came back fully enriched." Saichō, too, was very interested in the texts Kūkai had brought from China, and in 812 he asked Kūkai for an esoteric initiation and sent his student Taihan (778–837) to study the esoteric doctrines under him. However, Taihan eventually refused to return to Saichō and stayed with Kūkai. The tension between Saichō and Kūkai is apparent in a letter (known as *Fūshinjō*) sent by Kūkai. Saichō had borrowed texts concerning mantras and *siddhām* (Sanskrit letters), as well as the *Avataṣaka-sūtra*, and he further asked to borrow and copy Amoghavajra's commentary on the *Rishukyō* (*Prajñāpāramitā-naya-sūtra*; Path to the Truth Sutra, 243). Kūkai refused, saying that it was a text that required personal instruction and that actual practice was more important than writing and copying. Saichō broke off his relationship with Kūkai and their correspondence ceased.

Kūkai stood out among young intellectuals of his day for his systematic scholarship and powers of expression. His *Sangō shiiki* (Indications of the Goals of the Three Teachings; hereafter, *Three Teachings*), a fictional work written in 797 when he was in his mid-twenties, is clear evidence of his talents. Having betrayed his relatives' expectations by dropping out of the Daigakuryō and becoming a self-ordained priest, Kūkai poured into the work his earnest assessment of the three major ways of thought, together with his resolution and determination. It expresses his disillusionment with the government that had evolved under Prince Shōtoku's cap-rank system and the lack of opportunity for people outside the established elite to learn and grow. Where could a person go where ability alone would be valued?

Here, Kūkai fastened his gaze on Buddhism. The Buddhist world offered prospects, since intelligence and character were evaluated in terms of a person's knowledge and the power attained through religious training. Was Kūkai attracted to Buddhism not only for its philosophy but because the undesirable practices associated with an emphasis on family background did not yet extend to it? He must also have been well aware of priests like Genbō (d. 746) and Dōkyō (d. 772) who had held power at court as a result of royal patronage and then lost it.

Intelligence is what evaluates knowledge, but in the past, even as today, it was not easy to set due value on an eminent intellectual. In the Buddhist world, talent had the clearest currency in what is called the power of the Dharma (*hōriki*). It is possible to judge immediately the effectiveness of *hōriki*, the power displayed in magico-religious rites. Even if people do not understand it, they feel awe in its presence and so evaluate its effectiveness. This is a matter of spiritual power, rather than scholarship. It is a magical Buddhism of ritual practice, rather than an intellectual Buddhism that is an object of study—in other words, it is esoteric Buddhism.

By the end of the eighth century, some practices of esoteric Buddhism had begun to penetrate among the people. The goal of such practices was the healing of sickness and predicting future events through magical rituals, performed by popular Buddhist practitioners in answer to people's secular needs. The fact that Kūkai decided to throw himself in among such popular practitioners as a self-ordained priest rather than become an official priest tells of the degree of his misgivings and distrust of the "official" system. It was no good becoming an official priest, for the official priesthood was one of scholasticism and aristocratic cliques. It was among the self-ordained priests that *hōriki* lay.

How much were Kūkai's ideas and actions comprehended by his relatives? They must have been disappointed and angry, given the expectations they had had of him. Undaunted, he went against those expectations; for eleven years, far from the forefront of society, he constantly and persistently pursued both learning and practice. Did Huiguo immediately recognize the degree and intensity of this training when he met Kūkai for the first time at the Qinglong Temple? And did Kūkai perhaps acquire initiation to transmit the teachings by the free use of the funds at his disposal?

Kūkai's Rebellion and Commitment

There can be no doubt that Kūkai had been stung over and over by discrimination because of his low-ranking provincial origin. His attitude to the capital and the nobility can be seen as deriving from his entry to, and withdrawal from, the Daigakuryō. The *Three Teachings* reveals this tension in both style and content and was possibly born of the rebellion and commitment he felt at this time. The story starts with a criticism of Confucianism and the social system that underpinned it, continues with an invitation to the profundity of Daoism by Kyōbu, and ends with the argument in support of Buddhism by Kamei Kōji. Its three-part structure shows skillful development, and the young Kūkai's understanding of society, intellectual judgment, and statement of intentions give the work a masterly tension.

In the first section, describing the argument of the Confucianist, Tokaku, the host, asks the Confucian scholar Kimō to point out the errors of Tokaku's nephew Shitsuga, a profligate youth who "disgraced his father and elder brothers and in his arrogance humiliated well-learned elders," in order to bring him back to the right path. Why did Kūkai begin with a discussion on ethics?

Kūkai's description in the third section of Kamei Kōji, a mendicant priest so slovenly in appearance that villagers chased him away, is almost certainly a self-portrait. "His shaven head was like a round tray of copper, and his ashen face like an earthenware pot.... [H]is legs were long like those of a heron standing near a pond, and his sinewy short neck resembled that of a turtle in the mud.... He had a crooked nose [and] deep eye sockets." Such was his appearance that "if by chance he entered the market place, people showered him with pieces of tile and pebbles."[5] However, when he began to speak of the Dharma, his voice was clear and ringing, like a jewel. "Shaken, [the rings on] his golden staff tinkled; directed, his jewel-like voice resounded." Kamei Kōji composed four poems, "Lamentation," "Transciency," "The Ocean of Birth-Death," and "Clarifying the Three Teachings." They were "a golden staff" and "a jewel-like voice," full of the power of words (*kotodama*) and the Dharma (*hōriki*). Hearing it, Tokaku and the others were overwhelmed by the words and the discourse and became choked with tears; they promised faithfully to commit themselves to the Buddhist Way.

Three Teachings is a rare work of tremendous energy that combines dazzling rhetoric and clear logic. In composing such a work during the time he was undergoing religious training as a self-ordained priest, Kūkai was probably well aware of the persecution En no Gyōja had experienced and learned from his example not to pursue an antisocial form of Buddhism.

Indeed, Kūkai pursued a type of Buddhism that had an affinity with the state: to avoid being marked and repressed, he offered rituals to protect the state, a protection through a Buddhism that took a new, esoteric form. Kūkai later developed a very close relationship with Saga Tennō (r. 809–23), and his Shingon school was given royal recognition. Kūkai wanted to propagate the Dharma by protecting

THE NEW BUDDHISM OF THE HEIAN PERIOD

the capital on the one hand and studying Buddhism far from the city on the other. Thus he constructed a temple on Mt. Kōya as a training center and in 823 was invited by Saga to complete the Tōji Temple in Kyoto. What is of particular interest to me here is that at Mt. Kōya, he enshrined the local tutelary deities (*jinushi no kami*), Niutsuhime and Kōya Myōjin, within the temple precincts, and introduced elements from shamanistic folk beliefs and kami cults. Since Tōji, on the other hand, was a leading temple for conducting state protection rituals, there he enshrined such kami as Hachiman and Inari, which were connected with the state and with the Hata clan.[6] His two-pronged strategy proved skillful and shows that Kūkai was, besides being an eminent religious figure, an extremely able administrator with a high degree of organizational skill and know-how.

A new idea of the body

Special mention should be made of Kūkai's theory concerning the physical body and new techniques for achieving buddhahood through it. This theory is called *sokushin jōbutsu* (the attainment of buddhahood in this very body). It is a synthesis of theory and praxis developed by Kūkai so that a practitioner might become a buddha in his own physical body during his lifetime, rather than attaining it after "incalculable eons" of practice.

He introduced meditation techniques using images, such as the Ajikan (visualization of the character A [阿]) and the Gachirinkan (visualization of the moon-disc). Kūkai's esoteric meditation techniques shared elements in common with yoga and Hindu meditation. They were also similar to those of Tibetan Buddhism, which is fundamentally esoteric.

Kūkai's strategy was to bring about a physical transformation of the practitioner's body through the use of images, by visualizing the identity of one's own body with that of Fudō Myōō, or Fudō's original form, Dainichi Nyorai. This was called the practice of the three mysteries (*sanmitsu kaji*), through which the actions of body, speech, and mind of the individual are made one with the three mysteries of body, speech, and mind of Dainichi. Kūkai wrote in his *Sokushin jōbutsugi* (Attaining Enlightenment in This Very Existence) that "with the empowerment (*kaji*) of the three mysteries (*sanmitsu*), [our inborn three mysteries] will quickly be manifested."[7] Kūkai was a Buddhist practitioner who sought, true to his name, to expand himself into the sky (kū, 空) and the sea (kai, 海)—that is, into the vastness of the universe.

Kūkai wrote many works on doctrine and the use of language, including *Shōji jissōji* (The Meanings of Sound, Word, and Reality), *Unjigi* (The Meanings of the Word Hūṃ), *Himitsu mandara jūjū shinron* (Ten Abiding Stages on the Secret Mandalas), *Hizō hōyaku* (The Precious Key to the Secret Treasury), *Bunkyō hifuron* (a collection of excerpts from Chinese poetic treatises), and *Tenrei banshō meigi* (a dictionary of Chinese characters). Like Gyōgi (668–749), a popular Buddhist figure who was renowned for his construction and engineering skills, Kūkai's technical ability led in 821 to his involvement with repairs to the irrigation pond known as Mannō-ike in Shikoku. He also displayed his miraculous powers (*reigen*) in performing rainmaking rituals at the Shinsen garden in Kyoto and erected Abhiṣekha Halls called Shingon'in at Tōdaiji, the great temple in Nara, and inside the royal palace, for lay ordinations. In 822 he performed an esoteric initiation for the retired sovereign Heizei (774–824; r. 806–10) in Nara.

Heian-kyō, Capital of State Spiritual Protection

What we call Heian Buddhism has two sides. One side remained cozy with the state system, but at the same time it inquired deeply into the nature of original Buddhist practice and training. It was clearly for this purpose that Saichō laid out his *Regulations for Students of the Mountain School* that portrayed a new type of training different from what had pertained in Japanese Buddhism down to his time. In this sense, the Buddhism of the Heian period was not simply the Buddhism of the aristocracy; while remaining in accord and cooperating with the state, it also maintained a certain distance from it. It could well be called a new Buddhist reform movement. However, as time went by, Saichō's temple of Enryakuji on Mt. Hiei became increasingly tied to the state, and as royal sons and daughters entered associated temples known as *monzeki* ("noble cloisters"), the links between temples and the culture of the court grew ever closer.

This culture is described vividly in literary works of the time like the *Diary of Murasaki Shikibu* and the *Tale of Genji*. Murasaki Shikibu (ca. 973–ca. 1020) was a lady-in-waiting to Shōshi (Fujiwara Akiko, 988–1074), consort of Ichijō Tennō and the eldest daughter of Fujiwara no Michinaga (966–1028), the regent. She describes, for instance, how when Shōshi was in the middle of a very difficult labor, "living spirits" (*ikiryō*) and others flew around, and priests from Mt. Hiei and Tōji were called to perform esoteric rituals to contain these "possessing spirits" (*mononoke*) by the powers of their training. This was a time that also saw activities by magico-religious ritualists (*kitōsō*) and "yin-yang masters" (*onmyōji*). In this particular sense, Heian Buddhism was geared to the court and the nobility.

The work that more than any other describes in rich detail the spiritual world of the Heian period is the novel, the *Tale of Genji* (*Genji monogatari*), a depiction of the elegant court society of the time. When the Nativist scholar Motoori Norinaga wrote in his *Shibun yōryō* (The Essence of the Tale of Genji) that the *Tale of Genji* in its entirety could be described in the phrase, "to know *mono no aware* [the pathos of things]," he painted only half the picture—only the surface. Behind such poetic pathos Murasaki painted lives buffeted by fears of dangerous *mononoke* spirits. There are thus many scenes in the novel that describe the performance of esoteric rituals of exorcism. For example, we find the following in the chapter entitled *Heart-to-Heart* (Aoi):

> At His Excellency's, a spirit (*mononoke*), it seemed, was making the lady [Aoi] extremely unwell, and her family was alarmed. This was therefore no time for Genji to pursue adventures elsewhere, and it was only at odd moments that he even managed to visit Nijō. It pained him deeply that someone who so commanded his consideration should suffer this way, especially in her already delicate condition, and he had many prayers and rites (*misuhō*)[7] done for her in his own apartment

within the residence. Many possessing spirits (*mononoke*) and spirits of the living (*ikiryō*) came forth and identified themselves in one way or another, but one refused to move into the medium and clung instead to the lady herself, and although it did her no great violence, it never left her. Its persistence even to the most potent healers was extraordinarily stubborn.[9]

The Lady Aoi (Aoi no Ue) was Genji's wife. She was pregnant and had become ill through being possessed by *mononoke*. When the esoteric *misuhō* prayer ritual was performed, many *mononoke* and *ikiryō* left her body and went into the body of a young medium, identifying themselves. The spirit that refused to move appeared to be the "living spirit" of Lady Rokujō (Genji's jealous lover), who herself was not feeling well. Eventually Lady Aoi gave birth to a boy (Yūgiri), but she died shortly after. The circumstances of her death pointed to the work of a *mononoke*, seeing that she had been possessed many times, and exorcisms had been performed over and over again. The possessing spirit was more powerful than the rituals, which had no effect. Aoi's father, the Minister of the Left, and Genji were overwhelmed with grief, and her body was taken to the Toribeno cemetery to be buried.

While this is fiction, Murasaki appears to have witnessed such *mononoke* phenomena at various times in her own life. In her *Diary*, she describes events when Ichijō's consort Shōshi gave birth in 1025.

> At the moment of birth, what wails of anguish came from the spirits (*mononoke*). The Ajari Shin'yō had been assigned to the Lady Gen, a priest called Sōso to the Lady Hyōe, and the Master of Discipline from Hōjūji to the Lady Ukon. Miya no Naishi's enclosure was being overseen by the Ajari Chison; he was thrown to the ground by the *mononoke* and was in such distress that the Ajari Nengaku had to come to his aid with loud spells. Not that his powers (*gen*) were weak, it was just that the *mononoke* proved so very persistent. The priest (*egi*) Eikō, brought in to help Lady Saishō's exorcist, became

hoarse from shouting spells all night. There was further chaos when not all the women managed to accept the spirits to whom they had been assigned.[10]

Shōshi had been possessed at the time of her delivery. Murasaki describes vividly the perplexity of the exorcists when their efforts were of no avail. Shōshi eventually gave birth to a boy who later became Go-Ichijō Tennō.

Murasaki's description of the exorcism makes it clear that court ladies acted as mediums to receive the spirits from Shōshi. There was a great commotion when it was found the spirits could not be moved. The *egi* mentioned here refers to a mountain ascetic (*shugenja*) who supplicated spirits, but even his spiritual power was not enough to dislodge them. The esoteric masters (*ajari*) had already been overcome by them. A similar situation had occurred earlier in the pregnancy.

> Loud spells were cast in order to transfer the possessing spirits (*mononoke*). All the priests who had been at the mansion for the last few months were present, of course, but they were now joined by everyone worthy of the name exorcist (*genja*) from all the major temples. As they crowded in, you could imagine every Buddha in the universe flying down to respond. Those famed as yin-yang diviners (*onmyōji*) had also been asked to attend. Surely not a god in the land could have failed to prick up his ears, I felt. All day long there were messengers leaving to request the reading of sutras, and it continued throughout the night.[11]

The general mobilization of all these magico-religious specialists, including even *onmyōji*, was truly impressive. Today we cannot begin to guess the amount of spiritual strength and financial power required to exorcise *mononoke*. The Heian capital was a "city of apprehension," which could not be protected without the spiritual intervention of esoteric priests, *shugenja*, and *onmyōji*. Here vengeful spirits (*onryō* or *goryō*), *ikiryō* (spirits of living people), and *shiryō* (spirits of dead people) were constantly moving around and possessing its inhabitants, causing them distress. Curses and hauntings were also prevalent in this capital of fear.

From battles with spirits to battles among warriors

The Taira and Minamoto warrior clans emerged as members of the Northern Guard (*hokumen bushi*)[12] that protected Kyoto. Over time, as they became the dominant forces of the era, the battles with spirits gave way to battles among warriors, and ascendance came to be decided not by the spiritual power of the *shugenja* and esoteric exorcism but by the material factors of martial superiority, like how many warriors and weapons one possessed. The priest Jien (1155–1225), author of the *Gukanshō* (The Future and the Past, 1219), called this period the "age of warriors" (*musha no yo*), a time when spiritual power gave way before material (martial) strength. I might add that the age of the warrior has continued, in one form or another, down to the present.

Jien, the younger brother of the regent Kujō Kanezane (1149–1207) and head (*zasu*) of the Tendai school, saw the origins of the age of warriors in two conflicts, the Hōgen (1156) and Heiji (1159) disturbances. In the *Gukanshō*, he wrote:

> When the retired sovereign Toba died on the second day of the seventh month of Hōgen 1 (1156), the rebellions of the country of Japan broke out and the country's Age of Warriors began.[13]

The Hōgen-era conflict that broke out after the death of Toba Tennō (1103–56) had its origins in a factional dispute involving the court (between the sovereign and the retired sovereign), leading Fujiwara ministers, and the heads of the Taira and Minamoto warrior clans. It was a blood feud where fathers fought sons, brothers fought brothers, and uncles fought nephews. They murdered one another first in Kyoto, then on the battlefield. Jien regarded what had happened as belonging to an "age of chaos" characterized by the deterioration of relations between sovereign and regent. Before 1156, the rebellions and battles were all fought outside the capital; none took place within its limits. Jien's motive in writing the *Gukanshō* was to reveal the reasons for the outbreak of the Hōgen disturbance and to trace its course. He wrote that he hoped to achieve peace of mind by immersing himself in a consideration of these events.

Jien pointed out that what gave rise to the conflict in the capital was that fathers chose to favor younger sons over elder ones so they could control and manage political affairs for the father's own benefit. Specifically, retired sovereign Toba, instead of endorsing his son Sutoku's eldest son, Shigehito, as crown prince, chose rather Shigehito's younger brother Narihito (1139–55). Narihito, who later became Konoe Tennō, was probably Toba's own child and later adopted by Sutoku. Toba also decided that his fourth son, Masahito (1127–92), Sutoku's half-brother, should succeed Konoe (he in turn became Go-Shirakawa Tennō).[14] There was a similar rivalry between the two sons of the regent Fujiwara no Tadazane (1078–1162), Tadamichi (1097–1164) and Yorinaga (1120–56). Yorinaga was his father's favorite. This led to bitter resentment, hatred, and enmity between father and sons and among the brothers. Jien, incidentally, was a son of Tadamichi.

The Buddhist Dharma and protection of the state

Jien's entire perspective on history was based on the idea that vengeful spirits (*onryō*) brought disturbance to society, causing the downfall of individuals and bringing about pestilence and natural disaster.

> Since ancient times, there has been the Principle (*dōri*) that vengeful spirits ruin the state and destroy man.... The main point about a vengeful spirit is that it bears a deep grudge and makes those who caused the grudge objects of its revenge even while the resentful person is still alive. When the vengeful spirit is seeking to destroy the objects of its resentment —all the way from small houses to the state as a whole—the state is thrown into disorder by the slanders and lies it generates. The destruction of people is brought about in exactly

the same way. And if the vengeful spirit is unable to obtain its revenge while in this visible world, it will do so from the realm of the invisible.[15]

This type of malevolence is different from hatred in that it can be dispelled by unseen means. Jien believed a prescription is necessary for prayers to appease the *onryō*, and this prescription is to be found in the Buddhist Dharma.

For Jien, the Buddhist Dharma was a device for the spiritual protection of the state. He understood that through history, Tendai esoteric rites had been employed to exorcise vengeful spirits through magico-religious prayer rituals (*kaji kitō*). His was a historical philosophy, which called for the practice of rites such as spirit pacification (*chinkon*) and spirit-sealing (*onryō fūin*).

When political authority was restored to the traditional line of rulers of the court in Kyoto in 1868, one of the steps that Emperor Meiji took—perhaps in order to exorcise what had happened at the beginning of the "age of the warrior"—was to have the spirit of Sutoku recalled to Kyoto and re-enshrined at Shiramine Shrine. Sutoku had been exiled to Sanuki in Shikoku following the Hōgen disturbance and had died there full of bitterness in 1164. It is said that the exiled sovereign cut his finger and copied out the "five Mahāyāna sutras" in blood; when his donation of them to a temple in Kyoto was rejected, he took a terrifying form and announced:

> I, repenting my part in the struggles, have copied out these sutras to cleanse my heart from evil. However, when I cannot even place my handwriting in the capital, there is no help for it. I will devote the merit of copying these sutras to the three evil realms [hells, hungry spirits, animals], and become a great demon of Japan. I shall turn the Tennō into a commoner and the people I will make Tennō.[16]

Following the above statement, Sutoku "bit off the tip of his tongue and with the flowing blood wrote at the end of his sutras: 'May all, from the king of Brahman Heaven high above to the kami of the solid earth below, assist me.' He then had his vow sunk to the bottom of the sea with prayers." Of course, those prayers were curses, full of resentment and hatred.

People believed that the disturbances to society that followed the Hōgen conflict were caused by Sutoku's vengeful spirit. The statement that he would become a "great demon of Japan" and make the people rulers had the flavor of a prophetic curse. It may be read as predicting the warrior rule of the country. This may explain why Meiji had to pacify Sutoku's vengeful spirit by enshrining it in Kyoto in a particularly careful way: he wanted to break the curse implied in those words.

In 1168, the year after Taira no Kiyomori became chief minister of state (*dajō daijin*), the poet Saigyō (1118–90), a former member of the above-mentioned Northern Guard, visited Sanuki and the overgrown and neglected grave of Sutoku. There he composed three poems.

(1) A polished jewel-calyx
They have projected
On to a dew-deep plain
To see it is sad.[17]

(2) The ship he was on
crossed the waves to Matsuyama
and then suddenly
disappeared—as he too slipped
down below our horizon.[18]

(3) Let it be, my lord.
Surely this is nothing
like the jewel-floored
palaces of your past, but can
anything alter what's occurred?[19]

When Saigyō spoke, Sutoku's grave shook three times. The text suggests that "even the Venerated Royal Spirit may, by the recital of these poems, have relented in his design."[20] All the same, the fact that in 1868 Emperor Meiji again felt it expedient to placate the spirit means that the grudge was still thought to cast its long shadow over history as it entered the modern age. The ways and means of relieving the anger of vengeful spirits and pacifying them as respected entities was no simple matter.

Confucianism and Daoism in Japanese Religious Culture

Before continuing the discussion about the political, religious, and philosophical consequences of the rise of the "age of the warrior" in the next chapter, I would like to look at the influence that Confucianism and Daoism had exerted on Japanese religious culture down to this time.

Confucianism

The *ritsuryō* system that became the basis of the ancient state underwent various changes and was gradually hollowed out from within during the medieval period, but its basic framework remained, evolving into the two-tiered system of titular rule by the court (*tennō*, nobles) with practical authority exercised by the warrior-led government of the shogun and his vassals, the daimyo.

Confucianism developed in China around the same time Buddhism emerged in India, and it continues to be influential throughout East Asia in terms of both thought and institutions. If we consider that Buddhism shows the path to inner development, then Confucianism offers guidance on regulating the self and governing society. Confucianism looked on the legendary sage kings Yao and Shun, and kings Wen and Wu and the Duke of Zhou as ideal rulers because they were held to have systematized the way of human ethics, centering on virtues such as *ren* (humaneness, benevolence), *yi* (righteousness, justice), *li* (rituals and social norms), and music as the ideals at the core of good behavior and as providing the proper patterns for conduct. A highly developed moral order governs all society, from the actions of the individual to the conduct of the family, the nation, and the world as a whole. The vector to which Confucianism aspires is made clear in the *Great Learning (Da Xue)*, one of the classic "four books" of Confucianism.

> The person being cultivated, harmony is established in the household; harmony being established in the household, the state becomes well governed; the state being well governed, the empire becomes tranquil.[21] (*Da Xue* 5)

The research of the Japanese sinologist Shirakawa Shizuka and others suggests that Confucianism evolved from shamanistic funeral rites that used mediums (Ch. *wu*) to communicate with the dead and the spirit world. This eventually developed into the veneration of ancestors.[22] Ideas and practices related to central elements of this veneration, like *ren*, *li*, and music, were employed to bring under control the social turmoil of China's Spring and Autumn period (770 B.C.E.–481 B.C.E.), a time of wars between the various states. In this way, the condition described in the *Great Learning* could be achieved: "the state being well governed, the empire becomes tranquil." Particular mention should be made of the fact that the cultivation of ritual and music as ways to regulate society was considered to be at the core of the moral values belonging to a sage (Ch. *sheng*) and a gentleman (Ch. *junzi*, superior person). The conversations and discussions between Confucius (Kongzi) and his followers are recorded in the *Analects* (*Lunyu*). Traditional texts speak of six classics that make up the Confucian canon: *Book of Poetry (Shijing), Book of Documents (Shujing), Records of Rites (Liji), Book of Music (Yueji*, not extant), *Book of Changes (Ijing)* and the *Spring and Autumn Annals (Chunqiu)*. These, together with commentaries such as those on the *Record of Rites*, the *Book of Changes*, and the *Spring and Autumn Annals*, became the classical political philosophy of China and the basis of its political system.

Confucianism came to Japan around the fifth century when a Korean scholar named Wangren arrived with the *Analects*. Then in

513 the king of the Korean kingdom of Paekche sent a Confucian scholar of the Five Classics as tribute to the Yamato court. With the establishment of the *ritsuryō* system, Confucianism was taught through a course of study of the Confucian classics (Jp. *myōkyōdō*) at the Daigakuryō to train officials and as general learning. Kūkai studied this when he was a student there. Later, in his *Three Teachings*, he advocated the superiority of Buddhism over Confucianism and Daoism as a way to arrive at profound truth. The fact that the Chinese system of imperial examinations for the civil service was never introduced in Japan was one reason why Confucianism did not take institutional root in Japan the same way it had done in China and on the Korean peninsula. However, Neo-Confucianism, which entered Japan through Zen priests and other intellectuals from the fourteenth century onwards, had some influence on medieval Shinto, and in the early seventeenth century, it was adopted as the official orthodoxy of the Tokugawa shogunate as a result of the efforts of Fujiwara Seika (1561–1619) and his student Hayashi Razan (1583–1657). The office of Daigaku no kami (head of the state academy) was hereditary in the Hayashi family from the time of Razan's grandson, and the family was responsible for educational policy. Also at this time a Confucian-Shinto synthesis was developed by scholars like Yoshikawa Koretari (1616–94) and Yamazaki Ansai (1619–82).

Daoism

If Buddhism was concerned with the inner mind and Confucianism with the regulation of society, then Daoism can be characterized as a technique for achieving long life for the individual. It is a popular religion with a variety of elements born out of Chinese folk beliefs. At its core is the mysticism expounded by Laozi and Zhuangzi, integrated conceptually with the Dao (fundamental truth). Its practices include longevity techniques such as alchemy (Ch. *liandan*) and gymnastics (*daoyin*, lit., "guiding and pulling").[23]

Like shamanistic Confucianism, Daoism developed out of ancient magic (Ch. *wushu*) and "demonic arts" (*guidao*).[24] Since it

THE NEW BUDDHISM OF THE HEIAN PERIOD

incorporates a plethora of local folk beliefs and practices, it is not easy to define its characteristics clearly, but in terms of metaphysics, Laozi and Zhuangzi spoke of concepts like *dao* (the way), *xuan* (mysterious, profound), *wu wei* (non-doing), *ziran* (natural, spontaneous) and *zhen* (truth). It also avidly absorbed Buddhist ideas and practices concerning karmic retribution, transmigration, liberation, and the salvation of sentient beings. In the second century C.E., Zhang Jiao's Taipindao movement (the Yellow Turbans) and Zhang Ling's Woudoumi (Five Pecks of Rice) sect, also known as the Way of the Celestial Masters, were early examples of organized religious Daoism. In the Tang period, the emperor Xuanzong (685–762) was a keen supporter of Daoism and gave it precedence over Buddhism.

Daoism's presence in Japan is unmistakably indicated by the posthumous title of Tenmu Tennō: *Ama no nunahara oki no mahito no sumera mikoto* (Sovereign, the Perfected Man [*mahito*] of the deep ocean in the central marsh of Heaven).[25] "Mahito" (Ch. *zhenren*) is a Daoist term meaning "realized one." According to the research of Fukunaga Mitsuji[26] and others, the word *tennō*, which came to be employed as the title of the sovereign in Japan, was used in Daoism to signify a deity, Tianhuang. Many terms and concepts in the *Kojiki* and *Nihon shoki*, such as "heaven" (高天, Ch. *gaotian*), "high plain of heaven" (皇天原, Ch. *huangtianyuan*) and "Yomi" (黄泉, Ch. *huangquan*) are likewise thought to reveal a Daoist origin.

It is difficult to know when exactly, but Daoism probably entered Japan around the same time as Confucianism. The Onmyōryō (Bureau of Yin and Yang), a government department set up under the *ritsuryō* system, included officials concerned with astrology (*tenmon hakushi*) and with divination (*onmyōji*). Active in the tenth century were Kamo no Tadayuki (d. 960), his son Yasunori (917–77), and his student Abe no Seimei (921–1005). The Abe clan subsequently controlled astrology and divination, and the Kamo clan kept the calendar. Ideas about *fengshui* connected to both Daoism and mantic practices were incorporated into the layout and building of the royal capitals of Fujiwara-kyō, Heijō-kyō, and Heian-kyō. Another aspect of Daoist beliefs was the Kōshin cult, which was widespread in Japan, particularly during the Edo period. Members of Kōshin confraternities would meet to hold vigils every sixty (*kōshin*) days. Large numbers of stone steles and votive tablets were erected at roadsides or in temple grounds to commemorate the cult, and dedicated Kōshin Halls (Kōshindō) were built at some shrines and temples.[27]

The *Nihon shoki* recounts an incident with Daoist overtones that occurred in the autumn of 644.

> A man named Ōfube no Ōshi who lived in the vicinity of the Fuji river urged the people of his village to worship a caterpillar, saying, "This is the Tokoyo no kami, the kami of the everlasting world. Those who worship this god will have long life and riches. . . . People in the capital and in the countryside took the caterpillar of Tokoyo, placed it in shrines and prayed for good fortune singing and dancing. They threw away their valuables but to no purpose. The loss and waste was extreme. . . . Hata no Kawakatsu slew Ōfube no Ōshi.[28]

This seems to point to the Daoistic caterpillar cult of the *hayari-gami* ("faddish deity") type that was suppressed by the authorities.

Later a movement called Onmyōdō (Way of Yin and Yang) emerged around the tenth century out of the traditions of the Onmyōryō and was spread by the Kamo and Abe clans as a form of magic. The *Engishiki* (Procedures of the Engi Era, 927) includes a description of a ritual held by the Onmyōryō called the Nanomatsuri to exorcise evil spirits. It took place in the palace on the last night of the year. After the offerings were arranged, an *onmyōji* read a *saimon*, a written proclamation addressed to the deities. In it the word *oni* appears, using the characters 疫鬼, literally "pestilence demon." It speaks of "filthy demons" that are hidden around various villages, their dwellings just beyond the far borders in the four directions: specifically in Mutsu to the east (now Tōhoku), in Tōchika to the west (the island of Kagoshima), Tosa to the south (Kōchi), and Sado Island to the north. The Nanomatsuri is therefore a rite to drive the *oni* back to their distant domains in the borderlands of the four directions.

Spirit and Faith

The miraculous in the Nihon ryōiki

Two works that appeared early in the ninth century share a similarity in that the character *rei/ryō* 霊 (spirit) appears in the titles of both. The first is the *Shōryōshū*, a collection of poems, letters, and ritual documents by Kūkai. The second is the *Nihon ryōiki* (Record of Miraculous Events in Japan), the first collection made of Buddhist tales (*setsuwa*), compiled by Kyōkai, a priest at Yakushiji in Nara. It consists of 116 tales divided into three volumes.

The tale of the miraculous floating log that is mentioned in the *Nihon shoki* also appears in the *Nihon ryōiki* (I. 5).

> In the reign of Bidatsu Tennō, sounds of musical instruments were heard off the coast of Izumi province. There were sounds of flutes, *shō* [panpipes] and various types of stringed instruments, or others that sounded like rolls of thunder. They were heard in the daytime, and at night a bright light spread to the east. Lord Ōtomo no Yasunoko no muraji reported this to the Sovereign, but he was silent and disbelieving. When it was reported to his consort however she ordered him to investigate. He accordingly went to see and found that it was just as reported. While there, he came on a camphor log that had been struck by lightning. On his return, he reported to the consort, "While I was at the beach of Takashi, I have found this camphor log. I humbly request permission to make Buddha images out of it." The consort gave permission. . . . Shima no Ōomi [Soga no Umako] . . . commissioned Ikebe no atae Hita [Hita no atae] to carve three bodhisattvas. They were placed in the Toyura Hall [in Asuka].[29]

This is almost the same as the record that appears in the *Nihon shoki* dated Kinmei 14. What comes immediately next, however, differs. It is the story of the conflict between the Soga and Mononobe clans over the worship of Buddhist images.

However Lord Mononobe no Yuge no Moriya no Ōmuraji addressed the consort of Bidatsu saying, "These Buddhist images should not be displayed in our country. Put them away somewhere far away!" Hearing this, the consort said to Lord Yasunoko no muraji, "Quickly, hide these images!" Thereupon, he had Hita no atae [Ikebe no atae Hita] hide them among the rice sheaves. Lord Yuge no Ōmuraji eventually set fire to the hall and had the images thrown into the canal at Naniwa. He upbraided Yasunoko, saying, "The cause of our present trouble lies in keeping unauthorized images [客神] sent from a nearby country to our own land. Throw them away at once and let them flow back to the land to the west. ("Unauthorized images" means "Buddhist images.") But Yasunoko firmly refused. Yuge no Ōmuraji,

Figure 3.2. Seated statue of a female kami. Matsuo Taisha Shrine.

his mind deranged, began to plot rebellion, looking for a chance to carry out evil. But Heaven disliked him, and Earth too hated him. In the reign of Yōmei Tennō, he was at last overthrown, and the Buddhist images were brought into the open and handed down to later ages. At present, the image of Amida enshrined at the Hiso Temple in Yoshino and casting out its light is one of them.[30]

It is worth noting that the term Kyōkai used for the "unauthorized images" was *marōdo-gami* (客神, lit., "guest kami") and that he expressly included a note clarifying that it meant *butsu no shinzō*, literally, "Buddhist kami-images." What we refer to today as *shinzō* — images of kami — were a later development, made under Buddhist influence. At the time, there was no custom to make images of kami, even if shrines had objects acting as receptacles for the kami (*shintai*). Today the earliest known *shinzō* is a seated male figure kept at the shrine Matsuo Taisha in Kyoto that dates from the first half of the ninth century.

From the time Buddhism first arrived in Japan, buddhas were understood as being linked to kami and received as such. The "marōdo-gami" from a nearby country was identified as a "buddha," which had arrived upon the shores of Japan as a divine camphor log that had been hit by lightning, full of sacred energy and emitting sounds like "rolling thunder" along with a bright light.

The *Nihon ryōiki* includes a great number of stories that speak of mystery and power. For example, the first tale tells how "thunder" was caught and brought into the presence of Yūryaku Tennō.

> The god gave off a brilliant blast of light that dazzled and frightened the Sovereign. He made many offerings to it and then had it sent back to the place where it had struck, which is now called Thunder Hill.[31]

The tales in the *Nihon ryōiki* can be classified into a number of types: stories of natural wonders like the above, of supernatural creatures, like the story of the fox taken as a wife who gave birth to a child (Tale 1.2), of transformations and incarnations of buddhas and bodhisattvas, and of the miraculous merits of faith. There are also many stories that concern everyday life: disputes over irrigation and water rights, thieves selling stolen goods at market, and officials searching for people not settled in the area and exacting taxes from them.

Genshin and the "Essentials of Salvation"

In the tenth century, Genshin (942–1017; Eshin Sōzu), a priest at the Yokawa Shūryōgon'in at the Tendai complex of Enryakuji on Mt. Hiei, wrote the *Ōjō yōshū* (Essentials of Salvation), drawing attention to the Pure Land of Amida and methods of rebirth there. It was highly influential on the later development of the Pure Land school and faith in the power of calling upon Amida's name (*nenbutsu*). The work is a three-volume compendium of passages from scriptural and commentatorial sources concerning Pure Land rebirth; it contrasts leaving this polluted world (*onri edo*) and aspiring to rebirth in the Pure Land (*gongu jōdo*), giving detailed explanations about the Pure Land, hell, and rebirth. Genshin emphasizes here that there is no better way of reaching the celestial Pure Land than by chanting Amida's name with wholehearted devotion. He had been born into the Urabe family and entered the priesthood when he was nine years old. He was a student of Ryōgen (912–85; Ganzan Daishi), who revived the fortunes of Mt. Hiei and studied both the meditation (*shikan*) and tantric (*shana*) courses.

The next chapter will discuss how Buddhism and Shinto reacted to the gradual breakdown of the unity of the *ritsuryō* state and how they sought out the fundamental to establish what was correct. This search for the original characterizes the new intellectual movement and ethos of the medieval period.

CHAPTER FOUR

Kami and Buddhas in the Medieval Period

While the *ritsuryō* state centering on the sovereign was in decline by the twelfth century, its economic base—the *kōchi kōmin* system under which all land was regarded as property of the sovereign and all people as subjects of the sovereign—was already breaking down as early as the eighth. Though private ownership of land was not recognized, it had become a reality in the course of the Heian period, and the old system of land administration and taxation completely collapsed during the medieval period.

As the *ritsuryō* system declined, a form of government known as "cloistered rule" (*insei*) began in 1086 when Shirakawa Tennō abdicated in favor of his four-year-old son and exerted his authority in parallel to the regent as a retired monarch (*jōkō*). Successive retired monarchs had their own courts and their own warrior guards. Tensions inherent in the system led, as recounted in Chapter 3, to the outbreak of the Hōgen disturbance in 1156 and the Heiji disturbance in 1159, which had their origin in succession and factional disputes within the family of the *tennō* and the Fujiwara house. The Heian capital became a battleground as the nobles and the Taira and the Minamoto warrior clans allied themselves variously with one contender or another to gain advantage and power.

The Fujiwara were major players in these power games. Fujiwara no Tadamichi (1097–1164), the sponsor of the Onmatsuri at Kasuga Taisha who acted as regent (*kanpaku*) until 1158, sided with the sovereign Go-Shirakawa (r. 1155–58) during the Hōgen disturbance of 1156 against the retired monarch Sutoku (r. 1123–42). Sutoku, as mentioned previously, was defeated and banished to Sanuki province in Shikoku, while Tadamichi's brother Yorinaga (1120–56), who supported Sutoku, was killed in battle. However, three years later, in 1159, another armed dispute broke out, known as the Heiji disturbance.

The breakdown of the *ritsuryō* system was due to the development of manors called *shōen* that were exempt from taxes. *Shōen* extended private rights to areas that public authority could not reach, meaning that the "public" territory administered by the court was greatly reduced through the spread of land belonging privately to individuals, temples, and shrines. In modern terms, the momentum had moved from the center to the peripheries, from the centripetal court to the centrifugal *shōen*. As the area of land outside the direct jurisdiction of the central government increased, new power-holding classes emerged, in particular the warrior families that provided protection for these private holdings. An extraterritorial, pluralistic power structure came into being, where private lands and wealth were safeguarded by armed force.

The Hōgen and Heiji conflicts strengthened not only the power of the military clans but also their rivalry for dominance at court. The Minamoto clan emerged victorious over the Taira in 1185, and Minamoto no Yoritomo (1147–99) was granted the title of shogun by the sovereign, Go-Toba. He subsequently set up a warrior-led government (*bakufu* or shogunate) in Kamakura, and a bifurcated power structure emerged. The ethos that was to define myth in the new era was consequently very different from what had gone before. Whereas under the *ritsuryō* system, the court had been the sole political authority, after 1185 there was a parallel authority in the form of the Kamakura *bakufu*. The unipolar centralized rule of the *tennō* had become elliptical. Although there had been a duplication of power during the height of the Fujiwara's prominence, the Fujiwara had been indivisible from the sovereign; their relationship was like a two-headed eagle, two heads on one body.

The subsequent two-tiered government meant that shogunate officials like the *shugo* (military governor) and *jitō* (military estate steward) existed in parallel with the provincial and district officials appointed by the sovereign. As the medieval period progressed, the *shōen* system and land ownership by feudal lords increasingly encroached upon public (state) ownership, which fell into disarray. The medieval age was a time of successive battles for control of the land among rival warlords, particularly after the Ōnin War (1467–77), which reduced Kyoto to ashes. Outwardly, the *tennō* remained the supreme authority in terms of rank, but the shogun held the real power.

The Birth of a New Spirituality

At about the same time that social structures had begun to decay, the idea that Buddhism had entered an age of decline (*mappō*) was sweeping the country. This age of decline was widely considered to have started in 1052, when Fujiwara power was at its height with the regency of Fujiwara no Yorimichi (992–1074), son of the powerful regent Michinaga (966–1028). As the Fujiwara ascendancy began to wane, however, the capital, too, grew more disorderly, and the anxieties cast by the teachings of *mappō* began to seem ever more real. As the protection that had been assured by state power and authority disappeared, society was filled with fear and anxiety. What was the individual to do when the powers that had provided security were no longer around? This urgent existential question led to a search for "the primal, the One" in both the new Buddhist and the new Shinto movements of the Kamakura period (1185–1333). Thus, for example, Dōgen, seeking the original essence of Buddhism, looked to Zen and said in his *Shōbō genzō* (Treasury of the Eye of the True Dharma) that this essence was the "true Dharma"; Ise Shinto, similarly, sought the fundamental "One."

There was a growing conviction among people that the world had entered a time marked by the decline of Buddhism (*mappō*), an era that contributed to the prevailing lack of certainty within society.

Mappō thought was a kind of eschatology, and people accepted as reality the insecurity of the times in which they were living. Families became scattered, and the established social order throughout the country was shaken. No one knew what the future held. Large numbers of people left their villages, and illness and death from starvation were everywhere. What people had previously depended on was gone. In such a situation, there was no point in mastering Buddhism and propagating it unless it was a pure faith able to move people to follow it with all their being and had a genuine form of practice. The Pure Land movement, which taught absolute faith in "other-power" (*tariki*), depending on the Primal Vow (*hongan*) of Amida for salvation, met this need.

Pure Land faith had spread among the populace from the tenth century due to the efforts of priests like Kūya (903–72) and Genshin (942–1017). Kūya, initially a self-ordained priest who was later ordained on Mt. Hiei, spread devotion to Amida on the streets of the capital through music and dance as well as preaching, while Genshin was a scholar-priest who wrote, as we have seen, the *Essentials of Salvation*. Fujiwara no Yorimichi, seeking rebirth in Amida's paradise of Sukhāvatī, converted a Fujiwara villa in Uji, south of the capital, into the Byōdōin Temple in 1052, and its Phoenix Hall, housing an image of Amida, was built the following year.

Hōnen (1133–1212) and his student Shinran (1173–1263) were both trained on Mt. Hiei but left to propagate the recitation of the *nenbutsu*, a practice whereby one put one's faith in the salvific power of the Buddha Amida. Hōnen won the confidence of the regent Kujō Kanezane, who became his patron. Hōnen's famous *Senchaku hongan nenbutsu shū* (Passages on the Selection of the Nenbutsu in the Original Vow) was written at Kanezane's request in 1198. Both Hōnen and Shinran attracted the animosity of the Buddhist establishment, however, and in 1207 were exiled to Tosa (Kōchi, Shikoku) and Echigo (Niigata), respectively, just as En no Gyōja had been banished to Izu six centuries earlier and Nichiren (1222–82) was to be sent to Sado Island in 1271. Exile was a symbolic event, a sign of the violently changing times. Such men are known as *tonseisō*, or "reclusive priests," who focused on issues troubling ordinary people and formed the nucleus of the new religious movements of the twelfth and thirteenth centuries.[1]

These were intellectual movements responding to questions that myths of the ancient world could not answer. The secure base provided by the *ritsuryō* system was smashed, and the kami and the people were both searching for a new refuge and a new means of salvation. Suzuki Daisetsu (1894–1966), the author of many works on Buddhism, regarded this period as marking the awakening of a "Japanese spirituality."

A central concern of the ancient *ritsuryō* state had been to bring together all the various strands of mythology and history and create a matrix that would allow all the discrete parts to fit together. The collapse of this unity and the emergence of a two-tiered, *tennō*-shogun system of rule after the twelfth century posed a new issue for the post-*mappō* age: the impossibility of reintegrating the scattered pieces of society to render it stable again without introducing a third axis into it. The solution was to establish that which was fundamentally correct, to return to the source and enter the truest Dharma. This search for the original, "the One," characterizes the new intellectual movements of the twelfth and thirteenth centuries.

The word *senchaku* ("selection") best exemplifies this tendency. People engaged themselves in judging and interpreting the Buddhist teachings (*kyōsō hanjaku*), selecting one doctrine or one scripture from among the voluminous Mahāyāna sutras and the "eight thousand" teachings.

Particularly on Mt. Hiei, priests were questioning the basis of their faith, and they were strongly aware that Mt. Hiei had undergone institutional decay. Feeling that the traditional practices of the temple fell far from meeting the needs of the new age, they sought a fresh focus that would enable them to respond to the criticism and answer those needs. The Pure Land belief of Hōnen and Shinran, the Zen of Yōsai (1141–1215) and Dōgen (1200–53), and the Lotus teachings of Nichiren (1222–82) each represent the selection of a single teaching from among Tendai's traditional doctrines, refined and given purer form. In particular, the Lotus belief was regenerated and given a new monotheistic shape according to the One Vehicle teachings of the

Lotus Sutra by Nichiren to "establish the true Dharma to bring peace to the nation" (*risshō ankoku*). This he approached in a particularly aggressive way. Tendai meditation tradition was taken up by Yōsai and Dōgen, who centered their teachings on the practice of seated meditation (*zazen*). And predating them all was the Pure Land teaching of Hōnen and Shinran, characterized by the "selection of the Primal Vow [of Amida] and the sole practice of the *nenbutsu*" (*senchaku hongan senshū nenbutsu*). The effects of "selection" were felt also within Shinto, stimulating the formation of Ise Shinto and leading to the formulation in the fifteenth century of "One-and-Only" (Yuiitsu Sōgen) Shinto by Yoshida Kanetomo (1435–1511). Ise and Yoshida Shinto are discussed in more detail below.

Between the twelfth and thirteenth centuries, the word *reisei* (spirituality) began appearing in Shinto commentaries, such as the *Shintō hisetsu* (Secret Doctrines of Shinto), with a colophon of 1185, which has been attributed to Urabe Kanetomo, junior vice-director of the Jingikan (Ministry of Kami Affairs). These secret doctrines are described in passages such as "In the time before heaven and earth were divided, before the sun, moon, and constellations had appeared, and before the five elements of wood, fire, earth, metal, and water had come about, when the void penetrated all places and there was neither good nor evil, the Way was spirituality (*reisei*) itself, tranquil, uncreated, both perfect and empty: this is the secret doctrine of Shinto." Again, "Shinto is spirituality, both perfect and empty, and does not cross the two laws of birth and death. Of the two characters used to write Shinto, *shin* (神) is the kami beyond all kami and *tō* (道) is the Way beyond all Ways. *Shin* being the kami beyond all kami, *tō* is the quintessence of the divine light."

Here the secret doctrine is identified as "perfect empty spirituality" and "Shinto" adheres to it. Whereas "perfect" is an overabundance, "empty" is absence, the opposite concept. The text asserts that the mysterious workings of "spirituality" sublate this polarity. "Spirituality" is used frequently as a term of the utmost importance, expressing a fundamental view of the universe that forms the nucleus of the "secret doctrines" of "Shinto."

If the date of the colophon is accurate, the *Shintō hisetsu* was written around the time that Jien called the beginning of the age of the warrior, when the ancient world was collapsing and the age of chaos that characterized the medieval period, with its parallel systems of governance and its multiple manors (*shōen*) in place of state-owned land, was beginning. In 1184, Urabe Kanetomo, to whom the *Shintō hisetsu* is credited, became head, at his own request, of a shrine called Awata-gū dedicated in 1177 by the retired sovereign Go-Shirakawa to appease the spirits of Sutoku and Fujiwara no Yorinaga, which were thought to be bringing chaos to the land in revenge for the events of 1156.

Medieval Myth

Under the *ritsuryō* system, the Jingikan had control over all shrines and supervised a national system of shrine rites.[2] Over the course of the Heian period, it was degraded, and as it lost its supervisory power, local shrines set themselves up as independent institutions and constructed their own political theologies to support themselves. Both Ise Shinto and Yoshida Shinto developed their strong points and formed their own theologies and arguments in search of a "fundamental One," and in this way medieval Shinto mythology was created. The mythology was completely different from that found in the *Kojiki* and the *Nihon shoki*, where myths had been systematized to center on Amaterasu. That systematization lost substance and broke down in the medieval period. Medieval Shinto was characterized by a search for what lay at the root. Ise Shinto, for example, sought to find what was the most primal of all, asking where the "origin is the origin, the base the base," and finding it in its own kami. Priests created new, covert Shinto myths and theologies, such as found in Ise Shinto's *Five Books* and Yoshida Shinto's *Essentials of Terminology and Doctrine of Yuiitsu Shinto* (*Yuiitsu shintō myōbō yōshū*), as the true and secret myths and doctrines of their own tradition, in contrast to the overt state mythology found in the *Kojiki* and the *Nihon shoki*. They found the "original" in their own teaching and established a body of myth that had nothing to do with those earlier works. The underlying ethos of the myth had changed from a mediator to an ultimate progenitor.

The medieval myths did not function to support the *ritsuryō* state but were, rather, part of theologies and doctrines that sought a new foundation amid the political and economic changes of the time. Broadly speaking, they represent a compulsion to investigate and theorize about primordial, pre-*Kojiki* kami and to seek out what was "original" and "legitimate." The new movements and theologies that emerged at this time, like Ise Shinto and Yoshida Shinto, exemplify an esoteric tradition, in contrast to the exoteric mythology found in writings such as the *Kojiki*, *Nihon shoki*, and *Shoku Nihongi* that underpinned the *ritsuryō* system, and they found expression in "secret" texts like the Ise Shinto's *Five Books* and Yoshida Shinto's *Essentials*. The mythology they contained was basically "private" or "discrete," belonging to a particular family or lineage. For example, the Watarai clan serving the Outer Shrine at Ise proposed that their own kami, Toyouke, was the original deity of the cosmogony, and Yoshida Shinto propounded an original and primordial kami. Also part of this new Shinto movement were Shinto ideas put forward by Buddhists, not based on the *Kojiki* and the *Nihon shoki*. The *Shintōshū* (Collection of Kami; late fourteenth century) and the *Yōtenki* (Record of a Shining Heaven, 1223), for example, were compiled by Tendai priests.

Ise Shinto

As the institutional capabilities of the Jingikan drastically weakened both economically and politically, shrines all over the land faced ruin and, in a mood of self-preservation, sought out a rationale for their existence. Prominent here was Ise Shinto, born just outside the inner circle of Japan's most important shrine: Ise Jingū. Ise consists of two shrines, the Inner Shrine, dedicated to Amaterasu ōmikami, and the Outer Shrine, which worships Toyouke no ōkami. The priests of the Inner Shrine who served Amaterasu were of the Arakida lineage, an offshoot of the Nakatomi clan, while the priests of the Outer Shrine who served Toyouke were of the Watarai sacerdotal lineage. Since the theology of Ise Shinto was first proclaimed by the Watarai, it is also called Watarai Shinto. Under the ancient *ritsuryō* system both shrines were embraced within the belief of Amaterasu as paramount ancestor of the ruling line, with Amaterasu and the sovereign positioned as inclusive, mediating beings. The difference between Amaterasu and Toyouke was that one was the ancestral deity of the ruling house and the other was originally the local food kami Uka or Uke of the Tanba district that was later transferred to Ise, representing the deities of the land where food was grown for Amaterasu.

Medieval Ise Shinto saw in Toyouke the power to embrace the whole in place of Amaterasu. The Watarai priests argued that the element of *mi* in Miketsu-kami, another name for Toyouke, means water, and since water quenches fire, Toyouke must be the primal deity. Having the power of water (*suitoku*), Toyouke is the source of life, bringing forth all things in the universe. They thus reversed the order of precedence, positioning Toyouke as the primal deity, the fundamental cosmic god, older even than Amaterasu, and also held that Toyouke was identical with Kuni no tokotachi (in the *Nihon shoki*) and with Ame no minakanushi (in the *Kojiki*).

Figure 4.1. Entrance to the Inner Shrine, Ise Shrines.

CHAPTER FOUR

Raising Toyouke's status by means of linking the deity to the most exalted kami in the *Nihon shoki* and the *Kojiki* challenged traditional Amaterasu-centered ideology. At the root of the thinking of the Watarai priests was the concept of "primal," and they discovered a single primal deity in Toyouke, who, rather than being the oldest kami recorded in the *Kojiki* and the *Nihon shoki* and the state-supporting deity Amaterasu, they considered to be the source of all things in the universe. Such ideas derived from a view that transcended the framework of the *ritsuryō* state. Suzuki Daisetsu wrote in his *Nihonteki reisei* (Japanese Spirituality) that "Japanese spiritual history demonstrated its true significance for the first time upon reaching the Kamakura period. At that time, Buddhism's life spirit came into contact with the life-spirit of the great earth (*daichi-sei*)."[3] If Japanese Buddhism was now rooted in the "great earth" and not part of state Buddhism as it had been, this would encourage the search for a more heavenly and fundamental divinity. At the Outer Shrine, this primal deity was "water-powered," joining heaven and earth as rain falls from the sky to the ground. As Suzuki described it, "Though religion comes from heaven, its essence exists in the earth. Spirituality arises with its roots in the earth."[4] Medieval Shinto grew out of an aspiration for a primal deity that joined the two realms.

In the course of the thirteenth century, the Watarai priests produced a series of apocryphal "secret" texts, which they said predated even the *Kojiki* and *Nihon shoki*, to back up their claims, the best known of which are the so-called Five Books of Shinto: *Gochinza shidaiki* (Rituals of the Enshrinement of the Ise Deities), *Gochinza denki* (Records of the Enshrinement of the Ise Deities), *Gochinza hongi* (Authentic Record of the Enshrinement of Toyouke), *Hōki hongi* (Authentic Record of the Divine Emblems), and *Yamatohime no mikoto seiki* (Oracles of Yamatohime). The first three of these texts deal with the origins of the Inner and Outer Shrines of Ise and their deities, while the latter two speak of the construction and form of the shrines and the enshrinement of Yamatohime.[5] The overall intention of the Watarai here is to appeal strongly to the greatness of their own deity, Toyouke. These texts, with their clear political theology, presented a new ideology of the Watarai sacerdotal lineage that differed from that of the *Kojiki* and *Nihon shoki*. They declared that their way was where the "origin is the origin, the base the base," as found in the prophecy of Yamatohime in the *Oracles of Yamatohime*:

> Serve the great deity by not moving to the right that which is to the left, or to the left that which is to the right. Let left be left and right be right. Be correct in all things, whether turning to the left or to the right, because the origin is the origin and the base is the base.[6]

Yoshida Shinto

Yoshida Shinto, also known as Urabe Shinto and Yuiitsu ("one and only") Sōgen ("original") Shinto, was a new form of Shinto, that developed at Yoshida Shrine, situated at the foot of Mt. Yoshida in Kyoto. The Yoshida sacerdotal lineage of lower-ranking priests was a branch of the Urabe clan serving the Nakatomi family, who were in charge of court ritual. The Urabe split into two branches, the Yoshida and the Hirano. The latter lineage was in charge of Hirano Shrine, which appears among the shrines listed in the *Engishiki* and is located close to the well-known Kitano Tenmangū in Kyoto.

Yoshida Shinto borrowed ideas from the Shinto of the Outer Shrine and combined them with its own traditions and theology. It was brought to maturity by Yoshida Kanetomo (1434–1511), head priest at Yoshida Shrine, around the time of the Ōnin War (1467–77). This turbulent time also saw the emergence of distinguished Zen priests like Ikkyū Sōjun (1394–1481) of the Rinzai school and of Rennyo (1416–99), restorer of the Shin Pure Land school. It is easy for new religious movements to arise in times of intense social change, for they clarify the issues involved when people are asking how to survive in a destructive and uncertain situation.

Kanetomo has been both much praised and much maligned. He proclaimed that a numinous object, the spirit of the kami of the Inner Shrine at Ise (Amaterasu), had flown to his shrine, and that eventually, all of the 3,232 kami listed in the *Engishiki* had gathered there. In 1484, with the support of Hino Tomiko (1440–96), the wife of the shogun Ashikaga Yoshimasa (1436–90), he built the Daigengū on Mt. Yoshida as the "shrine of the great origin," venerating the entire pantheon, as the most important building for what he called his "true way," Yuiitsu Sōgen Shinto, the One-and-Only Original Shinto. It was an expression of Kanetomo's Shinto esotericism in concrete form.

Kanetomo had previously authored formularies, such as *Shinmei sangen godaiden shinmyōkyō* and *Sangen shintō sanmyō kajikyō*, attributing them to an ancient source, and continued to develop both doctrine and ritual. His major work is called *Yuiitsu shintō myōbō yōshū* (Essentials of Terminology and Doctrine of Yuiitsu Shinto), and in it he discusses the scriptural base of Yuiitsu Shinto:

> Question: On what scriptural evidence is [this claim] founded?
> Answer: Three primordial texts form the basis of the exoteric doctrine, and three divine scriptures form the basis of the esoteric doctrine. Yuiitsu Shinto is made up of these two doctrines.
> Question: What are the three primordial texts?
> Answer: They are *Sendai kuji hongi*, . . . *Kojiki*, . . . and *Nihon shoki* . . .
> Question: What are the three divine scriptures?
> Answer: They are [*Tengen jinben shinmyōkyō*] *The Subtle Sacred Scripture of the Divine Metamorphoses of the Heavenly Foundation*, [*Chigen jintsū shinmyōkyō*] *The Subtle Sacred Scripture of the Divine Supernatural Powers of the Earthly Foundation*, and [*Jingen shinryoku shinmyōkyō*] *The Subtle Sacred Scripture of the Divine Powers of the Human Foundation*.
> Question: Were those scriptures revealed by [the kami] or authored by wise men?
> Answer: They were revealed by [the kami] Ame no koyane no mikoto. In later generations they were translated into Chinese by the True Lord of the Polar Star. Thus did they come to be called the three divine scriptures.[7]

Kanetomo stated that two kinds of scriptures existed, the exoteric (*kenro*, "revealed," "manifest") and the esoteric (*on'yū*, "hidden," "discreet"). The three exoteric scriptures he cited were the well-known classics, the *Kojiki*, *Nihon shoki*, and *Sendai kuji hongi* (*Kujiki*; Chronicle of Old Things), but the three esoteric texts — the "three divine scriptures" listed in his "Answer" above — were fabricated, probably by Kanetomo himself. They were purportedly not known to the world at large but kept secret, to be passed on by secret transmission (*hiden*) as genuine texts. Kanetomo said they had been revealed by Ame no koyane no mikoto, the ancestral kami of the Fujiwara clan, whom he considered to be the ancestral kami of the Urabe clan, from which the Yoshida sacerdotal lineage was descended. Yoshida Shinto divided its teachings into two types and made free use of the scholarship of the "three teachings" to develop its own exoteric-esoteric symbolic dualism, which is laid out in the following chart.

Exoteric	Esoteric
the three primordial texts	the three divine texts
manifest (*kenro*) teachings	discreet (*on'yū*) teachings
outer purity	inner purity
light observance of taboos (*sansai*)	severe observance of taboos (*chisai*)
sacred site (*saitei*) for peripheral (ordinary) rites/outer site (*gejō*)	sacred space (*saijō*) for central (esoteric) rites/inner space (*naijō*)
sacred space for the kami of earth, the *suki* hall	sacred space for the kami of heaven, the *yuki* hall
kami of earth	kami of heaven
earth	heaven
Yin	Yang
even number	odd number
Inner Shrine	Outer Shrine
altar of Sources (*shogendan*)	altar of Original Spirits (*bansōdan*)
rear	front
north	south
Womb Realm	Diamond Realm

Kanetomo placed the Outer Shrine in the category of "discreet" and yang and said it was the "origin" (*sō*). The Inner Shrine on the other hand was the "source" (*gen*) and yin.[8] The most mystical Shinto is that which he himself transmits, Yuiitsu Shinto, which is the correct way.

Further, in his *Essentials,* Kanetomo divided Shinto into three categories: (1) the Shinto based on the scriptural transmissions of shrines; (2) Ryōbu Shinto (esoteric Shinto expressed through the two mandalas, the Diamond and the Womb); and (3) the Original and Fundamental Shinto (the Shinto transmitted through the Yoshida lineage). This Urabe-Yoshida Shinto was a secret transmission by the "founder (*sōgen*) of the rites of worship of the kami" and of the "rite of divination that has existed from the time of the kami," passed from Amaterasu to the ancestral deity of the Nakatomi, Fujiwara, and Urabe clans. This, Kanetomo states, is why his Shinto is called the "one and only, original Shinto."

Kanetomo further explains why his Shinto ("way of the kami") can also be written with an orthography meaning "true way."

> Question: But why is the term *shintō* written with the *kanji* meaning "true way" 真道 in this case, and not with those meaning "way of the kami" 神道?
> Answer: The term "kami" is the general denomination of all spirits (*reisei*) good and bad, false and true. In this particular case the term "true" (*shin* 真) is used so there can be no mistake that what is referred to is the One kami of the true origins that is unique and unadulterated.[9]

Here Kanetomo says that "kami" is a general term for the spirits (*reisei*) that underlie all things.[10] In order to differentiate this from the "unique and unadulterated kami of true origins," he uses the ideograph for "true" in place of "kami" to write Shintō. Through using this terminology, he asserts that the Shinto of his lineage is the true Shinto.

Kanetomo put enormous effort into forming Yoshida Shinto, receiving backing from both the royal house and the Ashikaga

Figure 4.2. Daigengū on Mt. Yoshida. Photo by Ōishi Takanori.

shogunal house and attaining great power thereby. He eventually assumed the role of "superintendent of Shinto," issuing licenses that certified the appointment of priests to shrines. Yoshida Shinto became the strongest of all the Shinto streams and remained very close both to the court and the *bakufu* right up to the Meiji Restoration in 1868.

Japan as the Land of the Gods

The daimyo (and "unifiers of Japan") Oda Nobunaga (1534–82) and Toyotomi Hideyoshi (1536–98) both incorporated Yoshida Shinto into their way of thinking. For example, the construction of Nobunaga's Azuchi castle is said to have been influenced by the One-and-Only ideas of Yoshida Shinto. Nobunaga also actively encouraged Christianity as a rival religion to weaken the power of the *sōhei* ("monastic warriors") of Mt. Hiei and the armed threat posed by followers (*monto*) of the Shin Pure Land school based at Higashi Honganji in Kyoto (Ikkōshū). This encouragement led to an increase in the number of Christian daimyo. His vassal and successor Hideyoshi at first continued Nobunaga's pro-Christian policy but in time reversed it, expelling the missionaries and finally banning the religion. The opening clause of his 1587 edict expelling Christian missionaries, "Japan is the country of gods," shows that the *shinkoku* ("land of kami") ideology found in Yoshida Shinto was also part of his worldview. Besides using this logic of Yoshida Shinto to defend the land, Hideyoshi also followed its version of the oneness of the three teachings, that Shinto is the root of the tree, Confucianism its trunk, and Buddhism its fruits and flowers. In the *Essentials*, Kanetomo had described the process of the fruits falling from the tree and returning to its root as the true meaning of Buddhism's eastward transmission, asserting that, in the end, Buddhism had grown out of Shinto:

> During the reign of the thirty-fourth ruler of our nation [Suiko], Shōtoku Taishi made to her the following secret declaration: "Japan produced the seed. China produced the branches and leaves, India produced the flowers and fruit.

Buddhism is the fruit, Confucianism is the leaves, and Shinto is the trunk and roots. Buddhism and Confucianism are only secondary products of Shinto. Leaves and fruit merely indicate the presence of the trunk and roots; flowers and fruit fall and return to the roots. Buddhism came east only to reveal clearly that our nation is the trunk and roots of these three nations." Since then Buddhism has remained in our nation. From Jinmu Tennō on and for more than two thousand years, Buddhism and Confucianism have never interfered with our history; all they did was to protect the root of this sacred nation and thus implement the fundamental vow of the kami. That is why it is common these days in the course of Shinto ceremonies to abandon the contemplation of the buddhas and the recitation of Buddhist scriptures.[11]

Here Kanetomo reveals the esoteric understanding that Prince Shōtoku was not only the patriarch of Buddhism in Japan but also the great disseminator of Shinto.

There can be no doubt that Kanetomo was influenced in his ideas by the *Jinnō shōtōki* (*A Chronicle of Gods and Sovereigns*, 1339) of Kitabatake Chikafusa (1293–1354), which said:

Japan is the divine country (*Ōyamato wa kami no kuni nari / Dainihon wa shinkoku nari*).[12] The heavenly ancestor it was who first laid its foundations, and the Sun Goddess left her descendants to reign over it forever and ever. This is true only of our country, and nothing similar may be found in foreign lands. This is why it is called the divine country. In the age of the gods, Japan was known as the "ever-fruitful land of reed-covered plains and luxuriant rice fields (*Toyoashihara no chiiho no aki no mizuho no kuni*). This name existed since the creation of heaven and earth. It appeared in the command given by the heavenly ancestor Kunitokotachi to the Male Deity and the Female Deity. Again, when the Great Goddess Amaterasu bequeathed the land to her grandchild, that name was used; it may thus be considered the prime name of Japan.

It is also called the country of the great eight islands. This name was given because eight islands were produced when the Male Deity and the Female Deity begot Japan. It is also called Yamato, which is the name of the central part of the eight islands. The eighth offspring of the deities was the god Heavenly-August-Sky-Luxuriant-Dragonfly-Lord-Youth (Ame no misora toyo akizune wake) [and the land he incarnated] was called Ō-yamato, Luxuriant-Dragon-Fly Island. It is now divided into forty-eight provinces."[13]

Medieval literature is full of apocryphal works, fabricated to reflect the views and purposes of their actual authors but attributed to some well-known personage or deity. Such works easily proliferate in times of uncertainty, and demagogues had the opportunity to do as they pleased. Just as medieval Christianity gave rise to many kinds of heresy, alternative views, and strange theories, esoteric doctrines of every description were widespread in medieval Japan. It was impossible to confirm them or to criticize them adequately. It was in this environment that Yoshida Kanetomo put in place the foundations that allowed Yoshida Shinto to ally itself to the political power of the day and to extend its own authority.

CHAPTER FIVE

Nativist Studies and a New View of Kami-Buddha Combination

So far I have discussed the basic differences between Shinto and Buddhism, and, more broadly, how deity is understood in Japan. I have also looked at the relationship between religious institutions and the state over the centuries, and described how new religious ideas grew as state authority declined. The many stalwart religious leaders that emerged out of the continuing chaotic times had changed society dramatically, offering people a religious vision in a period of national affliction and social crisis. The Pure Land school taught that the believer would attain rebirth in Amida's paradise (Sukhāvatī) by calling upon his name (*nenbutsu*), the Zen master Dōgen taught that a person could realize his or her buddha-nature and so achieve liberation through the practice of *shikan taza* ("just sitting"), and Nichiren proclaimed that the Lotus Sutra alone could save the country as the sutra of the One Vehicle (Ekayāna).

Shinto and Buddhism under the Tokugawa Shogunate

The early seventeenth century marked the beginning of "Pax Tokugawa" and the end of the dynamic political and religious flux of the medieval period. The secular rationalism of the Edo (or Tokugawa) period (1603–1867) stood in stark contrast to the religious passion and diversity of teachings and practices of the preceding era. Oda Nobunaga, Toyotomi Hideyoshi, and Tokugawa Ieyasu (1543–1616), the so-called "unifiers" of Japan, set about suppressing religious dissension and eliminating armed threats posed by religious institutions, like the warrior adherents (Ikkō *monto*) of the Shin Pure Land school and the *sōhei* (monastic warriors) of Mt. Hiei. Oda Nobunaga, intent on subduing those established Buddhist institutions that possessed a fighting capacity and strong religious convictions, ruthlessly suppressed their armed and economic strength, first razing the temple complex of Enryakuji on Mt. Hiei and slaughtering its inhabitants in 1571 and then subduing Ishiyama Honganji, the Shin Pure Land institution, in 1580. After Oda's assassination in 1582, his successor, Toyotomi Hideyoshi, destroyed the powerful Shingi Shingon Temple Negoroji in 1585. The religious landscape of Japan underwent a major shift.

New weapons and a new religion had arrived in Japan in the middle of the sixteenth century. Around 1542, Portuguese merchants landed on the island of Tanegashima, bringing muskets (*teppō*) with them, and within months muskets were being produced locally.[1] Christian missionaries began arriving by the end of that decade. Nobunaga, encouraged Christianity as a counter-balance to the powerful Buddhist institutions, and his armed forces were enhanced by the import of large numbers of firearms, which strengthened his aggressive and destructive power. A few of his vassals converted to Christianity, the so-called Christian daimyo, and very soon Christian influence was spreading, as was European (called "Nanban") culture generally, mainly through the merchants of the port of Sakai, near Osaka. Hideyoshi initially continued Nobunaga's religious policy regarding the strategic use of Christianity to weaken the influence of established religions, but the policy turned out to be a double-edged sword, as Hideyoshi became convinced that the Jesuit missionaries were plotting to rule the country through the Christian faith. With countries like India coming under the domination of the Christian-backed forces, the danger to Japan was evident. In 1587 Hideyoshi issued his edict expelling the missionaries.

It was Tokugawa Ieyasu who finally brought the country under unified rule. The political structure he established is called the *bakuhan* (*bakufu* government and domain) system. Ieyasu laid the foundations for the later policy of national seclusion (*sakoku*, "closed country") by issuing edicts banning the propagation and practice of Christianity in 1612 and 1613. This was Japan's first overall foreign policy and it remained in place for the next two hundred and more years. In terms of its results, it represented, from the point of view of world history, a bold policy reversal and a great experiment. The main reason for it was both to prevent the incursion of European countries and to secure internal stability. To contain European and Christian influence, Nagasaki and a part of Hirado were the only ports that remained open to foreign ships.

Unlike Nobunaga and Hideyoshi, who sought national and internal unification by weakening the influence of domestic religious institutions through direct confrontation and with the help of Christianity, Ieyasu set up the national isolation policy to exclude foreign interference and achieved political unification through the *bakuhan* system. In 1615 he promulgated codes such as the Kinchū Narabi ni Kuge Shohatto concerning the sovereign and the court nobility and the Buke Shohatto concerning warrior households, imposing strict restrictions on the scope of their activities. Also during his lifetime, a series of temple regulations (*jiin shohatto*) were issued separately to specific religious institutions, such as for Mt. Kōya in 1601, the Ise Shrines in 1603, and Sensōji (a temple in Edo) in 1613, as well as to sects and schools in general, like the codes for Shugendō in 1613, for the Tendai school in the Kantō region in 1614, and for the Shingon school in 1615.

All religious organizations were required to support the state and were rigorously controlled. The *danka* (parishioner) system was established under which all households were required to register with a temple, and this meant that every individual was affiliated with one Buddhist sect or another. Religious groups such as Christians and the Buddhist Fuju Fuse sect (which refused to accept anything from nonbelievers), were outlawed and severely persecuted. Religious institutions became subsidiary organizations within the government structure, complementing the state, and only those that supported the state system were allowed to exist. Thus a religious community that supported the state was formed.²

The beginnings of a restructuring of Shinto influence appeared during the early years of the Edo period. Toyotomi Hideyoshi had favored Yoshida Shinto and was posthumously enshrined according to its rites with the kami title of Hōkoku Daimyōjin (Great Shining Deity). Ieyasu, while inheriting Yoshida Shinto as a system, drastically reorganized it out of a wish to distance himself from a cult so closely associated with his predecessor. This resulted in a clash between Yoshida Shinto and a new Shinto school, called Tendai Sannō Ichijitsu Shinto, over the division of power and the differentiation of functions.

The creator of Sannō Ichijitsu Shinto was the Tendai priest Tenkai (1536?–1643). After Ieyasu's death the question arose concerning the rites according to which he should be enshrined. Tenkai advocated that the deified Ieyasu, Tōshō Shinkun (Divine Ruler Shining from the East), should be differentiated from Hideyoshi by being given the title of Daigongen (Great Avatar) according to the rites of the Sannō Ichijitsu Shinto school and considered an avatar of the Yakushi Nyorai. He devised a cult of Ieyasu as the tutelary deity of Tokugawa rule and the protector of the *bakuhan* system based on a network of shrines that extended all over the country and was centered on Ieyasu's mausoleum, the Tōshōgū Shrine at Nikkō. This contrasted with, and operated in parallel with, the shrine network of Amaterasu (Tenshō Daijin).³

This was a political theology concerning the peaceful unification of Japan that was produced by the Tokugawa house and supported by the warrior class. In this sense, we can say that the establishment of the Tōshōgū network was the articulation of an early modern mythology, a political mythology quite different from that of the ancient and medieval periods. During this time, too, warrior heroes who had performed distinguished service were venerated in many of the domains as kami. The Tōshōgū network represented a mythology of rule by bureaucrats backed by both military might and political acumen, and served as the ideology underpinning a secularized society.

Tōshōgū Shrines, headed by those at Nikkō and at Mt. Kunō in Shizuoka, were set up all over the country, built with political intent by Tenkai and others.

The creation of this new "fictional, inward-looking" myth of Tōshō Daigongen almost entirely stripped ancient myth of its authority[4] and circumscribed the power of the court and traditional religious institutions. The creation of this myth had the effect of secularizing the nobility and clergy, emasculating them so they became mere cultural figures—an idle educated class indulging in worldly pleasures. The secularized, "floating world" did not allow the survival of aggressive, radical figures who might object to the state of society or aspire to social change. By sealing off ancient myth, suppressing medieval myth, and raising a political deity to prominence, the new myth also placed a lid on folk shamanism, reformed Buddhism, Christianity, and other religious extremes.

Shinto under the *bakuhan* system was maintained by two lineages, Yoshida Shinto and Sannō Ichijitsu Shinto. In addition, there were Confucian Shinto streams (Suika Shinto), the Fukko (Restoration) Shinto (or Nativist Shinto), and Shirakawa (Hakke) Shinto, which had close connections with the court and its rituals. Tokugawa Mitsukuni (1628–1700) of the Mito domain and Hoshina Masayuki (1611–72) of the Aizu domain carried out a policy of separating Shinto and Buddhism and putting an end to combinatory practices, as well as regulating the number of temples and shrines in their territories. It was in this environment that Nativist Studies (Kokugaku) developed, focusing on the study of the Japanese classics (Nihon Kogaku) and criticism of the combinatory elements of Shinto, Buddhism, and Confucianism.

The Intellectual Environment of the Edo Period

The Edo period was a secularized age, with the "Tōshōgū network" nudging out all other religious initiatives. In this secularized environment, popular culture flourished. It reached a peak first in the Genroku era (1688–1704) and then in the Bunka and Bunsei eras

(1804–29). This was a culture of the urban dweller (*chōnin*): haiku, kabuki, the novels of Ihara Saikaku (1642–93) and the puppet plays (*jōruri*) of Chikamatsu Monzaemon (1653–1725) marked the development of a distinct Japanese popular culture. This culture, closely associated with public entertainment, encouraged the expansion of scholarship rather than religion. Influenced by the Chinese classical studies known as Ancient Learning (Kogaku) of men like Itō Jinsai (1627–1705) and Ogyū Sorai (1666–1728), Motoori Norinaga (1730–1801) and his "posthumous disciple" Hirata Atsutane (1776–1843) led a sudden flowering of Nativism. Confucianism, particularly the ideas of Zhu Xi (1130–1200) and Wang Yangming (1472–1529), was widely studied, as was Mitogaku, the historical studies associated with scholars of the Mito domain.

Edo period secularization of learning weakened the influence of religion and allowed urban culture to flourish. Both rural folk and urban dwellers had access to education through *terakoya* (local schools teaching basic literacy skills) and *juku* (private academies). The growth in numbers and the depth of the curricula of such schools raised the basic level of education on a national scale. Social stability encouraged the rapid expansion of literacy, in comparison with the uncertain times of the medieval period, when literacy was extremely low. This was a time when learning was most widespread and secularized, and this cultural and scholarly stockpile provided the intellectual support for the post-1868 Meiji state as it proceeded with its policy of "civilization and enlightenment" (*bunmei kaika*) and its adoption of Western material culture. If Japan had gone directly from the medieval period to the Meiji Restoration, Japanese scholarship would probably not have been able to catch up with the West, and without the ferment of intellectual inquiry and education of the Edo period, Japanese society might have experienced great turmoil following the Meiji Restoration, with a great disparity between the rich and the poor. More than two centuries of long-term social stability under the *bakuhan* system allowed the formation of a distinctive political and cultural system that paved the way for the subsequent acceptance of European culture.

The advent of "ancient learning"

The power of myth greatly weakened during the early modern period of Japanese history owing to the ban on Christianity, the policy of national isolation, and strict control of religious institutions. Scholarship flourished, though, and a movement arose among adherents of Kogaku, the neo-Confucianism of Zhu Xi, and classical Confucianism alike to look back to the past and effect a "return to origins" (*genten kaiki*). Thus, Itō Jinsai said that the *Analects* should be studied directly, not through Zhu Xi's annotations, and Motoori Norinaga developed a Nativist type of "ancient learning," encouraging the study of origins as represented in the *Kojiki*. He took the position that the deep study of the essence and values of Japan's distinctive culture was not to be made by seeing things with a "Chinese spirit" (*karagokoro*) but rather by rejecting its infection.

Motoori is famous for his studies of the *Kojiki* and the *Tale of Genji*. His teacher, Kamo no Mabuchi (1697–1769), had analyzed the *Man'yōshū*, while his "student," Hirata Atsutane, went on to create (or "restore") his own distinctive mythology. Of the three, it was Motoori who achieved the most as a scholar. His study of the *Kojiki* and the *Tale of Genji* became the cornerstone of later research into Japanese culture. He identified the aesthetic consciousness and spiritual sense of the court culture of Heian Japan as *mono no aware* (an awareness of the evanescence of things"). He wrote:

> If I were asked
> to explain the Japanese spirit [*yamatogokoro*]
> I would say it is
> wild cherry blossoms
> glowing in the morning sun.[5]

For Motoori, the wild cherry blossoms, their scent wafting on the early morning breeze, was the epitome of the Japanese spirit. A sensibility to subtle beauties of nature is at the core of *mono no aware*, the perceptivity to appreciate the subtle changes of all things. Motoori made this the very core of the Japanese spirit. And the essence of *mono no aware* is clearly expressed in the *Tale of Genji*.

Motoori did not, however, concern himself with what happened to the human soul after death. He wrote in the *Tōmonroku* (Record of Dialogues) that the absence of the assurance of peace of mind (*anjin*) in the afterlife is in itself reassuring. He did not believe that people should seek peace of mind by submitting their fate to the will of heaven, nor did he subscribe to the vague Japanese idea that the soul goes to the mountains after death to protect its descendants, or that it remains in an indeterminate state for 49 days before being reborn. In his mind it was better to have only an indefinite conception about what happened after death. Rather than being overly concerned with the afterlife, it was preferable to live in the now. In this sense Motoori's ideas were centered on the present life, and he asserted that for Shinto, peace of mind meant to live as the ancients had done, finding reassurance in the absence of assurance.

Hirata Atsutane, who declared himself a posthumous disciple of Motoori, was a Nativist scholar who, by contrast, spent his whole life intensively studying what happened to the soul after death and understanding the nature of the spirit world.[6] He was not satisfied with the literary emotivity exemplified by Motoori's *mono no aware*. What most interested him was evidence of spirituality, the destination and repose of an individual's soul after death and the true nature of the spirit realm. What happens to people when they die? How have souls come here, and where do they go after death? He believed that unless people understood the soul and the afterlife they could not understand the Japanese spirit (*yamatogokoro*) in the truest sense. In the process, he developed a view and discourse of Shinto completely different from that of his "teacher."

Hirata was deeply interested in *yōkai* (monsters) and *obake* (ghosts), subjects that had not until then been the subjects of scholarship. For him, such study was a matter of serious inquiry, connected as it was to questions about the kami and the soul and about the other realm and the spiritual world.

As we noted in Chapter 3, a perusal of the *Tale of Genji* and Lady Murasaki's *Diary* shows how regularly and assiduously magico-religious prayer rituals (*kaji kitō*) were carried out at the Heian court by esoteric Buddhist priests, *shugenja*, and *onmyōji*. Lady Murasaki vividly documented what she witnessed during the birth of the future Go-Ichijō Tennō: how various types of exorcists performed *kaji kitō* to extend the bounds of protection around Shōshi during childbirth and expel malevolent spirits (*mononoke*). She makes us feel we were present at the birth, as she recounts how the esoteric masters (*ajari*) were at their wit's end trying to expel the possessing *mononoke* with their magico-religious power. A similar scene is described realistically in the Aoi chapter of the *Tale of Genji*, where "a spirit (*mononoke*), it seemed, was making the lady [Aoi] extremely unwell."

The Heian court depicted there was by no means the world of beautiful and elegant feelings that Motoori portrayed with his phrase *mono no aware*. Of course we do find such sentiments in the literature of the time, such as the *Kokin wakashū* (A Collection of Poems Ancient and Modern)[7] and the *Shin kokin wakashū* (A New Collection of Poems Ancient and Modern).[8] However, behind the world that was to a large extent sublimated aesthetically in works of literature lay a hidden domain where *mononoke* ran rampant. Where there is light there is also shade. Hirata Atsutane asserted that reality could not be understood without looking properly into the domain of the dark. This darkness was unknowable territory for Motoori, who, not being concerned with it, could say that finding reassurance in the absence of assurance was the proper mindset of the Japanese. He thus never investigated the spiritual realm any further, finding value only in what caught the light and what was beautiful on the surface. His discourse therefore covered only the elegant outer surface of Shinto.

Hirata, by contrast, focused on the dark, developing a Shinto discourse based on *mononoke* and what was below the surface. His studies of *mononoke* centering on the spirit world were a form of Restoration Shinto (Fukko Shinto) that sought out a destination for the soul.

CHAPTER FIVE

The Japanocentric thought of Hirata Atsutane

The Hirata school of Nativist Studies had a strong impact on, and provided an important stimulus for, the grassroots Nativism of the Meiji period advanced by his followers. During the period of upheaval leading up to the Meiji Restoration of 1868, Hirata's ideas moved away from the spiritual world and focused on a Japanocentric national theology connected with the ideas of the Mito school (Mitogaku). Japanocentric thought was at the core of Hirata's ideas. He claimed that Japan was the first country created in the world and so was the center of everything. Japan's mythology likewise was seen as the source of all world mythology; it had been transmitted to all lands and all regions and had become part of all their myths. By this reckoning, the myth of Izanagi and Izanami was the origin of the myth of Adam and Eve. Japan was at the root of everything, and whatever existed abroad had flowed there from Japan.

Such nationalistic ideas naturally became linked with antiforeign, *sonnō jōi* (revere the emperor, expel the barbarian) concepts, fomenting an ideology backing the overthrow of the *bakuhan* system and restoration of the sovereign power of the *tennō*. Restoration Shinto-type *sonnō* ideas, operating under the banner of a just cause, saw the *tennō* as the legitimate ruler, standing at the apex of the Japanese government, with a legitimacy older than the Tokugawa shogunate. After all, it was the sovereign's right to formally appoint the *seii taishōgun* ("barbarian subduing general"). Thus the overthrow of the shogunate and its *bakuhan* system meant returning power to the *tennō*, the royal house of antiquity.

Hirata Atsutane's theology became the ideological basis for resisting the European powers and driving away enemies based on ideas of service to the sovereign (*kinnō*), reverence for the sovereign (*sonnō*), Japanocentrism, and the exclusion of foreigners. At first the elements of reverence for the *tennō* and expulsion of foreigners were linked, but when the scale of British and American naval power became apparent, expulsion of foreigners was put aside, and ideas about "civilization and enlightenment" took center stage. Following the Meiji

Restoration, Western culture and institutions were rapidly introduced. During the turmoil accompanying the end of the Tokugawa shogunate, Hirata was held up as a leading ideologue of Japanese ethnic nationalism (*minzoku shugi*). With attention being focused on his Japanism (*Nihonshugi*) and nationalism, which were driving forces propelling the Meiji Restoration, Hirata's studies on the spirit world received little attention.

Nevertheless, it was the study of the spirit realm that Hirata was keen on advancing. His achievements were later continued along two lines, in the "spirit studies" of Ōmotokyō and other new Shinto religious sects, and the ethnographical studies of Yanagita Kunio (1875–1962) and Orikuchi Shinobu (1887–1953). The legacy of Hirata's Nativism is apparent in the questions raised: how do the Japanese understand "god," what is "god"/kami, what is the human soul, and what is the nature of belief for the Japanese? Though many of Hirata's direct disciples, as well as their disciples, were directly involved in the political movements of the Meiji era and were at the center of national policymaking in the early years of the new government, they were not in a position to promote Nativist concepts like the spiritualism that Hirata advocated. This was left to the spiritual studies of sect Shinto, in particular Ōmotokyō, and to academia, including ethnography.

Kami and Buddhas in the Modern Period

A new unifying mythology again became necessary in the period of nation building that followed the Meiji Restoration. This took the form of reviving *ritsuryō* mythology in what was called the "restoration of imperial rule" (*ōsei fukko*) and "returning to the times of Jinmu Tennō" (*Jinmu sōgyō*), resuscitating the aspiration of the ancient state and returning to the "roots" to resist the encroachments of the West. In administrative terms, this meant the reconstruction of the Jingikan, the *ritsuryō* office in charge of rites for heavenly and earthly deities (*jingi*), with importance equal to that the Dajōkan, the Council of State. The myth created for the new political environment was for a "confrontational, outward-looking figure," replacing the "fictional, inward-looking figure" of the Edo period (see chapter 6).

The separation of kami and buddhas

The position of the Jingikan and of Shinto as state policy is reflected in the government offices set up to administer religion in the first two decades of the Meiji era. Administrative changes, particularly in the first decade of the new government, reflect the Meiji regime's uncertainty about basic policy on religion. The basis of the earliest policy was the separation of kami and buddha worship (which had already been carried out in the early Edo period in some domains, such as Mito and Aizu). A series of edicts to this effect were implemented in the third month of 1868, which scholars call the "kami-buddha separation edicts (*shinbutsu bunri-rei*), though at the time they were actually termed "clarification" not "separation." The first, enacted on April 9, 1868, forbade combinatory priests (*bettō, shasō*) from serving the kami; they were required to give up their status as Buddhist priests and "return to lay life" in order to take up duties as Shinto priests. The second, enacted on April 20, prohibited the use of "Buddhist" titles like *gongen* or *bosatsu* for kami and the placement of Buddhist statues and other items in sites of kami veneration. This legislation led in some places to a movement to eradicate Buddhism completely (*haibutsu kishaku*), and many important artifacts associated with combinatory religion were destroyed.

Through these measures, the state intruded on what the Japanese people believed. It was a religious reformation from above that was highly inconsistent with people's personal ideas about the kami and buddhas. For more than 10,000 years, people of the archipelago had thought of kami in terms of kami-kami combination. Within that combinatory structure, the kami, the buddhas and bodhisattvas, and all other spirits interpenetrated one another. Now, the government tried to forcibly divide this complex world of the divine into kami and buddhas and set about identifying the kami of all the shrines in Japan with those mentioned in the *Kojiki*. The new kami-buddha separation policy subjected the traditional understanding of the divine to an enforced divorce. People's fundamental understanding of kami did not essentially change as a result, but great changes came about institutionally. In shrine-temple complexes all over the country, Buddhist priests who had been reciting both the Heart Sutra and *norito* when conducting prayer rituals for the kami were now required to don the robes of a Shinto shrine priest.

And it was Shugendō that received the mightiest blow. This combinatory religion incorporating both Shinto and Buddhist elements was fatally compromised by the kami-buddha separation legislation and in 1872 was banned as a superstitious religion unfit for the new age. This was ironic, for the following year, the ban on Christianity was lifted, which meant Christianity was given official recognition, and the same year the Shin Pure Land priest Shimaji Mokurai (1838–1911) and his colleagues agitated publicly for religious freedom. Yet Japan's unique combinatory religion, founded by En no Gyōja, was banned. There was a clear contradiction in the religious policy of the new government. If the principle of religious freedom was to be upheld, Shugendō should not have been banned. It was rejected because it went against Meiji state ideology, whereas Christianity was formally accepted in the name of "religious freedom."

Shinto in the new government

Meiji religious policy proceeded by trial and error, tossed on the waves of "civilization and enlightenment" (*bunmei kaika*) ideas while a new state apparatus was being built. No consistent policy was ever hammered out, so matters proceeded by twists and turns. In its midst, Hirata school Nativist scholars rapidly retreated and were eclipsed. This occurred in the broader context of a government attempting a "renewal," grafting the most advanced forms of Western civilization onto institutions drawn from the model of Japan's ancient state. It was a path forged by combining diametrical opposites. A chronology of the main events involving the shrines and handling of religion follows.

April 1868[9] The Jingikan is created as a department within the Council of State (Dajōkan), and the following year is raised to the position of an independent office ranked above it. However, in September 1871 it is demoted to the Jingishō (Ministry for Kami Affairs), a new ministry within the Council of State, which is in turn replaced by the Kyōbushō (Ministry of Religion and Education) in 1872. This lasts until 1877, when its functions are taken over by the Shajikyoku (Bureau of Shrines and Temples) located within the Home Ministry. In 1900 this bureau is divided into the Jinjakyoku (Bureau of Shrine Affairs) within the Home Ministry and the Shūkyōkyoku (Bureau of Religion), established within the Ministry of Education.

1869 The American Board of Commissioners for Foreign Missions establishes the Congregationalist Nihon Kumiai Kirisuto Kyōkai in Yokohama.
Nakayama Miki (1798–1887), the founder of Tenrikyō, begins writing the *Ofudesaki*, the sect's most important scripture, which is made up of over 1,700 *waka*.
Emperor Meiji visits the Ise Shrines in February, the first visit ever by a reigning monarch.
The Tokyo Shōkonsha (renamed Yasukuni Shrine in 1879), commemorating those who had died in the Boshin War, is built at Kudan.

February 1870 Imperial edict announces the Great Promulgation Campaign (*taikyō senpu undō*), involving both Shinto priests and, for a time, Buddhist clergy as *kyōdōshoku* ("national evangelists"). This campaign, which aimed to make Shinto the state religion, is promulgated through the Daikyōin (Great Teaching Institute), succeeded in 1875 by the Shinto Jimukyoku, which is closely linked with the Ise Shrines. The campaign, however, encounters resistance and ultimately collapses.

1871 Koseki (Household Registration) Law is enacted, bringing to an end the Edo-period system of local population registers (*shumon aratame chō*) and compulsory temple affiliation (*terauke*).

In May, sacerdotal lineages associated with Shinto shrines are abolished; shrines are declared not private possessions of sacerdotal lineages but places for "state rites" (*kokka no saishi*). Hierarchical shrine and priestly rankings are also determined at this time.

1872 The Jingishō is abolished, together with the Shrine and Temple Section (Shajika) of the Bureau of Census Registration at the Ministry of Finance.

The Kyōbushō is established and takes over supervision of the "national evangelists," issuing them the "generalized Shinto ideology" called the Three Standards of Instruction (*Sanjō no kyōsoku*).[10] Buddhist priests are permitted to marry, grow their hair, and eat meat.

The Kurozumi Association (Kurozumi Kōsha) is given permission to proselytize (later this becomes the Kurozumikyō, one of the 13 Shinto sects).

Shugendō is banned; *shugenja* must affiliate either with Tendai or Shingon if they wish to maintain their priestly standing.

The Daikyōin is set up; temples, shrines and preaching places are designated "small" teaching institutes, where instruction is given based on the Three Standards.

January 1873 Folk shamanism is banned. *Azusa miko* (catalpa shamans), *ichiko* (traveling shamanic diviners), possession-prayer performers (*yorikitō*), fox exorcisers (*kitsunesage*), and the like are prohibited.

Christianity-prohibiting edict-boards on roadsides and street corners are taken down, lifting a centuries-old ban. This marks the beginning of religious freedom in the modern sense.

In March the government declares two national holidays, the first marking the accession of Jinmu (Kigensetsu, February 11) and the second the emperor's birthday (Tenchōsetsu, November 11). A further six are added in October: the court New Year festival (Genshisai, January 3), the New Year's feast (Shinnen Enkai, January 5), commemoration of Kōmei Tennō (January 30), commemoration of Jinmu Tennō (April 3), the harvest festival at Ise (Kannamesai, October 17), and the harvest festival (Niinamesai, November 23).

June 1874 The Kyōbushō prohibits healing by means of magic (*kin'yō*) and prayer rituals (*kitō*). The ban on folk healing practices coincides with the introduction of Western medicine.

1879 The Tokyo Shōkonsha is renamed Yasukuni Shrine and receives the ranking of *bekkaku kanpeisha* (special ranked imperial shrine).

1880 Tanaka Chigaku (1861–1939) founds the Rengekai, a lay Nichiren group; this later grows into the Kokuchūkai.

1881 Resolution of the so-called Pantheon Dispute (*saijin ronsō*), which had been brewing for a number of years. Shinto priests had set up their own private Shintō Jimukyoku (Shinto Office) in 1875, but a dispute broke out between the Ise- and Izumo-affiliated factions over which deities should be enshrined there. At first it was intended to enshrine the three creator deities that appeared at the beginning of the *Kojiki*—Ame no minakanushi, Takamimusubi, and Kamimusubi—together with Amaterasu. At the center of those proposing this was the chief priest at the Ise Shrines, Tanaka Yoritsune (1836–97). The Izumo faction, led by Senge Takatomi (1845–1918), chief priest of Izumo Shrine, advocated the enshrinement of five deities, adding the main deity of Izumo Shrine to the above four. Senge pointed to the existence of both unconcealed and concealed realms (*yūken ichinyo*), saying that Ōkuninushi, the lord of the invisible realm (*yūkai*), should be enshrined on the same basis as Amaterasu, the chief deity of the visible world (*kenkai*). The issue here was whether or not to enshrine Ōkuninushi, and this placed the Ise and Izumo factions in bitter opposition. The Izumo faction of course wanted their deity to be enshrined, while the Ise faction emphasized the superiority and special nature of Amaterasu as the ruler of both heaven and earth, governing both the visible and invisible realms. The dispute is settled in January 1881 at a national Shinto conference convened to settle the problem with the help of government officials: it was determined that the enshrined deities should be those venerated in the three shrines of the imperial palace, the kami of heaven and earth, Amaterasu, and the ancestral spirits. The Izumo faction experiences a strong and bitter sense of defeat.[11]

1882 Shinto priests are barred from acting as *kyōdōshoku* and from conducting funerals. In April, the Ise Shrines establish the Jingū Kōgakkan for research and the education of Shinto priests.
A number of Shinto groups become independent religious organizations: Shintō Jingū-ha (superintendent: Tanaka Yoritsune), Shintō Taisha-ha (superintendent: Senge Takatomi), Shintō Fusō-ha (superintendent: Shishino Nakaba [1844–84]), Shintō Jikkō-ha (superintendent: Shibata Hanamori [1809–90]), Shintō Taisei-ha (superintendent: Hirayama Seisai), and Shintō Shinshū-ha (superintendent: Yoshimura Masamochi [1839–1915]).
The Shinto Office establishes the Kōten Kōkyūjo (Center for the Study of Classical Culture) for the study of Japanese classical literature and the training of Shinto priests (this later becomes Kokugakuin University).

The dashed hopes of the Nativists of the Hirata school are vividly portrayed in the novel *Yoakemae* (Before the Dawn) by Shimazaki Tōson (1872–1943):[12] "The way to the restoration of antiquity (*fukko no michi*) has ceased to exist, and the Hirata school had already fallen into ruin," and "The activities of Nativist circles, with their dreams of a return to antiquity and their resolve to bring about the Meiji Restoration—what the many members of the Hirata school following Atsutane's death, including Hirata Kanetane, thought and did ended in a great failure." Shimazaki must have seen this sequence of events close up, as his father, Masaki, was a regional follower of the Hirata school, as was the father of folklorist Yanagita Kunio (with whom novelist Tōson was on close terms), who became a Shinto priest after the Meiji Restoration.

The one dream of these local Hirata Nativists and Shinto priests was that Japan would become a country of Shintoism. However, the religious policy of the Meiji government was complicated and obscure, meandering this way and that. The Hirata Shintoists apparently wanted Shinto to become the state religion, perhaps thinking of making Japan a state with a culture and religion found nowhere else in the world. However, as religious freedom progressed, the Hirata Nativists found themselves out of touch with the times and were rapidly ousted from influential positions. While "civilization and enlightenment" were moving forward on the one hand, there was also progress toward a state system that would ultimately center on the emperor, for it was this that was ultimately decided was the distinctively Japanese type of system that could stand up to the Western powers. By the late nineteenth century, a regenerated "emperor system" peculiar to Japan was rapidly being developed. This was the invention of the modern myth centered on what I call the "confrontational, outward-looking figure."

The chimera mythology

This new myth, created to complete the modern Meiji system, can be regarded as being chimerical. According to Greek mythology, the chimera was a grotesque creature made up of many parts. The Meiji state, too, was like a chimera, embracing the latest elements of Western civilization while seeking to revive ancient Japanese practices, as explicit in the slogan *ōsei fukko* (restoration of the monarchy). It was an attempt to both return to the Yamato past and to join the ranks of advanced Western powers. The state was shaping a renaissance, reviving the things of the past with its left hand while seizing what was newest with its right and attempting to buckle them together. This chimeric union of *ōsei fukko* and "civilization and enlightenment" characterized the myth guiding Japan's modernization drive.

Hirata Shinto gradually disappeared through the implementation of such policies as kami-buddha separation, restoration of the monarchy, "civilization and enlightenment" (*bunmei kaika*), "rich country, strong army" (*fukoku kyōhei*), "promotion of industry" (*shokusan kōgyō*), lifting of the ban on Christianity, religious freedom, and the principle of separation of state and religion. The freedom and popular rights movement (*jiyū minken undō*) emerged in the 1880s as well, and the settlement of the issues of that time came with the promulgation of the Meiji Constitution (Constitution of the Empire of Japan) on February 11, 1889, which established the emperor as the sovereign. With the issuing of the Imperial Rescript on Education the following year, Japan's course and overall framework as a nation under the rule of law was set.

The Meiji Constitution established two key points: that Japan shall be governed by a "line of Emperors unbroken for ages eternal" (*bansei ikkei*) and that the "Emperor is sacred and inviolable" (*shinsei fukashin*). The emperor was the sacred, inviolable ruler of Japan in a direct line from Ninigi no mikoto. This marked the beginning of the new myth of the national polity (*kokutai*)—the establishment of a "confrontational and outward-looking figure." Even in ancient times no claims about the sacred and inviolable nature of the ruler were made, and he was not deified in this way in the *ritsuryō* state. In stipulating that the emperor was divine and came from an unbroken imperial line, the Meiji Constitution created a distinctive Japanese state system that grafted a Prussian model of absolute monarchy onto the ancient *ritsuryō*-type system, in the process setting up a chimerical absolute monarchy.

CHAPTER FIVE

The shrine merger policy

In 1906 controversial legislation was passed to consolidate the nation's shrines, and this policy was implemented through the Jinjakyoku (Bureau of Shrine Affairs) within the Home Ministry.[13] The goal of the mergers was to have one shrine per village (*isson issha*). After the merger, the surviving shrine would absorb the assets of the other shrines. The reduced number of shrines was expected to make the system of state support feasible and to encourage greater alignment between the shrine and the local government. In practice, though, it led to the destruction of local culture, as large numbers of shrines with unique histories and traditions within their communities were forced to shut down.

Many of these old shrines were simple structures, but they were surrounded by forests, often with towering camphor trees among which people felt the presence of the divine. After the shrines were merged, some people cut down these old trees—quite valuable as lumber—and sold them for profit, leading to the loss of once-sacred landmarks of the community, aggravating wealth disparities, and breeding distrust among residents. The shrine-consolidation policy led to the decline of local culture, disrupted community life, and ultimately destabilized the very foundations of Japanese society. At least in terms of the social "ecology" of the community, the merging of shrines was a great mistake.

Naturalist and folklorist Minakata Kumagusu (1867–1941) was among the first to use the English word "ecology" to express his great opposition to the mergers.[14] A Diet member from Wakayama prefecture named Nakamura Keijirō read a letter from Minakata during Diet deliberations. In it, Minakata, who had studied in Michigan and London, argued that unlike forests that were planted for commercial exploitation, the groves in which shrines were situated had not been cut down for hundreds, sometimes thousands, of years and featured an "ecology" of close and intricate mutual relationships among the trees and plants. Supporting him in this campaign to end the mergers was the young Yanagita Kunio, who went on to become a famous folklorist and ethnologist. These protests led to the 1920 decision by the House of Peers to abolish this harmful policy.

The fate of local shrines aside, the Meiji government continued to insist that shrines serve as the sites for the performance of state rites and rituals and refused to consider them as centers of religious worship, unlike Buddhist temples and Christian churches. It did recognize as "religion" certain Shinto sects, though, of which thirteen were officially authorized, including Kurozumikyō,[15] Konkōkyō, and Tenrikyō. Shrines and shrine Shinto, however, were not classified as religion; they were identified as part of the government and tasked with performing rituals of the state. Shrine priests (*shinkan*), who had all been placed under the authority of the Jingikan at the time of the Meiji Restoration, were thus civil servants. This system gradually contracted until the term *shinkan* was applied only to the priests of the Ise Shrines and those ranked as national and imperial shrines (*kankoku heisha*). After 1894, *shinkan* legally applied only to Ise priests, and following the Shinto Directive of 1945, the term was abolished completely. *Shinkan* were not religious figures but worked for the state as bureaucrats. Buddhist priests, on the other hand, were religious figures. A strangely distorted system had come into being.

The system established meant that insofar as Izumo Taisha, which enshrined Ōkuninushi, was a shrine, it was deemed an organ of the state and responsible for performing state rites. Its chief priest, Senge Takatomi, was not satisfied with this role, however, and choosing rather to propagate Shinto as a religion, quit his *shinkan* position in 1882 to become superintendent (*kanchō*) of the Shintō Taisha-ha (later Shintō Taisha-kyō and now Izumo Ōyashirokyō), an independent Shinto sect. While both Izumo Taisha and Shintō Taisha-ha worshipped Ōkuninushi, one was not considered a religion, while the other was. This was clearly a paradoxical system. It would not have been such a problem if shrines had been recognized as being religious institutions: they would not have become the loci for the moral and ethical education of the nation. In the Meiji era, it was not a simple issue, however. Senge Takatomi was recognized as a religious figure not as the chief priest of Izumo Taisha but as the superintendent of his sect. In both roles, though, he revered and performed services for the same deity. Such a paradox was also inherent in the plan to apply the principles of religious freedom and the separation of state and religion imported from Europe to Japan's religious culture and its religious policy.

Growth of religious reform movements

In an earlier work I made a study of Hirayama Seisai (1815–90), who founded a Shinto sect called Shintō Taiseikyō.[16] In 1866, he was made magistrate of foreign affairs (*gaikoku bugyō*) by the Tokugawa shogunate and promoted to general magistrate (*gaikoku sōbugyō*) the following year, when Tokugawa Yoshinobu formally returned political authority to the *tennō* (*taisei hōkan*), signaling the beginning of the restoration of imperial rule. Early that same year, Meiji Tennō ascended the throne. In 1868 it was announced that rule would be according to a "unity of ritual and government" (*saisei itchi*). That was the same year as the implementation of the *shinbutsu bunri* measures and promulgation of the Charter Oath (Oath in Five Articles) at the Meiji ascension ceremony in April. Hirayama served as chief priest of Hikawa Shrine from 1873 and of Hie Shrine in Tokyo from 1875, but resigned from these posts to become senior instructor (*daikyōsei*) of the *kyōdōshoku*. In 1882 he became the superintendent (*kanchō*) of Shintō Taiseikyō and worked simultaneously as a professor at the Center for the Study of Classical Culture (Kōten Kōkyūjo) founded the same year.

A number of new lay religious movements based on the Lotus Sutra and new Shinto visions of the divine also developed, prominent among which were the Nichiren Buddhist Kokuchūkai (National Pillar Society) of Tanaka Chigaku (1861–1939) and the Ōmotokyō of Deguchi Nao (1836–1918) and Deguchi Onisaburō (1871–1948). The latter was a religious and social reform movement that looked to world-renewal (*yonaoshi*), that is, the reconstruction of society, based on a vision of kami rebuilding the world similar to that of Tenrikyō and Konkōkyō. This vision was expressed in the *ofudesaki* of both

Nakayama Miki of Tenrikyō and Deguchi Nao. The revelations in automatic writing received by Deguchi Nao in a kind of spirit possession (*kamigakari*) were linked with "spirit studies" (*reigaku*) by her son-in-law, Deguchi Onisaburō, who took Ōmotokyō to a new stage.[17]

Hirata Atsutane influenced the Meiji Restoration period in three ways. The first was his "learning of the ancient way" (Kodōgaku). This had an impact on Ōkuni Takamasa (1792–1871)[18] and Fukuba Yoshishizu (Bisei; 1831–1907) and the Japanocentric, nationalistic direction of their Restoration Shinto.[19] The second was his influence, as a pioneering ethnographer, on Yanagita Kunio and Orikuchi Shinobu (see below). The third was his effect on the "spirit studies" of Honda Chikaatsu (1822–83), Nagasawa Katsutate (1858–94),[20] Deguchi Onisaburō, Miyaji Suii (1852–1904), Miyaji Izuo (1847–1918), Asano Wasaburō (1874–1937)[21] and others.

Discourse on Shinto in the early Meiji period took up questions concerning the state and the national polity (*kokutai*). How should the national character be understood? This discourse drew on Hirata's Nativism and on Mitogaku and was very powerful around the time of the Meiji Restoration, influencing in particular the reestablishment of the Jingikan. Other questions concerned the emperor (*tennō*), the nature of the Japanese spirit, and the spirituality of the Japanese. This latter involved the study of *yōkai* (*tengu, oni, obake*) and of the kami and the concealed world. All of these topics were important in Hirata's Nativism.

The "New Nativism" of Yanagita Kunio and Orikuchi Shinobu

It was Yanagita Kunio and Orikuchi Shinobu who laid the foundations of *minzokugaku* (folklore studies)[22] as they delved deeply into the forms taken by Japanese religious belief. Here I would like to examine what Shinto meant for these two pioneers who spearheaded the study of Japanese folk culture. Yanagita was later to coin the term *jōmin* ("abiding folk") to refer to ordinary people as the carriers of this folk culture, and he set out to study their clothing, food, dwellings, and other aspects of everyday life in a comprehensive manner.

In the period following World War II, one of the most important questions facing Yanagita and Orikuchi was how the souls of the war dead could be consoled. For Yanagita, who published *Senzo no hanashi* (About Our Ancestors) in 1945 immediately after the war, this was a matter concerning the reaffirmation and reexamination of the form and meaning of venerating ancestors. In Buddhist terms, this would be how to venerate the spirits of *muenbotoke*, those who had died without anyone to pray for the repose of their souls, for example, through disaster or war. Orikuchi, who published his *Minzoku shikan ni okeru takai kannen* (The Concept of the Other Realm in Ethno-history) in 1952, called the young people who had died in the war "incomplete spirits" (*mikan seirei*), or those unable to gain buddhahood. How could these souls be made complete? Was it possible to console and venerate them?

Yanagita and Orikuchi, along with Deguchi Onisaburō, Asano Wasaburō, and Tomokiyo Yoshisane (1888–1952),[23] took up the subject of spirituality that Hirata Atsutane had studied so deeply and gave it a new outlook and methodology. As I have written elsewhere in detail,[24] Suzuki Daisetsu criticized Hirata as the evil nemesis who paved the way toward militaristic nationalism, State Shinto, and ultimately defeat in World War II. I would raise the point here that in his *Japanese Spirituality*, Suzuki intentionally or unconsciously overlooked the question of spirituality that Hirata took so seriously. Many later Nativist scholars likewise remained silent on the matter. Suzuki condemned Hirata unilaterally without giving him credit for this line of research.

I would now like to examine what Yanagita called the culture of ordinary people (*jōmin bunka*) for insights into what lies at the core of popular culture.

Yanagita Kunio and minzokugaku

Yanagita Kunio was born in 1875 in the village of Tsujikawa in Hyogo prefecture. He graduated from the First Higher School and enrolled in the elite Faculty of Law at Tokyo Imperial University, after which he joined the Ministry of Agriculture and Trade, specializing in agricultural policy. In 1914 he became the chief of the Secretariat of the House of Peers but left the government in 1919 and began working for the daily *Asahi Shimbun* as an editorial writer while pursuing his studies in local history and folklore. In the course of his work in agricultural policy, he had always been interested in how country people managed to live in a stable and comfortable way and what constituted their happiness. Yanagita thus personally embodied an awareness of both political and policy issues and *minzokugaku*.

Yanagita believed that his studies of local culture should be aimed at contributing to local development, such as through village revival (*mura okoshi*) and community building (*machi zukuri*). To put this into effect, it was first necessary to study the local area, which provided the raw material of the fundamental culture. It was necessary to gain a firsthand understanding of the locality. Books alone could not achieve this, since the overwhelming majority of the books had been written from the standpoint of those in power or by intellectuals. In times past, most ordinary people were illiterate, and so what was most important was to inquire into Japanese beliefs and lifestyles through the oral culture and trace the wisdom and legacy inherent there to appreciate and recognize it anew.

While still serving as a bureaucrat concerned with agricultural policy, Yanagita began his local studies (*kyōdo kenkyū*) in order to promote government countermeasures for rural villages in crisis and to preserve local culture. These studies eventually grew into his *minzokugaku*. For him, the purpose of *minzokugaku* was to study the political economy (*keisei saimin*)[25] and bring relief to society. It was a field of study for the benefit of both society and people that sought to bring ordinary people (*jōmin*) happiness. He felt that scholarship should be useful to society and linked to protecting the family and the community, and by extension to society and the country as a whole. Japan was not preserved by the state from above but by the people's own local communities. For Yanagita, *minzokugaku* was what would protect and preserve the native locality (*kyōdo*)[26] by rediscovering, retransmitting, and recreating the fundamental culture.

Orikuchi Shinobu and minzokugaku

Orikuchi Shinobu, who became Yanagita's foremost follower and colleague, was quite a different sort of folklorist. Essentially, he was a poet, continually pursuing the question of the individual's soul, writing novels as well as poetry. He was born in Osaka in 1887. From his early years he had felt a certain uneasiness about his upbringing, and from around the time when he was 14 and a student at the Tennōji Middle School he became convinced that he was not the child of his parents but of his father and his mother's younger sister. This would explain, he thought, the coldness of his mother and why his parents did not seem to love him. The death of his father at that age brought to the fore his doubts about the circumstances of his birth, and he suffered a nervous breakdown, twice attempting suicide.

The collection of Orikuchi's *tanka* poetry published in 1947, *Kodai kan'aishū* (Archaic Love), contains a poem called "Itokenaki haru" (Spring of My Youth):

> Detested by my father,
> Unloved by my mother,
> In my youth
> I was treated differently
> From my brothers and sister.

In another poem in the same collection, "Kotsugaishō" (The Face of a Beggar), he wrote:

> And so, this is the face
> Of someone destined to become a beggar,
> Who emerged in this world,
> At arms' length from his mother and father.
> . . . .
> Well then, in the image on my mirror
> Nonetheless there it is.

Orikuchi's three elder brothers all had one-character names (静, 順 and 進), while he and two younger brothers (twins) had two-character names (信夫, 親夫 and 和夫). The twins, born seven years after Shinobu, were the children of his father and Yū, the younger sister of his mother, Kō. Therefore, he thought that he himself must be the illegitimate child of his father Hidetarō and Yū. This would explain why his mother disliked him so much. Haunted by an existential anxiety, he could not find his place in the family. Thinking that he had been born unwanted into the world, he developed a strong inferiority complex and tendency for self-negation.

During this tormented time, his youngest maternal aunt, Ei, took him to visit his grandfather in Asuka, the ancient capital near Nara where the *ritsuryō* state was born. This journey represented a great escape for the boy, who loved the *Man'yōshū* and had been writing poetry from a young age. Wandering around Asuka like a ghost, Orikuchi felt nostalgia for the distant past, and a small hope grew within him.

Orikuchi's grandfather had been a member of the family of priests of one of the oldest shrines in the Asuka valley, Asukanimasu Shrine. In Asuka, the 15-year-old Shinobu, plagued by the mystery surrounding his birth, experienced firsthand the landscape of the *Man'yōshū* and found salvation and hope in it. A stronghold of history and fantasy, the *Man'yōshū* became all the more familiar to him. He saw the world of the Japanese classics as if it was a dream of another realm. Later he entered Kokugakuin University and studied Japanese literature. Returning to his home in Osaka after graduation, he taught Japanese and Chinese classical texts (*kanbun*) at Imamiya Middle School.

Just before Orikuchi's graduation in 1910, Yanagita Kunio published his groundbreaking *Tōno monogatari* (Tales of Tōno), and in 1913 he founded the journal *Kyōdo kenkyū* (Native Place Studies). Orikuchi read Yanagita's essays published there and knew intuitively that here was the course he wished to pursue. The "classics of living" (*seikatsu no koten*) were to be found within the living local oral culture, among the various legends, tales and rites. Classics like the *Man'yōshū* that he had studied so closely were living within the oral culture of nameless people and mingled in the soil of the local culture. He was determined to spend the rest of his life searching for the links between the literary classics that he had studied and the "classics of living" revealed through folklore studies. That search became his life's work; he burned with the desire to create a "new Nativism."

Orikuchi is particularly noted for introducing such concepts as *marebito* (outsider, mysterious visitor, stranger, guest),[27] *okina* (old man, visiting deity), and *kishu ryūritan* (the exiled, wandering noble). All of these, however, indeed everything he studied, fundamentally relate to *chinkon* (spirit pacification):[28] This is evident in his collections of poetry (such as *Umi yama no aida* [Between the Mountains and the Sea, 1925], *Kodai kan'aishū* [Archaic Love, 1947] and *Kindai hishōshū* [Modern Grief, 1952]) and his brilliant novella *Shisha no sho* (Book of the Dead). For example, in his first poetry collection, *Between the Mountains and the Sea*, he wrote:

> The cloud-filled sky above the mountains is lonely / Sounds disappear in the dense woods in all directions.
> I haven't yet stopped feeling loneliness / I wander alone on a small island in the sea.

Here Orikuchi writes of a feeling of loneliness (*sabishisa*) he cannot shed, always an underlying current in his poetry. As he searched for the origin of this "loneliness," he had a deep and internal motive to "pacify and purify" (*chinkon*) it.

The *Book of the Dead*[29] is actually a story of kami-buddha combination. Set in eighth-century Japan, it concerns a beautiful girl named Fujiwara Iratsume who calls back the soul of the executed Prince Ōtsu (called Shiga Tsuhiko in the novel) and forges a bond with it. The spiritual vision she receives is woven into the Taima Mandala. Here Orikuchi has written a tale that mixes the ancient Japanese understanding of the spirit realm and the Buddhist idea of the Pure Land of Amida Buddha and rebirth in paradise (Sukhāvatī).

Orikuchi also superimposed the motif of the *marebito* on the original form of kami. *Marebito* are mysterious visitors from Tokoyo, the land of eternal life across the sea, who visit communities seasonally to bring fertility and happiness. In the performing arts, this figure developed into the *okina*, the old-man role, and in tale literature into the motif of the exiled, wandering noble (*kishu ryūritan*). Tales of noble *marebito* like Susanoo, Yamato Takeru, Prince Genji and Minamoto no Yoshitsune wandering around various regions are examples of this latter motif.

Orikuchi never married, but in 1945 he adopted Fujii Harumi (1906–45), a former student who had entered Kokugakuin University in 1925 and became a professor in the Japanese Literature department there in 1933. Fujii was the son of the priestly family of Keta Taisha, an ancient shrine (mentioned in the *Engishiki*) in Hakui, Ishikawa prefecture. He, like so many of Orikuchi's students, was killed during World War II, at Iōjima (Iwo Jima). Orikuchi's greatest concern during the last years of his life was how to console and pacify the "incomplete spirits" (*mikan seirei*) who had died as soldiers in the war.

In terms of their interest in how people viewed the kami, spirits, and the spirit realm, Yanagita and Orikuchi were the heirs of Hirata Atsutane. Whereas Orikuchi understood the divine presences he called *marebito* as spirits visiting from the beyond, Yanagita was concerned with the question of the family, ancestral spirits, and the ancestors themselves. He considered that ancestor veneration was at the heart of the beliefs and culture of ordinary people (*jōmin*). The ancestors would become deified several decades after their death and become ancestral spirits who watched over their descendants from their abode in the mountains. These mountain deities (*yama no kami*) descended to the fields in spring to become the deities of the rice fields (*ta no kami*) to ensure their fertility and returned to the mountains after the harvest. This was a circulatory construct whereby the ancestors watched over their descendants in the village from both field and mountain.

A contemporary of Yanagita and Orikuchi who also had a considerable impact on the development of *minzokugaku* was the aforementioned Minakata Kumagusu. He was born in Wakayama in 1867 and, from the end of 1886, spent many years abroad, principally in the United States and Britain, engaged in advanced study of the latest in anthropological, biological, and folklore studies research. On his return to Japan in 1900, he lived at Nachi in Kumano and then at Tanabe, Wakayana prefecture. He did not establish a formal affiliation with any institution but soon became renowned as a biologist, anthropologist, and folklorist. He studied slime mold and made world-class discoveries in this field. As mentioned above, he also actively opposed the policy to consolidate the nation's shrines, drawing on his expertise as an ecologist. He met Yanagita Kunio in 1911, and the two corresponded after that, exchanging ideas about anthropology and *minzokugaku*.

Fiction of the living spirit

Orikuchi's fiction, written throughout his lifetime, makes up volume 24 of his collected works. Two of his earliest novellas are the unfinished works *Kuchibue* (The Whistle, 1914) and *Kami no yome* (The Divine Bride, 1922). *Kami no yome* is the story of a shamanistic woman of the Fujiwara clan who served the kami. His later *Ikiguchi o tou onna* (The Woman Who Called a Living Spirit) is a masterwork that vividly depicts phenomena associated with the kami and spirit possession experienced by an ordinary old man and woman living in Osaka. It is a realistic portrayal of how possession occurs in the daily lives of ordinary people.

Ikiguchi o tou onna is about a merchant of the Senba area of Osaka who keeps a lover. When he drops by to visit her, the living spirit of his wife comes flying down, getting in the way of his pleasure. He realizes that something is strange, and in an attempt to get back on track, he sets out with his lover for Dōtonbori, Osaka's entertainment district. As they walk, their passage is described like the "traveling" scene (*michiyuki*) in *Love Suicides at Amijima*—the bunraku play by Chikamatsu Monzaemon. The story skillfully describes the psychological changes experienced by the bewildered couple.

Orikuchi was a surprisingly good novelist, perhaps among the finest that Japan has produced. In *Ikiguchi o tou onna*, considered one of his best novels, he is not attempting to depict *miko*, mediums, or other people with special shamanistic abilities but rather ordinary people and situations—like the man and his lover—in out-of-the-ordinary situations, describing them in the minutest detail. I wonder where he cultivated such descriptive powers? How was it that Orikuchi, a homosexual, was able to express so realistically the bonds between men and women and the realm of the *mononoke*?

Orikuchi's powerful maiden work, *Kuchibue*, is an unfinished work full of sadness and loneliness (*sabishisa*). The protagonist is a thirteen-year-old boy named Yasura who takes no interest in school. He deceives his aunt in order to be allowed to go to Asuka, saying he would go with a school friend and not alone. It is the story of his upbringing, reflecting the torment of an unloved child and perceived ostracism within the family.

Orikuchi carried that feeling of loneliness throughout his life. He grew up to become a renowned literary scholar and folklorist, but the trauma of his youth remained with him, as revealed by the poem written soon after the end of World War II, "The Face of a Beggar," quoted in part above. The beggar's face he sees is that of himself, reflected in the mirror. This is my fate, he is saying, my karma. This trauma, however, enabled him to intuitively grasp what Japanese literature was desperately seeking.

The theme of loneliness recurs both in his poetry and in his fiction. Almost unconsciously, he came to assert that loneliness is what is to be found at the very root of the Japanese mentality. He also observes that such fundamental loneliness was alleviated with the entry of Buddhism into Japan and that the haiku poet Matsuo Bashō (1644–94) played a central role in freeing literature of this essential loneliness; these, for Orikuchi, were negative developments, as he was persuaded that both Buddhism and the haiku of Bashō were disconnected from what flowed at the depths of Japanese literature. It was of the greatest importance to him to rediscover the loneliness that he believed existed before Buddhism introduced the idea of transience. Orikuchi constantly mused on his own state of unhealed loneliness. His research and his creative work emerged from this superimposition of his own emotional state upon the fundamental mentality of Japanese literature.

When Orikuchi himself was taken to Asuka by his two maternal aunts (one of whom may have been his real mother), he had wondered what sort of place it was, what he would see there. Asuka was his grandfather's native village, but Orikuchi's family had little contact with the place. Why did they have no connection with the relatives there? There must have been complicated issues in the background. Both his father and his grandfather had been adopted into the Orikuchi family of merchants, marrying the daughters to carry on the family name. As a child, his grandfather had been adopted into the family of the priests of the Asukanimasu Shrine, while his father was the son of a village headman (*shōya*) in Osaka. When Orikuchi visited his grandfather's village, he felt a strong sense of the ancient and of the kami there.

In *Kuchibue*, Orikuchi found the Asukanimasu Shrine, now remote and dilapidated.

> Asuka in Takechi-gun in the province of Yamato—that ancient province and that ancient village, and there was his ancient family with its two thousand years of history. This was where Yasura's grandfather was from. Realizing that, Yasura became aware that his body was tingling; he felt a mysterious power spread out to the tips of his fingernails and to the ends of his hair.... The great shrine whose powerful authority was repeatedly mentioned in the classics was now a small rustic shrine amid grassy fields, leaning in a way that reminded him of the demise of ancient Shinto (Koshintō).
>
> Yasura knelt down before his ancestral kami and closed his eyes. As he was doing so, the expansive spirit of the deity infused warmth into his heart. "We have always done the same things that you have done. Before me, none of these things are seen as sins." He felt that a voice was whispering to him, saying that what he had to do was right before his eyes.

Yasura returns to his home briefly and then, encouraged by his family, goes to spend some of the summer holidays with relatives in Kawachi. He uses the opportunity to visit a friend who was staying in a mountain temple in the vicinity and ends up staying there with him. The boys nurse homosexual feelings for one another. Finally, deciding to die together, they throw themselves off the top of a cliff. There the novel ends.

Kuchibue was serialized in the newspaper *Fuji shinbun* between March 24 and April 19, 1914. The theme of homosexual youths attempting suicide together was a highly unusual topic in newspaper serials at the time, and only the first part of the novel appeared, with the rest remaining unfinished. Perhaps the second part would have dealt with what later happened to Yasura, who survived. What kind of life would a young man who had attempted a love suicide lead in the future? It is easy to surmise that the path of someone who had failed in suicide would not have been ordinary. Was this in fact the story of Orikuchi's own life? Like *Ikiguchi o tou onna*, *Kuchibue* was never completed. In any case, its depiction is truly electrifying, as neither work pulls any punches. Orikuchi Shinobu, the novelist, was very gifted. He portrays complex intricate folds of feeling and the deeply buried darkness of the heart. In the hands of an author of such profound sensibilities, the depths of the human heart are realistically and vividly drawn. He would probably have been able to even portray what went on in the minds of child murderers like Sakakibara Seito, a 14-year-old boy who claimed two victims in Kobe in 1997.

Orikuchi's expression of kami-buddha combination

Toward the end of his life, Orikuchi wrote his last novel, *The Book of the Dead*, also unfinished, in the sense that he intended to write a sequel. The first part is finished in terms of narrative, but only part of the opening section of the sequel was completed, a draft that was not published until it was included in his collected works.

It tells of the spirit possession of Iratsume, a daughter of the Southern (Nanke) branch of the Fujiwara clan, one of the four branches founded by Fujiwara no Fuhito, son of Fujiwara (Nakatomi) no Kamatari.

The eldest daughter of Fujiwara no Toyonari of the Southern branch, Iratsume, has a vision of a man and, in a trance state, finds herself in a temple in the district of Taima. The "man" in her vision is Amida Buddha, but it is not just him. Rather, superimposed on the image of Amida is Prince Ōtsu (called here Shiga Tsuhiko), who had died more than fifty years before.

Yamato is famous for its mountains: Mt. Miwa in the east and Mt. Nijō (Futakamiyama), Mt. Katsuragi and Mt. Kongō in the west. And located in the middle of the Nara basin are the three hills of Yamato (*Yamato sanzan*): Mt. Kagu, Mt. Unebi, and Mt. Miminashi. The sun rises in the east over Mt. Miwa, and sets in the west over Mt. Nijō. Mt. Nijō has two peaks, Odake (male) and Medake (female). In between the two is a depression called Hoto (*yin*). Since *hoto* means the female genitals, this hollow in the valley between the two peaks may be considered the vulva or the uterus. The sun appears to set here at the spring and autumn equinoxes. Beliefs from ancient times surrounding the setting sun and the western paradise may have originated here. Mt. Miwa in the east is the site of Ōmiwa Shrine, a sacred shrine where Shinto flourishes, while Buddhism thrives in the west at the Taima and other temples. The Nara Basin configures a cosmology of yin and yang, with Shinto in the east and Buddhism in the west. Kami and buddhas coexist while inhabiting their own environments. This small universe was the world of Yamato.

Iratsume lived in Nara, but one day for some unknown reason suddenly wandered off in the direction of Mt. Nijō. When she came to her senses she found herself inside the precincts of the Taima Temple, a place forbidden to female access. When she was discovered, there was a great commotion, and she was placed in isolation. While walking in a trance, she had a vision of being guided along by the soul of a deceased person.

Prince Ōtsu (663–86) was a tragic figure who had been involved in a political dispute and executed. The gifted third son of Tenmu Tennō, he was expected to succeed his father. However he was accused of rebellion by Tenmu's consort Jitō (Ōtsu's mother's elder sister) who wanted the succession to go to her own son, Prince Kusakabe (Ōtsu's half-brother), and was executed. It was a political murder. Prince Ōtsu's full sister, Princess Ōku (661–702), was the first *saiō* to serve at the Ise Shrines. Both brother and sister were very talented, and though they were her nephew and niece, they posed a threat to Jitō.

The *Man'yōshū* includes a poem written by Ōku as she looked up to Futakamiyama (as Mt. Nijō was known at the time), where the grave of her dead brother was.

> From tomorrow, ever
> Shall I regard as brother
> The twin-peaked mountain of Futakami—
> I, daughter of man![30]

She would always think of the mountain as her beloved brother. It is an eloquent elegy, expressing a poignant message of consolation to the spirit of the dead.

Orikuchi quotes many poems and events that appear in the *Man'yōshū*, brings in the legend of Princess Kaguya who returned to her home in the moon as told in the *Taketori monogatari* (The Tale of the Bamboo Cutter), and uses as background Nara period political disputes like the struggle between the factions of Junnin Tennō and the former sovereign Kōken involving Fujiwara no Nakamaro of the Southern branch (706–64) and the priest Dōkyō of the Yuge clan. Amid the great changes of the period, the eldest daughter of the Fujiwara Southern branch, who held to the old traditions, fell into a trance and communicated with the soul of a dead person, and her vision turned out to be of Amida Buddha and his Pure Land.

This story is based on a legend of the Princess Chūjō, who went to the Taimadera Temple and wove into a harmonious whole the Taima Mandala, a depiction of Amida and his Pure Land. Orikuchi wrote *The Book of the Dead* as a tale of spirit pacification, interweaving the Taima legend and its theme of rebirth in paradise and

Amida's welcome (*raigō*), historical facts about Prince Ōtsu, the *Tale of the Bamboo Cutter*, and a great variety of Japanese myths, legends, and historical incidents.

This is a superb creative expression of kami-buddha combinatory culture. That this work does not occupy its rightful place in Japanese literature may be attributed to the fact that the Meiji policy of separating kami and buddha worship has prevented an understanding of the subtleties of the interweaving of Shinto and Buddhism. It is very necessary to look again at the world Orikuchi wanted to portray from a broader and deeper historical and substantive viewpoint.

CHAPTER SIX

Epilogue: Toward a New Kami-Buddha Combination

Looking broadly at the religious and cultural history of the Japanese archipelago, we see first the broad stream of ancient kami-kami combinatory culture that evolved into kami-buddha combination from the time of the *ritsuryō* state. This socio-religious culture underwent a major shift as a result of the kami-buddha separation policy of the Meiji government and was discontinued following Japan's wartime defeat in 1945. The future may bring a new period of kami-buddha interaction, guided by a longing for a diverse, co-active unifier. This is because, recognizing religious coexistence and diversity, there is a need to construct a large map of cooperation and harmony. As a means of clarifying the direction Japan is headed, an overview of the religious and political myths created over history to facilitate or legitimize the rule of the nation's leader is helpful. The myths surrounding the unifying figure (*issha*) in whom the myth is embodied may be characterized as follows.

Ancient period: Mediation and shared rule
Medieval period: Search for the primal and emphasis on the individual
Early modern period: Fictional and inward-looking
Meiji period: Confrontational and outward-looking
Postwar period: Symbolic and integrated
Future: Coexistence and diversity

Myth is a way of understanding things by attaching meaning and value to the world. Myth and "unifying figure" are used here in a broad sense, myth being the distinct sense of values belonging to a particular period, the period's specific current of thought, the values attached to that current when considering things, and the identity of the period. Myth can therefore be understood as representing the "ethos" of the age.

The Five Myths and Their Modern Meaning

Let us review these five myths.

(a) Ancient period: *The myth centered on mediation and on shared rule*. This ethos took concrete form as the *ritsuryō* system, the centralized state centered on the *tennō* (sovereign). Although legally all the land and all the people belonged to the sovereign, actual power was in the hands of the Fujiwara clan. The mythology of the time is contained in two eighth-century chronicles, *Kojiki* and *Nihon shoki*, the former a type of private lore and the latter an official history. The myths appearing in the *Nihon shoki* included variants—a style of compilation distinctive to this work.

The *tennō* was placed as the pivot around which the powerful clans (*gōzoku*) in different parts of the country were grouped. The system resembled in many ways the post-World War II regime in which the emperor is the symbolic head of state. Under the sovereign, the Fujiwara clan held the political reins in the same way the Liberal Democratic Party has through most of the postwar period. The ancient sovereign, like the emperor of modern times, functioned as a conduit of myth and symbol.

The *ritsuryō* system may have been modeled on institutions and practices of Sui and Tang China but it formed a distinctively Japanese order; this has continued to underlie society down to the present in its overall framework. The *ritsuryō* system, in other words, forms the foundation of all subsequent systems in Japan. The word *tennō* ("heavenly sovereign") came into use during its formative period[1] and it remains effective today as an important and legally prescribed concept. Before the term *tennō* was adopted in the late seventh century, Japanese monarchs were called "great kings" (*ōkimi*). But whatever the title used, the fact remains that the institution itself has continued down to the present without fundamental change from the time of the *ritsuryō* state.

(b) Medieval period: *Myth of the primal and the individual.* The effectiveness of the *ritsuryō* system broke down after the twelfth century, and political power became a two-tiered structure of court and shogunate, the latter preserving the unity of the state by armed might. With the appearance of privately owned manors called *shōen*, governance according to the established law codes became impossible, so the shogunate imposed centralized rule over the fiefs held by the *jizamurai* (small local samurai landholders) through officials such as *shugo* (military governors) and *jitō* (estate stewards). Under this two-tiered system, the warriors protected their own lands themselves and collected the taxes and the agricultural products (mainly rice) associated with them, circumscribing the power of the court. The *shōen* system eventually turned into a feudal arrangement based on lord-vassal relationships. The *tennō* was allowed to remain at the pinnacle of the state while actual power was firmly held by the shogun and his warrior (*bushi*) government. This was the time when apocryphal Shinto literary works, such as the *Five Books of Shinto* and the texts of Yoshida Shinto, appeared.

(c) Early Modern Period: *The fictional and inward-looking myth.* The warrior class-led government of the medieval period continued into the early modern period with the Tokugawa shogunate, prevailing from the seventeenth to the mid-nineteenth centuries. Religion was rendered virtually powerless and used as an apparatus of the state to provide stability within communities and ensure the unification of rule. Shinto had originally been the religion of the community, but within the new political system it, along with Buddhism, was completely secularized as a vehicle of community life. It was observed by household or village units, and its rites were absorbed into secular folkways and customs. Qualities associated with religion, such as the power to bring about change in society or deliver a sense of personal liberation were considered threats to the state system, and thus the dangerously transcendental elements were all suppressed. The Tokugawa shogunate was particularly concerned about the Ikkō leagues associated with the Shin Pure Land school, about the extreme wing of the Lotus school of Nichiren, and about Christianity. The Christian faith in particular had a transcendent, foreign character and the power to threaten the unity of the Japanese state. National isolation (*sakoku*) was decreed, based on the logic that Christianity had to be eliminated, and stabilizing mechanisms were strengthened. Religion was completely dominated by the shogunate. Nobunaga and Hideyoshi set Mt. Hiei ablaze, quelled the Ikkō leagues, and suppressed the Shingon priest-warriors of the Negoro Temple, cutting off the power of religion at its root. Under the *bakuhan* system, religious institutions were placed under the supervision of the shogunal magistrate for temples and shrines.

(d) Meiji and prewar periods: As encroachments from foreign powers became increasingly hard to repulse, the Meiji and prewar period came to require a *confrontational and outward-looking figure*. Situated as they had been within the state political system during the Edo period, temples and shrines under the new Meiji government were without the power to challenge its authority. Rather, the so-called new religions that fundamentally resisted the modern state with a reformist spirit. Tenrikyō, Konkōkyō, and other such founder religions that preached a "joyous life" (*yōki kurashi*) belonged to the thirteen sects of Shinto that were recognized by the government as "religions."[2] The traditional Buddhist sects and Shinto shrines fundamentally lacked the power to confront the state.

One of the most important policies of the Meiji government was to abolish the domains (*han*) through which the Tokugawa shogunate had ruled the country and replace them with prefectures in the framework of the modern state. Land reforms were also put into place. With the abolition of the shogun and daimyo, a centralized state was established centering once again on the emperor. The advisory and political supportive role for the sovereign once played by the Fujiwara house was taken over in the Meiji era by the lower-ranking samurai of the Satsuma and Chōshū domains who had emerged as the driving force in the new government, men such as Ōkubo Toshimichi (1830–78) and Itō Hirobumi (1841–1909), whose efforts contributed to the formulation of the Imperial Rescript to Soldiers (1882), the Meiji Constitution (1889), and the Imperial Rescript on Education (1890). The Meiji Constitution established in law that the emperor was sacred and inviolable and was of an unbroken line stretching back to Amaterasu. As discussed above (p. 131), this was something new in Japanese history; the Meiji Constitution can be said to have deified the emperor to the greatest possible degree.

The defining myth of the age that set Japan's direction as a modern state followed a route that promoted "civilization and enlightenment" and Westernization, since Japan was determined to join the company of the Western powers. Having avoided colonization, Japan embarked on an ideology guided by the slogan "rich nation and strong army" as the foundation for its policy of industrial development. For Japan to tread its own distinctive path, Ōkubo Toshimichi, Itō Hirobumi, and others who had been part of the Iwakura Mission to Europe and the United States in 1871–73 clearly realized that it was useless to make shrine Shinto and its myriads of deities the pivot of the new state. Neither could Buddhism play such a role, since government policy, which included the separation of Buddhist and Shinto elements in temples and shrines, was to prevent it from gaining influence. Shinto and Buddhism alike were fundamentally powerless as forces to buttress the state. The only recourse, then, was to use the emperor system.

Many people have the image of Shinto as being the same as "State Shinto." This is inaccurate in view of the fact that followers of the Hirata school were ousted from the political mainstream in the early years of Meiji (see p. 125). Those who truly thought that shrine Shinto was important were frustrated, and their movement collapsed. What emerged was a bureaucratized shrine system tamed by political leaders for ease of state supervision and control. The story of the Hirata Nativists told in Shimazaki Tōson's *Before the Dawn* shows that they had no wish for a system of shrine supervision that sought to merge and consolidate the nation's shrines. A misunderstanding of history seems to have made the Nativists, and the Hirata followers in particular, the scapegoats for Japan's nationalistic path.

(e) Postwar period: The defining myth of the postwar period revolves around *symbolism and integration*. This is discussed in the sections below.

The role of religion and the rise of militarism

Great insight on the position of Buddhism in the rise of the *symbolic and integrated* ethos of Meiji and prewar Japan is offered by Miyasaka Yūshō (1921–2011), a much-respected Buddhist scholar who taught for many years as a professor at Kōyasan University and Nagoya University and also served as the head of the Chisan branch of the Shingon school. With great courage, he wrote an opinion piece in the *Chūgai Nippō*[3] about the role of Buddhist scholars in the future, which I would like to summarize in detail. Despite the anti-Buddhist (*haibutsu kishaku*) campaign of the early Meiji era, during the tumultuous years leading up to the outbreak of Japan's war in Asia, he observed, Buddhism was largely passive, "Why did sectarian Buddhism remain silent? Why did Buddhism always go along with the government of the time?" he asks.

Miyasaka believed that the motive force behind this was Nativist ideology. To bring about the restoration of the monarchy, Nativist-influenced leaders had deemed it necessary to separate Buddhism, which had been the state-authorized religion until then, from the statist religion of Shinto and to destroy it. Miyasaka describes the 1872 edict that declared that Buddhist priests could henceforth do as they liked about the restrictions against eating meat, having wives, and growing their hair as having transformed Buddhism from a monastic faith (*shukke bukkyō*) to a lay religion devoid of ideological power. There were, however, sects of Buddhism that retained their monastic traditions unchanged from the Edo period. Miyasaka chronicles the weakening of Buddhism as a result of the secularization decreed

EPILOGUE: TOWARD A NEW KAMI-BUDDHA COMBINATION

by the Meiji government, whose aim was to institutionalize Shinto as State Shinto and use it to bolster the emperor system, legitimizing the divine role of the sovereign in the modern state. In order to compete with the advanced countries of the West, the new government adopted the "rich nation and strong army" policy. At this juncture, Miyasaka notes, the leaders of the Buddhist world ironically concluded that Buddhism should work for the benefit of the state (*bukkyō kokueki ron*), catering to the views of the government despite its persecution of the religion.

After Japan's victory in the Russo-Japanese War of 1904–1905, the great powers recognized Japan as the only modern state in Asia, much emboldening its military leaders. After the Pearl Harbor attack, overseas expansion gained momentum, and war escalated on the continent. In 1942, Miyasaka recalls the government confiscation of bells and all other metal objects from temples in the name of collecting materials to be made into weapons. A second round of collections targeting all Buddhist images made of metal was planned, he writes, but luckily the war ended before it could be put into effect.

Miyasaka also reports that the government was preparing to issue a proclamation that the funerals of the war dead would be required to be held according to Shinto rites, not Buddhist, and that there was even a debate in the Diet regarding the famous "Iroha" phonetic alphabet song when a bill was introduced calling for it to be banned because it was Buddhist. Sectarian Buddhism did not protest these various stratagems against the traditional role of Buddhism, saying they were matters of national policy. However, Takagami Kakushō (1894–1948)—Buddhist scholar of the Chisan branch of the Shingon school and Miyasaka's teacher—was an outspoken opponent of the funeral plan, asserting that "The kami is the father and the Buddha the mother. The oneness of the kami and the buddhas is our country's traditional culture." The passage of the bill through the Diet was subsequently blocked. Miyasaka believed that if the war had gone on longer, Buddhism might have faced a second round of persecution.

Miyasaka places responsibility for Japan's rampant militarism and defeat in World War II on the Nativist ideology of the period before and following the Meiji Restoration, and he indicts sectarian Buddhism for only the feeblest statements on behalf of society. Buddhism was not entirely without influence on society as a whole, but it was still negligible. The underlying cause of this, Miyasaka believed, was the subordination of Buddhism, which ought not to be concerned with mundane affairs, to the secular in the form of the state or society. Its assurance to the government that it could benefit the state was a form of self-defense following the depredations of the anti-Buddhist movement in the early Meiji years.

Miyasaka asserted that even at the time of writing in 2004 not much had changed. Statements or messages concerning social or religious matters made by Buddhist groups were often for internal consumption and rarely reached the general public, though he noted that there were some organizations like Ōmotokyo and its secular branch ULBA (Universal Love and Brotherhood Association), the National Christian Council (NCC) in Japan, the Federation of New Religious Organizations of Japan (*Shinshūren*), and Rissho Kosei-kai that sent out social and antiwar messages globally. By comparison, while there are some groups from within traditional Buddhism that have criticized worsening social conditions and offered prayers for world peace, such messages tend to be sectarian and represent the standpoint of the particular sect, so they are powerless and have no social effect. He noted, however, that given their freedom from political parties and political ideologies, religious leaders were in a position to issue plain and socially relevant messages.

Miyasaka cited a *Chūgai Nippō* editorial encapsulating his ideas that stated "The views and messages of people of religion have to reach the general public. We have to let people know that we have a message we want to send out. . . . I hope that by stating more openly that we are concerned about society we can lessen the gap between ourselves and society." As an example, he mentioned how Ōe Kenzaburō, while accepting the Nobel Prize for literature from the king of Sweden, declined to accept the Order of Culture from the Japanese government because it is conferred personally by the emperor, which he could not do as a proponent of postwar democracy. Does this make all the other recipients of the Japanese award enemies of democracy? The media glossed over the remark, but this is a point that should have been highlighted from a Buddhist perspective.

Regarding the visits of Japanese prime ministers to Yasukuni Shrine, which enshrines the country's war dead, Miyasaka observes how the visits provoke outcry from Korea and China, but pointed out that Article 3 of the Treaty of Peace and Friendship between Japan and the People's Republic of China states that there will be no interference in each other's internal affairs. China's statement was clearly in contravention to the treaty's terms, he argued, so why did not Japanese politicians make that clear? He declares that, if politicians do not react, surely it is up to the National Federation of All Buddhist Sects (Zennichibutsu) to make this point. He further protested the 2004 dispatch of Japan's Self-Defense Forces to Iraq as a blatant violation of Article 9 of the Constitution.[4]

Miyasaka noted that the Asian Buddhist Conference for Peace (ABCP) continues vociferously to demand that Japan uphold its Three Non-Nuclear Principles, that all nuclear and chemical weapons be abolished and that armaments be reduced, but its efforts have not been supported by Buddhist organizations in Japan. Many Buddhists, he observed, are indifferent to the Five Precepts and Five Virtues[5] — also based on the five precepts and ten virtues taught by Shakyamuni. "Surely the time will come," he urges, "when the National Federation of All Buddhist Sects, taking Shakyamuni's fundamental stand, will appeal to all sects and subsects to strongly promote a universal Buddhist peace movement as the practice of Buddhist ethics."

Recalling the events that led to war, Miyasaka recounted how on September 18, 1931, the Mukden Incident was engineered by the Japanese military as a pretext to invade Manchuria. The government announced on September 24 a policy of non-expansion, though, saying it would withdraw troops from Manchuria. It continued to proclaim that policy and should have started to withdraw troops from the continent. But after the Marco Polo Bridge Incident of July 7, 1937, the military forces spread the conflict to Shanghai, and all-out war between Japan and China broke out on August 15. All five of Miyasaka's cousins were war casualties, and only he survived.[6]

More than half of his classmates and acquaintances, he recounts, are enshrined at Yasukuni. Miyasaka concludes his essay with words that ring with great immediacy:

> Military expansion is the fate of history. Expenditure on the Self-Defense Forces, which ostensibly is exclusively for self-defense, now ranks fourth highest in the world. Do people know the true scale of Japan's military?
>
> As a Buddhist, I am filled with misgiving about how the history of past military expansion repeats itself over and again. In a situation where the world seems to have begun to retrogress, much of sectarian Buddhism, as well as the National Federation of All Buddhist Sects, remains silent and feigns disinterest.
>
> What messages should we be transmitting to society in order to enable it to renounce war based on Shakyamuni's injunction that Buddhists should not even watch military parades and strictly prohibits the taking of life?
>
> Japanese sectarian Buddhism again stands at a crossroads of history.

Miyasaka's courageous and candid argument represents the wisdom of a Buddhist leader with the backbone to stand up to the trends of the times. There is a pressing need, I believe, for discussion about the type of world we want, based on values that go beyond particular religions and sects, to be transmitted far and near.

Factors determining militarism

While I agree with the majority of points Miyasaka raises and with his conclusions, I cannot concur with his statement that the Nativist ideology of the period before and following the Meiji Restoration was to blame for Japan's participation and defeat in World War II. I do not think that, as a whole, it is possible to say that Nativism was the prime ideological mover in the reckless march toward militarism.

It was not committed to any clear political position when it began in the eighteenth century. Motoori Norinaga, who sees the essence of the Japanese spirit as knowing *mono no aware* (the pathos of things) and described it as "wild cherry blossoms glowing in the morning sun," may have criticized the "Chinese spirit," but he was no militarist thinker and certainly not a prime mover in the ideology of militarism. Hirata Atsutane, a pioneer of studies of *mononoke* and spirituality, among other topics, was forced by the shogunate to return to his native village in the Akita domain (a form of exile) toward the end of his life for writing a treatise on the rule of the *tennō* and forbidden to publish. Embittered, he spent his last years dreaming of the dawn of Shinto based on his investigations into spirituality.

Miyasaka no doubt had in mind some of the government-hired scholars and militarist forces influential in the new Meiji state who had been Hirata followers or were their students and were working together with Itō Hirobumi and others involved in creating the apparatus of the Meiji state.

It may be said that Confucian ethics and Confucian theories about the state played a greater role than Nativism in the path toward nationalism and militarism. Confucianists and scholars of the Mito school, such as Aizawa Seishisai (1781–1863), who developed the idea of a distinctive Japanese *kokutai* (national polity) based on Confucianism, and his teacher Fujita Yūtoku (1774–1826), as well as Yoshida Shōin (1830–59) of the Hagi domain, were influential ideological sources in the formation of the modern state. We may say that Mito learning provided the ingredients of Restoration Shinto while Nativism merely added the flavoring.

Men who succeeded to Hirata Atsutane's ideas on Shinto certainly were part of the power behind the Meiji Restoration, but by 1873 they had been largely ousted from the political center as the Confucian proponents of the Mito school, and followers of Yoshida Shōin intensified their influence on the ideology of state formation. Compromising with the "civilization and enlightenment" policy, these Confucianists played a part in the compilation of the Meiji Constitution and the Rescript on Education. These documents have nothing to do with Shinto. Nowhere is a Shinto-type spirit to be found in them. They clearly express a Confucian ethical code; the Meiji Constitution provides for a modern emperor system that is based on a Confucian ethical code and ideology.

Miyasaka wrote how during the war his teacher Takagami Kakushō bravely opposed proposals to ban Buddhist funerals for the war dead as well as the "Iroha" song and emphasized the unity of buddhas and kami. Professor Takagami was a Buddhist scholar at Taishō University in Tokyo who, with Tomomatsu Entai (1895–1973), in 1934 founded the magazine *Shinri* (Truth) and developed a Buddhist enlightenment movement called the Movement for Religious Truth (*Shinri undō*). Takagami was also the author of many widely read books, including an introduction to esoteric Buddhism and a lecture series on the Heart Sutra.[7]

Takagami's formulation of the kami as father and the Buddha as mother and about the oneness of the kami and the buddhas being Japan's traditional culture is easy to understand, but it could also lead to misunderstanding. Can kami really be characterized as being paternal and buddhas as maternal? Both deities at Ise—Amaterasu of the Inner Shrine and Toyouke of the Outer Shrine—are female, so Japanese kami might rather be considered to have strong female and maternal characteristics.

This is not a straightforward matter, for kami and buddhas have given rise to complex and diverse combinatory forms. One problem is that people tend to oversimplify their logic and expression in order to make their arguments easier to understand. To indict Nativist studies as the prime ideological mover of militarism is a case of such oversimplification.

Making War and Making Peace

My father was a kamikaze pilot who was sent to Manchuria. However, he contracted tuberculosis and was repatriated to Japan, where he was recuperating when the war ended. He thus survived. Most other "special attack" pilots died on their missions. Only one other man from my father's class in military school survived. He became a commercial pilot after the war but was killed in a plane crash on the island of Yakushima.

Returning to Japan, my father was eventually cured and married my mother. He died suddenly when I was 16, though, killed in a motorbike accident. It happened two days after my graduation from junior high school. When I think about the deaths of my father and his comrades, I cannot help being aware how fortunate I am to be able to live a settled and peaceful life. I also cannot help feeling at the same time that their deaths should not have been in vain, that I should do what I can to protect the peace we now enjoy and help build a more prosperous world. This will be a way of praying for the repose of those who died in anguish in the war.

When I was a child, my father often spoke to me about the war and the kamikaze pilots, of which he had been one. He would always recall his fellow airmen, tears running down his cheeks, to a recurring refrain, "I'm just living out what remains of my life." I realized then, that I was the product of the "remains" of his life. As I grew older, though, I came to understand his feelings and the strong sense of guilt he felt for having survived.

Everyone else had sacrificed their lives for the war, he felt, but it so happened that he contracted tuberculosis and was sent back. He thus not only survived but even became a father. When he thought about the pilots who had been his contemporaries, he was overcome with indescribable sorrow and grief. At such times, all he could do was to drink and sing songs. This trauma and emotional turmoil had haunted him continually. Because of his sudden death, I never had the chance to talk with him in detail about the war. I often remembered what he did share with me, however, and wondered what he had hoped for in postwar society.

In 2003, hearing of the Koizumi Cabinet's decision to deploy the Japanese Ground and Air Self-Defense Forces in Iraq and listening to reports about the prime minister's press conference, I was deeply disappointed. It seemed to me, as I wrote in an article in the *Tokushima Shimbun* on December 16, 2003, that Japan's politicians were totally ignorant of people's wishes and had learned nothing from history. There was nothing about sending troops to Iraq that constituted an "international contribution" or served the national interest.

The deployment was nothing but a "contribution to the United States" that served U.S. interests. How can acting as an agent of American imperialism to turn Islamic societies into enemies be considered an international contribution? The government was totally lacking in long-term vision.

As the son of a kamikaze pilot who survived the war, I am unconditionally against any kind of warfare. Human history clearly shows that war solves nothing. We have no time to be fighting with one another when our environment, our culture and civilization, our education system and livelihoods, in fact, the entire human race are all facing a crisis. Our first concern must be to eliminate all kinds of war.

The idea of world peace

My study of Shinto has been undertaken as part of my pursuit of promoting world peace and renewal. I believe we must consider what means are available to us to eliminate war. Buddhists, Shintoists, and all religious scholars must join together to work out ideas and methods of doing so and put them into practice.

In 1989, when Japan's era name changed to Heisei (平成, "establishment of peace") on the accession of the present emperor, I felt intuitively that the meaning of the name notwithstanding, the world was about to fall into the maelstrom of war. To a student of Japanese history like myself, it inspired only foreboding, and I expressed my protest to the politicians and authorities who had chosen that name. Some might find it a bit bizarre, but in Japan's long history, there has been only one other era name that starts with the character *hei* (平, peace). That was the Heiji era, which is well known for the bloody Heiji disturbance of 1159 between the Taira and Minamoto clans.[8] Both then and now people have longed for peace, but instead both periods were marked by war. As the Heiji era changed from one aspiring to peace to one dominated by war, the trend of the Heisei era has changed from one of peace to one that seems determined to inspire conflict.

On January 7, 1989, I was thoroughly disheartened. Chief Cabinet Secretary Obuchi Keizō had announced that Heisei would be the new era name, and I could not help thinking that those who made the decision must have a very shallow understanding of history. As I was walked home with my five-year-old from daycare, I caught my breath, thinking of the difficult times and the social hardships children of the same age were going to have to live through. "It's going to be a difficult time ahead. Will I be able to protect these children? Will we even be able to raise them?" I had absolutely no confidence, but I made up my mind to do whatever I can for them.[9]

With the beginning of the Heisei era, I immediately thought that history seemed to be repeating itself. An epoch of transition and social change reminiscent of the medieval period was at hand that surely would lead to an age of great turmoil.[10] Japan's medieval period was a cataclysmic time of natural disasters, war, famine, earthquakes, tsunami, and flooding. The killing continued as warriors wrested land from one another, members of aristocratic families fought among themselves, and people quarreled over religious differences.

Today, too, fighting continues over land, family, and religion. What can we do to resolve these conflicts and build true peace and stability? As I pondered such questions, I became convinced that resolving these fundamental issues required the invocation of the spiritual dimension, where spirit takes precedence over the physical. A spiritual solution to these issues involves prayer, meditation, and artistic creation.

I had an opportunity to pursue such endeavors in earnest in 1998 when Okinawan musician Kina Shōkichi[11] called on me to assist him in holding a festival centering on prayer in Kobe—a city devastated by a severe earthquake in 1995 and haunted by a series of child murders in 1997. I resolved to make every effort to bring this about in the belief that prayer, meditation, and artistic creation were indispensable to bringing fundamental peace to a disordered world.

To me this would be a large-scale ritual to venerate the ancestors of everyone there and take a step toward building true peace in our time. On August 8, 1998, "Full Moon Concert: A Prayer from Kobe" was held at Kobe's Meriken Park, and on October 10 the same year "Tokyo Ohiraki Matsuri Concert: A Prayer from Kobe" was held in front of the Great Buddha at Kamakura.

It happens that Kobe is the port where Taira no Kiyomori moved the country's capital for six months in 1180. Kamakura, meanwhile, is the port where Minamoto no Yoshitomo and his son Yoritomo lived and where the Kamakura shogunate was later established. Holding a gathering marked by prayer and artistic creativity in places with such karmic connections might also be said to be an attempt to bring about a great reconciliation between the warring Taira and Minamoto clans of the past.

We issued a call for true peace and a community based on friendship through prayer and cooperation. We sought widespread support for the sake of the future of our children.

A new encounter between kami and buddhas

Making associations between the past and present based on the character for "peace" (平) was intuitive on my part. I see the present as a time experiencing the same kind of problems that Japan experienced during the middle ages in terms of social structure and direction.

Kina Shōkichi and I appealed to both traditional and new religious groups, sending our message to all and asking for their contribution and participation. We are grateful for the support we received from Kidlat Tahimik, the Filipino film director who has made films about the Ainu, Okinawa, and the Philippines, native American Dennis Banks, and native American spiritual leader Leonard Crow Dog, and a large number of Buddhist and Shinto priests. We also received 15 million yen in donations from the private sector, which we used to cover the costs of the two concerts. Kina and his band volunteered their services to appear at the ceremony of song, dance, and prayer. Transportation fees, lighting, and stage preparation required a great deal of money. We enlisted sponsors to cover expenses like

EPILOGUE: TOWARD A NEW KAMI-BUDDHA COMBINATION

Figure 6.1. The prayer ceremony before the Great Buddha at the Kōtokuin Temple in Kamakura, October 10, 1998.

accommodations of performers and the production of leaflets. Everybody volunteered their time to put together these two large events, even paying for their own meals. I learned a great deal through the experience, and I believe that such events offer a model for a new kind of interplay and collaboration between Shinto and Buddhism.

I have called for the building of a community based on fraternity and to this end have published books and been involved in various projects, like the Rainbow Festival at Hakusan, the Flame Festival at Gassan, and World Peace and Prayer Day. Nevertheless, I cannot help thinking that the world is not going the way we had hoped, but rather, is going in quite the opposite direction.

Political and economic developments today may appear to unfold in ways that have nothing to do with trends in the spiritual community. But there may yet emerge a confluence of these disparate currents. I remain hopeful that the highest values and ideas we carry within us will be heard and shared by all.

The Postwar Myth: Spirituality and the New Nativism of Yanagita Kunio and Orikuchi Shinobu

The defining myth of the postwar period may be said to revolve around the "Peace Constitution" and its Article 9. Also important were the postwar agricultural land reforms, which like the Land Tax Reform of 1873, changed the very structure of Japanese society. Just as early Meiji-era reforms abolished the old social hierarchy and the domain system, changes in the landholding system brought about far-reaching changes in the basic conditions of life and livelihood.

The core principle of the postwar Constitution was the upholding of basic human rights. This was expressed in terms of the sovereignty of the people, and it provided for the democratic administration of the state by popular sovereignty. It was at the same time supplemented by historical features particular to Japan. Popular sovereignty did not take the form of a republic but was structured as a constitutional monarchy with the emperor as the symbol of the state. This I have referred to as the symbolic and integrating myth. The position of the emperor is defined in Article 1: "The Emperor shall be the symbol of the State and of the unity of the People, deriving his position from the will of the people with whom resides sovereign power." What constitutes the "will of the people," though, is not clearly defined.

The Fundamental Law of Education was drawn up based on the Constitution. Calls have been made in recent years to revise both the Constitution and the Fundamental Law of Education, with the latter being thoroughly amended on December 15, 2006. I believe, however, that there is no need for any fundamental change in either law. The objectives of education are now defined as:

> (i) having students acquire wide-ranging knowledge and culture, fostering the value of seeking truth, and cultivating a rich sensibility and sense of morality as well as building a healthy body;
> (ii) developing individuals' abilities, cultivating creativity, and fostering a spirit of autonomy and independence by respecting the value of the individual, as well as emphasizing the relationship between one's career and one's everyday life and fostering the value of respect for hard work;
> (iii) fostering the values of respect for justice, responsibility, equality between men and women, and mutual respect and cooperation, as well as the value of actively participating in building our society and contributing to its development, in the public spirit;
> (iv) fostering the values of respecting life, caring about nature, and desiring to contribute to the preservation of the environment; and
> (v) fostering the value of respect for tradition and culture and love of the country and regions that have nurtured us, as well as the value of respect for other countries and the desire to contribute to world peace and the development of the international community.[12]

New emphasis has been placed on "public spirit," "respect for tradition and culture," and "love of country and regions." The preamble of the 1947 law, meanwhile, stated:

> Having established the Constitution of Japan, we have shown our resolution to contribute to the world and welfare of

humanity by building a democratic and cultural state. The realization of this idea shall depend fundamentally on the power of education. We shall esteem individual dignity and endeavor to bring up the people who love truth and peace, while education aimed at the creation of culture, general and rich in individuality, shall be spread far and wide. We hereby enact this Law, in accordance with the spirit of the Constitution of Japan, with a view to clarifying the aim of education and establishing the aim of education and establishing the foundation of education for new Japan.

The aim of education was stipulated in Article 1:

Education shall aim at the full development of personality, striving for the rearing of the people, sound in mind and body, who shall love truth and justice, esteem individual value, respect labor and have a deep sense of responsibility, and be imbued with the independent spirit, as builders of peaceful state and society.

Article 2 stated the principles of education:

The aim of education shall be realized on all occasions and in all places. In order to achieve the aim, we shall endeavor to contribute to the creation and development of culture by mutual esteem and cooperation, respecting academic freedom, having a regard to actual life and cultivating a spontaneous spirit.[13]

No one would deny the importance of "public spirit," "respect for tradition and culture," and "love of country and regions" in and of themselves. However, if moves toward a constitutional revision are made with insufficient regard for the common understanding of the people, including a perception of history, I fear that further confusion and conflict will occur in the future. The issue concerning the

Fundamental Law of Education resides, I believe, in the practical action necessary before making express statements about public spirit and promoting patriotic sentiments. The old law was fully adequate to deal with this.

Specifically, if we have respect for academic freedom and a "regard to actual life," if we cultivate a spontaneous spirit and have mutual esteem and cooperation, public spirit and patriotic sentiments should both arise. If the spirit of the former Education Law was correctly realized, then a "love of country and regions" and a "public spirit"—along with the notion of world peace—should naturally result.

In an age when harmony was lacking, Prince Shōtoku began his Seventeen Article Constitution with "Harmony should be valued." His words have since shone brightly in Japanese history. Ironically, though, he himself suffered a reversal of fortunes and lost hope in his later years, and his family fell into ruin after his death. An age that needs to emphasize public spirit and patriotic sentiments is surely an ill-fated one, since it suggests that such sentiments are in decline in society.

The new "age of the warrior"

The modern Constitution, embodying what I call the postwar myth, is known as the Peace Constitution. Some complain it was written by Americans during the Allied Occupation and imposed on Japan, but regardless of who wrote it, it displays a spirit and vision unparalleled in human history and principles of magnificent integrity. It is possibly the first instance in history where the renunciation of armed force, based on a reflection of past wars, has been so clearly expressed. Article 9 states: "Aspiring sincerely to an international peace based on justice and order, the Japanese people forever renounce war as a sovereign right of the nation and the threat or use of force as means of settling international disputes." No other Constitution makes the renunciation of war its cornerstone. It goes on: "In order to accomplish the aim of the preceding paragraph, land, sea, and air forces, as well as other war potential, will never be maintained. The right of belligerency of the state will not be recognized."[14] The Constitution, in other words, seeks to come to grips with the country's historical experience and to use that understanding as a stepping stone to building the future. This is not an issue for Japan alone. When people as a whole ask what kind of society needs to be formed in the future, these constitutional principles can serve as a model, with tenets and criteria based on important historical experience. Whether or not the Constitution was written by the United States is irrelevant; what is good is good. In fact, it is a perfect example of the merits of a combinatory culture. The spirit expressed in Article 9 is so important that I think a lot about the best ways to broaden and strengthen it.

The situation that gave rise to the modern myth appears to have encouraged a dark, ominous tale superseding all preceding myths. The current Heisei era may be seen as a new medieval age, with the era name meaning not "establishment of peace" but rather its homophone, 兵制 (military system). I am extremely apprehensive that we have entered a new "age of the warrior" like that Jien described in his *Gukanshō* in regard to the Heiji disturbance. At that time, the ties between land, communities, and people—social ties in general—had weakened, and the social structure was heading for collapse. Today, the relationship between people, nature, and the environment is likewise heading toward an irreparable breakdown, and we have no clue how to deal with the situation. We are truly living in an age of benighted myth, enveloped by darkness.

Assessing the focus and sense of values at each point of Japanese history over its long course, can we tell what direction it has taken in the modern period down to the present? Can we tell what direction is it likely to take in the future? The Meiji era was marked by such policies and events as the institutionalization of kami-buddha separation, restoration of the monarchy (*ōsei fukko*), "civilization and enlightenment" (*bunmei kaika*), "rich country, strong army" (*fukoku kyōhei*), "promotion of industry" (*shokusan kōgyō*), lifting of the ban on Christianity, religious freedom and the implementation of the principle of the separation of state and religion, the freedom and popular rights movement (*jiyū minken undō*), and the establishment of a parliamentary democracy. The modern period saw the formation of a strong imperial state peculiar to Japan, a "heteromorphic monarchy" (*igyō no ōken*),[15] formed out of the chimera-like combination of the "restoration of the monarchy" and "civilization and enlightenment," in other words, out of Japan's surviving ancient system and modern Western institutions. From the point of view of Shinto, this was also a process that destroyed the ideas and ideology of Nativism (Kokugaku).

A reconsideration of Japanese culture

Yanagita Kunio and Orikuchi Shinobu called for a reconsideration of Japanese culture from its very roots, saying that Nativism had to be retrieved and brought to the minds of the Japanese as a way for them to reflect upon themselves. They formulated *minzokugaku* (folklore studies) as their methodology and showed great determination in promoting a new Nativism through it.

As mentioned in Chapter 5, Yanagita was a bureaucrat in the Ministry of Agriculture and Commerce with an interest in political economy and addressing the crisis in rural villages. He attempted to reconsider the oral structures and systems that were at the core of the culture of ordinary people (*jōmin*), the culture and history of the local place that were not recorded in books. This he set out as "local studies" (*kyōdo kenkyū*) and *minzokugaku*, the study of local lore. Yanagita considered the purpose of folklore studies to be basically for the benefit of ordinary people and society, aimed at bringing happiness to the *jōmin*. By extension, it sought to create a cognitive paradigm to elucidate the cultural underpinnings of such institutions as the household, community, and state. Yanagita was therefore greatly attached to, and had great hopes for, *minzokugaku* as an essential field of learning that would buttress the foundations of Japanese culture.

In the closing days of World War II, when the seventy-year-old Yanagita had almost finished writing his *Senzo no hanashi* (About Our Ancestors),[16] Tokyo was subjected to heavy air raids, and he often took refuge in his shelter, clutching the manuscript to him.

He had hoped to publish the book as soon as the war was over, but was unable to do so because of paper shortages and censorship by the Occupation authorities. It finally came out in 1946.

A *tour de force* that was considered by Yanagita to be his final testament, the book links the question of what happens when people die and what becomes of the souls of the dead to the issue of family continuity, in other words, souls and their veneration within the family. The family or household (*ie*) was a major concern for Yanagita, as the core unit of the community. It is a book that I hope all Buddhist and Shinto priests, as well as laymen, would read.

Yanagita, born Matsuoka Kunio, had been adopted into the Yanagita household when he married the family's daughter. He thus understood the question of family succession as fundamental to community formation and the social order. This understanding probably developed also in the process of his own studies and interests, which had a strong political and administrative perspective. At the base of his thinking was not the "individual" but the "village" and "community," centered on the family.

Orikuchi Shinobu, by contrast, was consistent in his concern for the "individual" and the "personal." His was a "personal" and literary *minzokugaku*. His theories, like those about the outsider (*marebito*) and wandering performers, were all about unusual individuals, about what was private or secret (*watakushi*) and heteromorphic (*igyō*). This describes Orikuchi himself. Though completely dissimilar in temperament and outlook, Yanagita and Orikuchi both gave shape to *minzokugaku*, complementing one another in the early period of Japanese folklore studies while following different vectors in both sensibility and thought.

Death and rebirth

At the beginning of *About Our Ancestors*, Yanagita rhetorically asks what people think of when they hear the word *senzo* (先祖, "ancestor"). Some think of just the founder of their family as the "ancestor." Such people represent the modern way of thinking, who interpret the word by the characters with which it is written. Since 祖 means "forefather" or "progenitor," it is reasonable that they should understand *senzo* in this way. However, those who have not been influenced by the orthography regard an ancestor as the object of veneration within the family, to whom offerings of rice and incense are made. The traditional understanding hinges on an attitude of "venerating" (*matsuru*), an attitude apparent whenever people use "ancestor" in the personified form of *gosenzosama*. For those who have absorbed this usage without knowledge of its written form, therefore, the ancestor is an important object of veneration. This understanding lies at the core of Yanagita's *minzokugaku* and has come to be called his "ancestral theology," a methodology deriving from an inquiry into the actuality behind the words when they are transmitted orally rather than by writing. Yanagita used this to reflect on the culture of lore passed down among ordinary people, whom he called *jōmin*.

At the very end of the book, Yanagita took up the matter of spirituality in a dramatic fashion. He began by asking about what kind of image people held of ancestors and finished with the question of rebirth. From ancient times, he said, Japanese have believed in rebirth, but this was different from the idea of reincarnation in Buddhism, where transmigration occurs not only among human beings but also among animals and other forms of life. At the root of the Japanese ideas of rebirth was that ancestors return eventually to be reborn in the bodies of their own descendants, grandparents being reborn within the families of their grandchildren or great grandchildren. Ideas about rebirth represented hope for the continuation of the family. In *About Our Ancestors*, the phenomena of rites for ancestors and rebirth, and ideas about them, frame the discussion. This is because for Yanagita the subject of family continuity was linked with how people thought about the ancestors, how they were venerated, and how rebirth should be understood.

Let us look at an example of this practice from the Fujiwara clan. Their genealogical chart reveals that grandsons were given one character of their grandfather's name. For instance, the eldest son of Fujiwara no Michinaga was called Yori*michi*, and his grandson was called Moro*michi*, his grandson was Tada*michi*, and his grandson was Moto*michi*. The grandson of Moromichi's son Tada*zane* was

Moto*zane*, and his grandson was Ie*zane*. This was a custom of long standing. My name of Kamata Tōji takes one character from the name of my grandfather Kamata Tōsuke. Since I was the second-born son, the second character of my name is *ji* (two). This very simple naming method that was applied by my grandfather, the head of the family, is one of ancient tradition. Yanagita pointed out in About Our Ancestors the importance for Japanese that the family line develop and survive through a continuing series of death and rebirth.

Invigorating the soul, restoring life

Orikuchi Shinobu, on the other hand, was a man who never felt that he belonged to his family nor that his birth was wanted. So he never arrived at ideas about the necessity for the continuation of the family as Yanagita did. At the center of his way of thinking was not the family but what connected the individual to the community and society. He understood this connection in terms of his concept of *marebito*, the outsider, the guest from afar. He felt himself to be such an outsider, the strange being who arrived like a traveler and shared curious words and deeds before departing for somewhere else. Orikuchi considered the primary conception of Japanese beliefs about the kami to be the *marebito*, the beings who came from the other realm, brought fortune to this world, and then departed. He understood such beings to be kami. He thought that what gave the community strength, the mechanisms of *chinkon* (spirit pacification) and *tamafuri* (spirit reinvigoration) that invigorate the life force, was not a matter of the family but of the structure of social dynamics, as expressed through the individual. The motifs of *marebito*, *okina* (old man), and the wandering, exiled noble were for him essential elements in literature as the metaphors and prototypes of this dynamism.

The *marebito* uttered spells or incantations (*jugen*), transmitting divine words, and it was such words that evolved into performing arts, songs, epic poetry, and literature. Yanagita Kunio wrote poetry when he was a student at Tokyo Imperial University, but he gave it up later. Preferring to read books about agricultural administration, he became a bureaucrat in the Ministry of Agriculture and Commerce.

He was thus a poet who gave up literature; for him, poetry and literature were something to be abandoned.

For Orikuchi Shinobu, on the other hand, to give up literature would be like committing suicide or dying from a fast. He would have perished without it. Literature was as necessary to him as food, providing him with the driving force in his life and activities. From this point he set out to consider anew matters concerning the souls of the dead and spirit pacification (*chinkon*), how it was possible to regenerate and strengthen the soul, and how, and for what purpose, did the power of the performing arts and all the various festivals passed down in villages serve to act as a force to accomplish this. Orikuchi thought of his *minzokugaku* as a new type of nativism (*kokugaku*). If a new Nativism can be established in the course of modernization, this surely means that Nativism was not the prime ideological mover of militarism, as Professor Miyasaka asserted. To make such an accusation would negate the spirit of the new Nativism of Yanagita and Orikuchi. Was it possible, they wondered, to rediscover a way of thinking of value from within the culture and attitudes of the Japanese people? This was the spirit and orientation of the field they called new Nativism and *minzokugaku*; they saw in it a fresh perception of a type of popular theology, a liberation theology. Both men sought to use it to enhance the self-perception and happiness of the Japanese public.

An impending sense of crisis in the state

The course of postwar culture, however, flowed in directions increasingly removed from the *minzokugaku* and new Nativism of Yanagita and Orikuchi. The wellspring of its course lay first of all in the religious policy of the early Meiji era, when the government forcibly separated kami and buddha worship by decree. Second, that early policy had created a double standard concerning religion, as a belief in and veneration of the same kami might in some circumstances be considered religious and in others not. If veneration of the kami was deemed to be religious, then government certification was required, and if not, it came under different criteria. The classical example of

CHAPTER SIX

this, as mentioned above (see page 133) was the split between Izumo Shrine in Shimane prefecture and Izumo Ōyashirokyō, which exhibited all the contradictions of this separation between state ritual and religious worship: a shrine was not religious but the sect to which it belonged was.

It was out of this situation that there arose in the prewar period what might be called shamanic Shinto, which sought to bring about "world renewal" (*yonaoshi*) and to restore the kami to their original position. It was a theological movement that insisted on the necessity of reconstructing society from its very foundations, a movement to create a new people's myth, unlike the Meiji state myth, that embodied an impending sense of crisis in the state. Such movements, beginning with Ōmotokyō, were suppressed by the government from the 1920s.

Tenrikyō and Ōmotokyō incorporated values and ideas that refuted the ethos of the modern Japanese state system. Because of their strong popular support, the government saw them as potential threats to state security and therefore cracked down on them. The basis for the state myth created by the government was the Meiji Constitution and other laws. Tenrikyō and Ōmotokyō, though, embodied principles and strengths that transcended the law. This the state clearly realized and, impelled by a sense of fear, moved to suppress them.

A regime may feel threated by myths that stand outside the state myth structure, as was seen on June 4, 1989, when the Chinese army opened fire on students and other protestors gathered in Beijing's Tiananmen Square to demand greater liberalization and democratization. Many were killed or wounded. What happened there closely resembled the incidents of government suppression in pre-World War II Japan. In 1999, again, the Chinese government tried to eradicate the Falungong movement as a potential threat, and it has shown the same attitude toward Tibet and Tibetan Buddhism and to the Uyghurs of Xinjiang and Islam. The Falungong movement does not seem all that dangerous, but the Chinese government's rather strong reaction means it viewed the differences in thought between itself and the organization as being of such great import that people's lives should be put on the line. Its reaction was a sign of fear of its authority being undermined.

It is true that certain ideas and religions possess an unfathomable and unpredictable power. The law determines social rules, and the state has the power to enforce them, just as ethics has the power to set out rules about morality, and clinical psychology has the power to treat mental illness. However, religion goes beyond law, ethics, and psychology in its power to embrace people, to support them by being with them. Whatever words we use when referring to religion—kami, buddha, bodhisattva, belief, faith, love, compassion, forgiveness—religion crosses the line of social rules and represents actions of acceptance. I regard spirituality to be the foundation of this sort of religion.

Suzuki Daisetsu and Japanese Spirituality

The beginning of ideas about spirituality in Japan can be found, as discussed above (p.100), in the writings of Urabe Kanetomo. However, it was the publication of *Nihonteki reisei* (*Japanese Spirituality*)[17] by Suzuki Daisetsu in 1944 that brought the word "spirituality" (*reisei*) to wider notice. Suzuki said that Japanese spirituality existed in its purest form in Zen and Pure Land thought and concluded that Shinto was an immature religion in terms of its consciousness of spirituality. After the war, Suzuki published three more works on the subject in rapid succession: *Reiseiteki Nihon no kensetsu* (The Building of Spiritual Japan, 1946), *Nihonteki reiseiteki jikaku* (The Awakening of Spiritual Japan, 1946), and *Nihon no reiseika* (Spiritualized Japan, 1947). These represent a powerful outpouring, intensely criticizing Shinto and reevaluating Kamakura Buddhism.

In the preface to the second edition of *Nihonteki reisei*, Suzuki roundly criticized Nativism and Nativist ideology.

> [Speaking of] narrow-minded and conservative nativist scholars—there is just one thing we are forced to bear in mind about the historical view of Nativism, and that is that it cannot be understood either as a science or philosophy or

religion. Nativists overpowered and suffocated opinions other than their own by various means. Their power is symbolized by what is called militarism, imperialism and totalitarianism. The Shintoist ideology of bigoted, narrow-minded, and imprudent Nativist scholars supplied the ideological backdrop for all those doctrines. . . . I believe that the most important factor in Japan's collapse lies in our lack of understanding of the nature of Japanese spirituality.[18]

He severely condemned Hirata Atsutane and his followers, saying "Should we not censure their ideological "war crimes?" Professor Miyasaka, whose writing is summarized above, carried on this position.

All the same, long before Suzuki, the idea of spirituality had already been developed by Urabe Kanetomo, Yoshida Kanetomo, and Hirata Atsutane, and even in the modern period, works by J.W.T. Mason and Deguchi Onisaburō preceded Suzuki's publications in this field.

In 1933, Mason published *Kannagara no michi: Nihonjin no aidentiti to sōzōsei no saihakken* (The Way According to the Kami: A Rediscovery of Japanese Identity and Creativity) in a translation by Imaoka Shin'ichirō. The English version, *The Meaning of Shinto*, followed two years later.[19] In this work, he spoke of "Nature's spirituality" and "universal spirituality."

> Shinto has never lost th[e] first knowledge of Nature's spirituality. (203)
> Shinto however still comprehends the spiritual character of Nature and so makes no . . . artificial separation between man and divinity. Nature, not man, enlarges Shinto Shrines into sanctuaries of universal spirit. (203–04)
> The Shinto conception of universal spirituality confers spiritual equality on all. (230)
> The creative aspect of Shinto, its universality of spiritual conceptions, its broad-minded tolerance, its influence

> of Japanese culture and on racial co-ordination all require conscious elaboration, not as a religious doctrine but as the national spiritual culture of the Japanese people. (240)
>
> The Shrines are concentration centres for man's renewal of his understanding of the spirituality of all existence. Spirituality expands from the Shrines with the all-inclusiveness of Nature. (204)

For Mason, shrines are "places where people go to pay respect to divine spirit and give 'salutation' to universal divinity." (238)

Suzuki advocated his own views about Japanese spirituality, overlooking Shinto ideas either intentionally or out of ignorance. Nevertheless, a Shinto type of spirituality was already being discussed before the Kamakura period, when, according to Suzuki, the term *reisei* (spirituality) first appeared. Surely we cannot ignore the intellectual developments and activities associated with such ideas and discussions about the term *reisei*. It could be said that Suzuki neglected the Shinto discourse on spirituality in order to strengthen his own thesis. If his argument is shown to lack academic impartiality, it should be criticized from the viewpoints of both intellectual history and cultural theory.

According to Suzuki, the classical manifestation of Japanese spirituality was found in medieval Zen and Pure Land thought. This understanding is too narrow. There is a need to widen the study of spirituality to see clearly the universal base underlying it.

Japanese Spirituality Today

If we admit the presence of a Japanese type of spirituality within Japanese culture, this takes the form of ways of sensing and perceiving the manifestations of that immense power called kami within the regeneration and workings of phenomena. The diversity of these manifestations is termed the "myriad deities." Spirituality takes shape through prayers, rituals, and deities. These deities, however, have no single unifying principle of goodness: having two aspects, one peaceful and calming (*nigimitama*) and one fierce and harsh (*aramitama*), they are considered to be benevolent or violent according to their function.

Human recognition of the workings of superhuman powers as "divine" or "god" is thought to have been present as early as the Paleolithic Age. That archaic, primitive way of thinking is embedded in views of the divine held by people living in the Japanese archipelago. In 538 Buddhism entered a culture where the fusion of deities already had a long tradition, and what resulted was the flowering of a culture of kami-buddha combination that has continued down the course of history to the present. Its blossoming was as diverse as the patterns in a kaleidoscope, but the Meiji-era edict ordering the separation of the kami and buddhas ripped its components apart. It was like forcing a loving couple to divorce—wholly unacceptable and inviting a backlash.

However, this very unacceptability has created the opportunity for people to reconsider the nature and roots of kami-buddha combination and to ask why the kami and buddhas coexisted In Japan, standing side by side. It allowed them to think about this idea in a deeper and clearer way.

There is a wide gap between the underlying thought patterns of Buddhism and Shinto. Shinto is more naturalistic, deriving from an awe of what exists in nature, while Buddhism begins from "right views," correctly understanding human suffering as it actually is. It is thus basically humanistic, in comparison to Shinto, which born from the plainest of origins, means living with awe of nature, sensitive to the beauty, harmony, and sacred energy within it.

Spirituality to solve the human problem

As civilization developed and large states came into being, society grew more complex and people's sufferings more acute. World religions like Buddhism and Christianity flourished against such a backdrop, conscious of the need to respond to the problem of universal human suffering. Human issues were at their core. Seeking a fundamental resolution of the social problems created by people themselves, Christianity preached salvation through love and Buddhism taught enlightenment.

Today, however, we are not concerned just with solving human suffering. We are confronted with problems relating to nature and life as a whole. We seek solutions to issues involving human beings within the natural world, beyond the type of human problems that Buddhism and Christianity have focused on, and must find a fuller solution. It is my belief that no true solution can be achieved unless Shinto and ancient religious spirituality, with their focus on the wider world, join hands with religions like Christianity and Buddhism to address human issues.

A new kami-buddha combination—a new coworking between Shinto and Buddhism—may be necessary. It is not enough for the "father" alone to be engaged in gainful employment; the household income needs to be supplemented with earnings by the "mother" and even grandparents. Only when the various religions and organizations all work together can the problems facing humanity be solved.

In this sense, the formulation of combinatory ideas must be premised on the common ownership of a universal spiritual foundation that acts as a cornerstone. Without it, we would be forcing religions holding dissimilar ideas to get along together, and this would never work. Searching for a common human base and bringing it to life represent, I believe, the future of spirituality and the spiritual movement.

Before we talk about Japanese spirituality, we have to consider the dimension of universal or global spirituality (perhaps we could even say cosmic spirituality). The Dalai Lama has pointed out that we all possess "universal spirituality," and this provides us with a hint when we come to discuss this topic. If human beings possess a universal spirituality, we also have a universal responsibility. It is the spirituality of each individual that allows us to recognize this responsibility. Based on such a recognition, we should then ask what kind of peace and reassurance we can establish.

Based on this point of view, I have discussed in a number of works, such as *Shintō no supirichuariti* (Shinto Spirituality, 2003), the meaning of spiritual ideas in a modern context. There I wrote that spiritual ideas are oriented toward universality and impartiality and are impelled to seek a super- or pan-religiosity. Their strength is that they are free from the exclusivity that often characterizes religious institutions. At the same time, however, their very universality and pan-religiosity may result in ambiguity, since *spirituality* may be used vaguely and imprecisely. Care should be taken against this.[20]

I believe that the spiritual perspective is all the more effective today as a common frame of reference when intensifying one's attention toward a deeper dimension of one's spiritual nature and the deepest levels of consciousness. I would suggest three further constituents of spirituality: entirety, rootedness, and depth—a capacity to change and grow. Spirituality allows us to plumb the depths of thinking about ourselves and the totality of existence, by means of which we change in a fundamental way.

Spiritual ideas have the power to approach those states that the late Buddhist scholar Tamaki Kōshirō spoke of as the "maturation of karma" (Pa. *kamma-vipāka*) and "transcendent." They also encompass not only the encounter of kami and buddhas but also the interaction of various religious cultures. I hope in the future to deepen my understanding of spirituality as a compass showing us the way to better live our lives.

Notes

CHAPTER ONE

The Mechanism of Combination

1 *The Threefold Lotus Sutra.* Quotes from introductory chapter, p. 42; "The Parable of the Magic City," p. 155; "The Story of the Bodhisattva Medicine King", p. 311; "Encouragement of the Bodhisattva Universal Virtue," p. 343.
2 *The Larger Sutra on Amitāyus* (Taishō 12: 360), p. 4.
3 Translator's note: Refers to Kūkai's *Shōji jissōgi* (The Meanings of Sound, Word and Reality). Hakeda 1972, pp. 234–45.
4 *Shugen sanjūsan tsūki* SS 2: 413. Translation by GS.
5 I discuss the mutual relationship that developed as a result of the encounter of the native deities (kami) of Japan and the buddhas and bodhisattvas of Buddhism in detail in Kamata 2000a.
6 *Nihon rettō no shizenshi.*
7 Translator's note: These are known to scholarship as *honji suijaku* (original forms and local traces) and *han honji suijaku* (inverted *honji suijaku*), respectively. For a good discussion, see Teeuwen and Rambelli 2003.
8 Translator's note: In Japan, most characters have two pronunciations, the Sino-Japanese (e.g., *shin*) and the native Japanese (e.g., kami). The Sino-Japanese form is usually used in compounds (e.g., *seishin*).
9 Translator's note: The *Kojiki* (Record of Ancient Matters) was completed in 712 as an account of the origins of the ruling clan.

10 *Kojikiden* III. Translation of this passage is based on Havens 1998, p. 234.
11 Translator's note: "The *wakamiya*, a type of secondary shrine usually dedicated to the child of a kami venerated in the principal sanctuary, symbolizes youthfulness and rejuvenation." Grootenhuis 1998, p. 14.
12 Translator's note: The waka Saigyō wrote at Ise: *Nanigoto no / owashimasu ka wa / shiranedomo / katajikenasa ni / namida koboruru*. Translation from Barnhill 2010, p. 175.
13 Translation slightly adapted from Wilson 2013.
14 Translator's note: These are posts buried beneath the main sanctuaries of many shrines.
15 *Nihon shoki* II, vol. 68. See also the translations in Aston 1972, vol. 2, p. 106, p. 195, p. 226.
16 Translator's note: Literally, "raising the voice" to speak to the kami. This brings *kotodama* into play. It may have originated as an invocation to the kami for rain, etc. *Kotodama* is defined as the "magico-religious efficacy of certain words" (Commons 2009, p. 172). For its connection with poetry, see Ebersole 1989.
17 *Man'yōshū*, Vol. 6, No. 3,253. Translation here adapted from Plutschow 1990, p. 90.
18 Translator's note: The custom of royal posthumous names is said to date from the late eighth century, when the scholar Omi no Mifune (722–85) chose Chinese-style names for all the Tennō from Jimmu down to his time. The *Nihon shoki*, which predates this, was later revised to include these posthumous names.
19 Translator's note: This refers to the six histories compiled by imperial order during the eighth and ninth centuries. They are the *Nihon shoki* (720), *Shoku Nihongi* (797), *Nihon kōki* (840), *Shoku Nihon kōki* (869), *Nihon Montoku Tennō jitsuroku* (879) and *Nihon sandai jitsuroku* (901). See Sakamoto 1991.
20 *Kojiki*. For the standard English translation consulted here, see Philippi 1968.
21 Translation from the *Nihon shoki* is adapted from Aston 1972.
22 *Fudoki*. Translator's note: Some of the *fudoki* have been translated into English. 1. *Harima Fudoki; A Record of Ancient Japan*

Reinterpreted. Translated, annotated and with a commentary by Edwina Palmer (Leiden: Brill, 2016). 2. "Hitachi fudoki," *Traditions* 1:3-4 (1977). 3. *Izumo fudoki*, Michiko Y. Aoki, Tokyo: Sophia University, 1971. 4. *Records of Wind and Earth*, translated with an introduction and commentary by Michiko Y. Aoki, Ann Arbor: University of Michigan Press, 1997 (all five extant *fudoki*).

23 Translator's note: This phrase appears for the first time in the *Shinjō sōmoku jōbutsu ki* by the Tendai priest Annen (ninth century). See Stone 2009, particularly pp. 214–16.

CHAPTER TWO

The Encounter of Shinto and Buddhism in the Early Japanese State

1 Endō 1996, p. 191. For English translation see Gessel 1994, p. 118.
2 Hearn 2009, p. 141.
3 Hearn 2009, pp. 169, 170.
4 Translator's note: *Kongengo* 根源語 was used to translate Martin Buber's "primary words," which he says are "not isolated words but combined words." (Buber 1937). It is also a neologism invented by Kōyama Rokurō to refer to certain basic syllables that are associated with particular elements (like water, stone, etc.).
5 Translator's note: For a good discussion of the meaning and typology of festivals, see Hardacre, 2017, pp. 422–507. See also Havens 1988 and other articles in Ueda ed. 1988.
6 Translator's note: The *hime-hiko* system was "rule by a closely-related female and male . . . in which the female acted as a shaman in charge of ritual matters while the male held secular power" (Inoue ed., 2003, p. 21). The *onari-ukeri* system was associated with the spiritual predominance of sisters (*onari*) over their brothers (*ukeri*), who governed the community. It was described by Yanagita Kunio in 1926 (Yanagita 1989-2015, vol. 11, pp. 7–304).
7 *Amagandha Sutta, Suttanipāta* 2.2 (PTS: 239–252). Translator unknown.
8 *Sammaparibbajaniya Sutta, Suttanipāta* 2.13. Translated by H. Saddhatissa. Saddhatissa 2013, 41.

9 *Tuvataka Sutta, Suttanipāta* 4.14 (PTS: Sn 915–934). Translated by Thanissaro Bhikkhu.
10 Translator's note: The *Atharvaveda* is the Veda of charms and spells. Its incantations are not only to appease the "secret powers" but to use them in the material service of people. See Gadkari 1996.
11 *Vesala Sutta, Suttanipāta* 1.7. (PTS: Sn 116–142). Adapted from the translation by Piyadassi Thera.
12 *Pūra āsa (Sundarika bhāradvāja) Sutta, Suttanipāta* 3.4.
13 Translator's note: *Hwarang*, literally "flower youths," refers to military bands led by young aristocrats that existed in Silla, a state on the Korean peninsula. Part of their training was wandering in the mountains. See McBride 2008, pp. 20–21, 54. For Shugendō, see Blacker 1999; Miyake 2005; Sekimori 2011; Grapard 2016.
14 In later times, the *Nihon shoki* was accorded far more importance by Japanese scholars than the *Kojiki*, which drew little scholarly attention until Motoori Norinaga published the *Kojikiden*, his commentary on it, in the eighteenth century.
15 Translator's note: Awa was a province in Shikoku.
16 Masuda 1968.
17 Translation from the *Kogoshūi* slightly adapted from Kato and Hoshino 1926.
18 Philippi 1968, p. 138, note 7 (slightly adapted).
19 Philippi 1968, p. 91 (slightly adapted).
20 Interestingly, while the tenth month of the year is traditionally known in most parts of Japan as *kannazuki*—the "month when the deities are absent"—in Izumo, it is called "the month when the deities are present" (*kamiarizuki*). Every year in the tenth month, it is said that kami from all over Japan gather in Izumo to make plans for the following year.
21 There is an inconsistency with the dating of the introduction. The *Nihon shoki* says that King Sŏngmyŏng (r. 523–54) of Paekche sent the Japanese monarch Kinmei (509–71) a present of "a gold and copper statue of Sākyamuni Buddha, together with several banners and canopies, and several volumes of sutras and treatises" in the tenth month of 552 (Kinmei 13). *Jōgū Shōtoku hōō teisetsu*

(Biography of Shōtoku Taishi, ca. 701) and the *Gangōji garan engi narabi ni ruki shizaichō* (History of Gangōji with a list of its treasures, 747), however, record the year as 538 (Senka 3). The date is thought to have been deliberately altered by the compilers of the *Nihon shoki*.

22 Bowring 2005, pp. 15–16.
23 Aston 1972, vol. 2, p. 68 (slightly adapted).
24 Aston 1972, vol. 2, p. 122.
25 Aston 1972, vol. 1, p. 156.
26 Aston 1972, vol. 2, p. 129.
27 Bowring 2005, p. 21.
28 Translator's note: *Ubasoku*, from the Sanskrit *upāsaka*, Buddhist layman, was the term applied to a "shamanistic Buddhist," an "ascetic, magician, healer, and medium." They had "no formal training in Buddhist doctrines; although they were known for unusual spiritual power, they were not recognized by orthodox Buddhist schools as regular clergy" (Kitagawa 1990, p. 39).
29 Watson 2013, pp. 47–48.
30 *Shoku Nihongi* (VIII, Yōrō 3: 7: 13), Snellen 1934, p. 179 (slightly adapted).
31 *Kogoshūi*. Adapted from Kato and Hoshino 1926, n.p.
32 Translator's note: Fusasaki (681–737) founded the Hokke (Northern) branch, Maro (685–737) founded the Kyōke branch, Muchimaro (680–737) founded the Nanke (Southern) branch, and Umakai (694–737) founded the Shikike branch.

CHAPTER THREE
The New Buddhism of the Heian Period

1 Translator's note: Otherwise his trainees would have to go to Nara and take full ordination in the old style, not in the Mahāyāna style that Saichō advocated.
2 Saichō, *Regulations for Students of the Mountain School* (*Sange gakushō shiki*). T 74: 2377. In *Dengyō Daishi zenshū*, vol. 1. Translation according to Groner 1984, p. 116.

3 Translator's note: *Nyūjō* refers to the belief that later grew up that Kūkai had not died but was in a state of meditation (suspended animation) on Mt. Kōya.
4 Translator's note: *Shidosō*, "those who independently proclaimed themselves priests and nuns, thereby violating the Sōniryō code. From the government's point of view, shidosō were criminals who . . . [hid] behind the privileges given only to officially ordained priests and nuns" (Abe 2000, p. 78).
5 *Indications of the Goals of the Three Teachings*. In Hakeda 1972, p. 121 (slightly adapted).
6 Translator's note: The Hachiman cult was closely connected with Tōdaiji and state protection in this period. Inari was the clan tutelary deity of the immigrant Hata clan, which had settled in nearby Fushimi. The Inari cult had grained great popularity by Kūkai's time.
7 Hakeda 1972, p. 230 (slightly adapted).
8 Translator's note. Also pronounced *mishuhō* and *mishihō*, a general term for Shingon rituals that involved reciting sutras at a varying number of altars. They could be ordered according to purpose and the sutras chosen accordingly. In the case cited in the extract, a belief in the power of words is clear, and the readings could be regarded as spells.
9 Tyler 2003, pp. 171–72 (slightly adapted).
10 Bowring 1996, p. 11 (slightly adapted).
11 Bowring 1996, p. 8 (slightly adapted).
12 Translator's note: An elite private guard serving the retired sovereign. Literally, "northface warriors" (from the fact that their quarters were on the north side of the palace).
13 Brown and Ishida 1979, p. 89 (slightly adapted).
14 Translator's note: By so doing, he deprived Sutoku, as the cloistered ruler with power, of control of the (child) sovereign.
15 NKT 86: 339. Brown and Ishida 1979, pp. 218, 220–21 (slightly adapted).
16 *Hōgen monogatari*.
17 *Migakareshi / tama no utena o / tsuyu fukaki / nobe ni utsushite / miru zo kanashiki*. Translation by Wilson 1971, p. 153.

18 *Matsuyama no / nami ni nagarete / koshi fune no / yagate munashiku / narinikeru kana.* Translation by Lafleur 2003, p. 33.
19 *Yoshiya kimi / mukashi no tama no / yuka totemo / kakaran nochi wa / nanika wa sen.* Translation by Lafleur 2003, p. 34.
20 Wilson 1971, p. 154.
21 Gardner 2007, p. 5.
22 See Shirakawa 1972.
23 Translator's note: Gymnastics include physical exercise and self-massage, which, with breathing exercises, serve to cure diseases and prolong life. See Engelhardt 2000, p. 101.
24 Translator's note: *Guidao* "appears to have involved the evocation of minor deities or spirits, followed by the reception of the spirits' oracles through the speech of spirit-mediums." Pregadio ed. 2008, Vol. I, p. 56.
25 Translated by Ooms 2015, p. 41.
26 Fukunaga 1982.
27 Translator's note: For the Kōshin cult, see Kohn 1993, 1995.
28 Aston 1972, Vol. 2, pp. 188–89 (translation adapted).
29 Watson 2013, pp. 21–22 (slightly adapted).
30 Watson 2013, p. 22 (slightly adapted).
31 Watson 2013, p. 14.

CHAPTER FOUR

Kami and Buddhas in the Medieval Period

1 Translator's footnote: "Reclusive priests" were founders of new orders or groups whose main task was to respond to the individual needs of believers and who participated in personal religion. See Matsuo 1997.
2 Translator's note. "The national system of shrine rites . . . focused on a public role for shrines, shrine ritual and shrine priests, uniting the realm in reverence for the monarchy through reverence for the Kami, not as a matter of personal religious faith, but *as a necessary function of government.*" Hardacre 2017, pp. 111–12.
3 Suzuki 1972, p. 54, slightly adapted. Translator's note: Suzuki used the metaphor of "great earth" to refer to a culture of those whose

roots were in the country, that is, the Kamakura bushi (warriors). For Japanese original, see Suzuki 1968.
4 Suzuki 1972, p. 40.
5 Translator's note. According to the *Nihon shoki*, Yamatohime, daughter of Suinin Tennō, brought Amaterasu to Ise (Aston 1972, vol. 1, 176–177).
6 Bowring 2005, p. 388.
7 *Yuiitsu shintō myōbō yōshū*. Grapard 1992, p. 139.
8 Translator's note: According to the *Essentials*, the sacred space for the kami of heaven is the *yuki* hall, which contains the altar of Original Spirits of the Ten Thousand Phenomena (*bansōdan*) and the sacred space for the kami of earth is the *suki* hall, which contains the altar of Sources of All Living Beings (*shogendan*). The Outer Shrine is equated with the first, and so "original," while the Inner Shrine is equated with the second, and so the "source." They correspond to the twofold aspect of Yuiitsu Shinto. Grapard 1992, pp. 140–41.
9 Grapard 1992, p. 158.
10 I previously pointed out Kanetomo's use of the word reisei in the *Essentials* (Kamata 2003).
11 Grapard 1992, pp. 153–54.
12 Translator's note: The Japanese reading of this passage, "Ōyamato wa kami no kuni nari," would suggest "Japan is a country of the gods," whereas the Sino-Japanese reading, *Dainihon wa shinkoku nari*, could be taken as "Japan is the divine land." Most translation follows the second rendering. For issues concerning the translation of this sentence, see Bowring 2005, pp. 386–87.
13 de Bary et al., eds 2001, Vol. 1, pp. 358–59.

CHAPTER FIVE

Nativist Studies and a New View of Kami-Buddha Combination

1 Translator's note: On the introduction of firearms to Japan, see Lidin 2002.

2 Translator's note: On the *bakufu* policy towards religions in the seventeenth century, see Nosco 1996.
3 Translator's note: For the deification of Ieyasu, see Boot 2000.
4 Though in one sense, ancient myth was revivified when Commodore Perry's "black ships" forced open the country for trade and diplomatic intercourse.
5 *shikishima no / yamatogokoro o / hito towaba / asahi ni nihofu / yamazakurabana*. Shirane 2002, p. 613.
6 For an in-depth study of Hirata Atsutane, see Kamata 2002a.
7 Translator's note: For an English translation, see McCullough 1985, Rodd and Henkenius 1984.
8 Translator's note: For an English translation, see Rodd 2015.
9 Translator's note: Japanese chronologies until 1873 follow the lunar calendar. Dates here are translated into the Gregorian calendar.
10 Translator's note: The Three Standards concerned "reverence for the kami and love of the country" (*keishin aikoku*), "heavenly principles and human ethics" (*tenri jindō*), and "reverence for the emperor and adherence to the court's wishes" (*kōjō hōtai, chōshi junshu*). For a summary of the Great Promulgation campaign and its effects, see Sawada 2004, 110; Hardacre 1989, 42–59.
11 Translator's note: For Izumo in the Meji period, see Zhong 2016, Chapter 5.
12 Translator's note: For the full English translation of *Yoakemae*, see Naff 1987.
13 Translator's note: For a study of shrine mergers, see Fridell 1973.
14 Translator's note: For a study of Kumagusu, see Blacker 2000.
15 Translator's note: For a study of Kurozumikyō, see Hardacre 1986.
16 Kamata 2002b. Translator's note: See also Sawada 2004, 194–201; Inoue ed. 2003, 179–81.
17 Translator's note: For a discussion of Deguchi Onisaburō, see Stalker 2008.
18 Translator's note: For a discussion of Ōkuni Takamasa, see Breen 1996.
19 Translator's note: For Ōkuni and Fukuba, see Breen 2000.
20 Translator's note: For a discussion of Honda and Nagasawa, see Staemmler 2009, Chapter 2.

21 Translator's note: For a discussion of Asano, see Hardacre 1998.
22 Translator's note: For the problems associated with the translation and concept of *minzokugaku*, see, for example, Christy 2012, pp. 6–10.
23 Translator's note: For Tomokiyo Yoshisane, see Staemmler 2009, p. 135 and passim.
24 See Kamata 2003 and Kamata 2002a.
25 Translator's note: According to Confucian thought, the ruler had the moral obligation to "order the realm and save the people" (*keisei saimin*). The modern Japanese term for "economics" (*keizai*) is a contraction of this phrase.
26 Translator's note: The term *kyōdo* is an elusive concept to translate. It refers to the local or native place. According to Kären Wigen, "native place" studies emerged in the late nineteenth and early twentieth century as a counter to Westernization and modernization. She states that *kyōdo* should be understood as "a site of reverence as well as recreation and as a locus of devotion as well as development." Prewar "native place" studies were appropriated to promote patriotic sentiment, to resist cultural standardization, and to boost local, rural economies (Wigen 1996).
27 Translator's note: For a study of the concept of *marebito*, see Hori 1980; Falero 2010.
28 Other terms with a similar meaning include *tamafuri* (reinvigorate a soul by shaking a ritual object or the body itself), *tamafuyu* and *tamashizume* (pacify and settle a spirit in the body). Translator's note: According to Orikuchi, the word *furi* in *tamafuri* does not mean to shake but refers rather to possession or being touched by an external spirit. It also connotes *fuyu*, to reproduce or multiply and *tamafuru*, to bestow. See Encyclopedia of Shinto, Basic Terms: "Tamashizume, tamafuri." Kokugakuin University Digital Museum, http://k-amc.kokugakuin.ac.jp (accessed November 12, 2016).
29 English translation: Angles 2017. The Japanese original was first published in 1939 with revisions in 1943 and 1947. Translator's note: for a discussion of the *Book of the Dead*, see Liman 2005, pp. 183–91.

30 *Utsusomi no hito naru ware ya / asu yori wa / Futakamiyama o / irose to waga mimu. Man'yōshū*, Vol. 2, No. 165. Nippon Gakujutsu Shinkōkai, p. 22.

CHAPTER SIX
Epilogue: Toward a New Kami-Buddha Combination

1 For a discussion on the term *tennō*, see Piggott 1997, pp. 144 and 361–62, nn. 57–60; Barrett 2000, pp. 23–24; Bowring 2005, p. 3.
2 Ōmotokyō, which taught of "world renewal" (*yonaoshi*), shared many similarities with the 13 sects but was never recognized as one of them. Twice, in 1921 and 1935, its leaders were arrested and imprisoned, first for printing materials disrespectful of the emperor as defined in the Newspaper Law, and then for *lèse-majesté* and for violations of the Public Security Preservation Law. The Kokuchūkai, the lay Buddhist organization that developed out of the Nichiren school, and other Buddhist new religious groups were also influential, and during the war leaders of Hitonomichi, Reiyūkai, Risshō Kōseikai, Sōka Gakkai, and others were also imprisoned.
3 *Chūgai nippō*, January 20, 2004.
4 Translator's note: Article 9 of the Japanese Constitution renounces war as a means of settling international disputes. Japanese Ground and Air Self Defense Forces were dispatched on a peacekeeping mission to post–Saddam Hussein Iraq in January 2004, authorized by a special law passed in 2003.
5 Pañcasīlāni (abstain from harming living beings, stealing, sexual misconduct, lying, and intoxication).
6 One of them, Uehara Ryōji (1922–45), who was killed in action as a kamikaze pilot, left a letter for his parents that appears at the beginning of a volume called *Listen to the Voices from the Sea: Writings of the Fallen Japanese Students* (*Kike wadatsumi no koe*). Compiled by Nihon Senbotsu Gakusei Kinen-Kai (Japan Memorial Society for the Students Killed in the War—Wadatsumi Society). Translation in Yamanouchi and Quinn, 2000.

7 *Mikkyō gairon* (Tokyo: Daihōrinkaku, 1989, revised edition); *Hannya shingyō kōgi* (Tokyo: Kadokawa Bunko, 1942).
8 See an account of this era at the beginning of Chapter 4. Japan's medieval period can be thought of as beginning with the Hōgen (1156) and Heiji (1159) disturbances. Minamoto no Yoshitomo, head of the Minamoto clan, together with Fujiwara no Nobuyori, abducted retired sovereign Go-Shirakawa while Taira no Kiyomori was away from the capital on a pilgrimage to Kumano. In the Hōgen insurrection, Yoshitomo had sided with Kiyomori in support of Go-Shirakawa, but was left greatly dissatisfied with the paltry rewards following victory. Whereas Kiyomori was granted a fief of four provinces, including Harima, Yoshitomo was compelled to behead his own father—who had supported the retired sovereign Sutoku against Go-Shirakawa—while his younger brother Tametomo was exiled to Ōshima in Izu. To add insult to injury, he merely received the relatively minor title of Sama no kami (captain of the Guards of the Left). Yoshitomo felt deep resentment toward Go-Shirakawa and Kiyomori.

The Hōgen disturbance broke out as a result of succession disputes within the ruling house and the Fujiwara clan. The royal and aristocratic rivals enlisted the services of members of the military clans to defend their cause. It was a cruel and bloody conflict in which fathers fought sons, brothers fought brothers, and relatives were aligned against one another. Jien, head of the Tendai school, stated in his *Gukanshō* that the Hōgen insurrection marked the beginning of the age of the warrior.
9 Kamata 1999.
10 My sense of foreboding perhaps stemmed from my personal ties to the bloody history of the Heiji era. My ancestor, Kamata Masakiyo, was the son of Yoshitomo's wet nurse. Following Minamoto's defeat in the Heiji disturbance, he took refuge with Yoshitomo at the home of his father-in-law, Osada Tadamune, in Owari province. They were betrayed during the New Year period, being killed when they lowered their guard while drinking sake. As a result, a tradition has remained within my family never to drink

alcohol during the New Year holidays, during which all alcohol is removed from the house. I worry over what I should do to unravel the karmic bonds of my ancestors, and most of the work I have done is related to this.

11 Kina Shōkichi is a singer-songwriter from Okinawa and the leader of the band Champloose; he is the composer of the well-known song *Hana—Subete no hito no kokoro ni hana o* (Flowers in the hearts of all people), famous for the line "Cry, laugh, someday, someday let flowers bloom from our hearts." For a time he was a member of the House of Councilors affiliated with the Democratic Party of Japan. On August 8, 1998, we held a concert and prayer ceremony together at Awaji Island and Meriken Park in Kobe, and repeated it on October 10 the same year before the Great Buddha in Kamakura.

12 Article 2. Translation according to www.japaneselawtranslation.go.jp, downloaded December 19, 2016.

13 Translation according to *Education in the New Japan*, vol. 2, pp. 109–111.

14 Translation according to http://japan.kantei.go.jp/constitution_and_government_of_japan/constitution_e.html, downloaded December 16, 2016.

15 Translator's note. This expression was first used by the historian Amino Yoshihiko to refer to the regime of Go-Daigō Tennō, known as the Kenmu Restoration (1333–36). *Igyō* connotes the abnormal or extraordinary. Amino 1986.

16 In vol. 10 of Yanagita 1989–2015. English translation: Mayer and Ishiwara 1970.

17 Suzuki 1968; for English translation, see Suzuki 1972

18 GS translation.

19 Mason 1933. For English edition, see Mason 1935. The numbers in parentheses refer to the page numbers in the English edition.

20 Kamata 2003.

Bibliography

Abe 2000
  Ryūichi Abe. *The Weaving of the Mantra: Kūkai and the Construction of Esoteric Buddhist Discourse.* New York: Columbia University Press, 2000.
Amino 1986
  Amino Yoshihiko. *Igyō no ōken* (A Heteromorphic Monarchy). Tokyo: Heibonsha, 1986.
Angles 2017
  Angles, Jeffrey trans. *The Book of the Dead*, by Orikuchi Shinobu. Minneapolis: University of Minnesota Press, 2017.
Amagandha Sutta
  Amagandha Sutta, Suttanipāta 2.2. Oxford: PTS, 2001.
Aston 1972
  W. G. Aston, trans. *Nihongi*. Rutland and Tokyo: Tuttle, 1972.
Barnhill 2010
  David Landis Barnhill. *Bashō's Journey.* New York: SUNY Press, 2010.
Barrett 2000
  Tim Barrett. "Shinto and Taoism in Early Japan," in *Shinto in History, Ways of the Kami*, ed. John Breen and Mark Teeuwen, pp. 13–31. Richmond, Surrey: Curzon, 2000.
Blacker 1999 (1975)
  Carmen Backer. *The Catalpa Bow.* Third edition. Richmond, Surrey: Curzon Press, 1999.
Blacker 2000
  Carmen Blacker. "Minakata Kumagusu, 1867–1941: A Genius Now Recognized." In *Collected Writings of Carmen Blacker*, pp. 235–47. Richmond, Surrey: Curzon, 2000.
Boot 2000
  W. J. Boot. "The Death of a Shogun: Deification in Early Modern Japan." In *Shinto in History, Ways of the Kami*, ed. John Breen and Mark Teeuwen, pp. 144–66. Richmond, Surrey: Curzon, 2000.

Bowring 1996
　Richard Bowring, trans. *The Diary of Lady Murasaki*. London: Penguin, 1996.

Bowring 2005
　Richard Bowring. *The Religious Traditions of Japan, 500–1600*. Cambridge, UK: Cambridge University Press, 2005.

Breen 1996
　John Breen. "Accommodating the Alien: Ōkuni Takamasa and the Religion of the Lord of Heaven." In *Religion in Japan, Arrows to Heaven and Earth*, edited by P. F. Kornicki and I. J. McMullen, pp. 179–97. Cambridge, UK: Cambridge University Press, 1996.

Breen 2000
　John Breen. "Ideologues, Bureaucrats and Priests: On 'Shinto' and 'Buddhism' in early Meiji Japan." In *Shinto in History, Ways of the Kami*, ed. John Breen and Mark Teeuwen, pp. 230–51. Richmond, Surrey: Curzon, 2000.

Brown and Ishida 1979
　Delmer M. Brown and Ichirō Yoshida, trans. *The Future and the Past. A Translation and Study of the Gukanshō: An Interpretive History of Japan written in 1219*. Berkeley, CA: University of California Press, 1979.

Buber 1937
　Martin Buber. *I and Thou*, trans. Walter Kaufman. Edinburgh: T. & T. Clark, 1937.

Christy 2012
　Alan Christy. *A Discipline on Foot: Inventing Japanese Native Ethnography, 1910–1945*. Plymouth: Rowman and Littlefield, Publishers Inc., 2012.

Commons 2009
　Anne Commons. *Hitomaro, Poet as God*. Leiden: Brill, 2009.

de Bary et al. 2001
　William Theodore de Bary et al., eds. *Sources of Japanese Tradition*, 2nd edition, 2 vols. New York: Columbia University Press, 2001.

Ebersole 1989
　Gary L. Ebersole. *Ritual Poetry and the Politics of Death in Early Japan*. Cambridge MA: Harvard University Press, 1989.

Education in the New Japan
　Education in the New Japan. 2 vols. Tokyo: General Headquarters, SCAP, CIE, 1948.

Endō 1996
　Endō Shūsaku. *Fukai kawa* (Deep River). Tokyo: Kōdansha, 1996.

Engelhardt 2000
: Ute Engelhardt. "Longevity Techniques and Chinese Medicine." In *Daoism Handbook*, ed. Livia Kohn, pp. 74–108. Leiden: E. Brill, 2000.

Falero 2010
: Alfonso Falero. "Origuchi Shinobu's Marebitoron in Global Perspective: A Preliminary Study." In *Classical Japanese Philosophy. Frontiers of Japanese Philosophy* 7, eds. James W. Heisig and Rein Raud. Nagoya: Nanzan Institute for Religion and Culture, 2010.

Fridell 1973
: Wilbur M. Fridell. *Japanese Shrine Mergers, 1906–12: State Shinto Moves to the Grassroots*. Monumenta Nipponica Monograph Series. Tokyo: Sophia University, 1973.

Fudoki.
: *Fudoki*. In vol. 2 of *Nihon koten bungaku taikei* (Complete Classical Literature of Japan). Tokyo: Iwanami Shoten, 1958.

Fukunaga 1982
: Fukunaga Mitsuji. *Dōkyō to Nihon bunka* (Daoism and Japanese Culture). Kyoto: Jinbun Shoin, 1982.

Gadkari 1996
: Jayant Gadkari. *Society and Religion, from Rugveda to Puranas*. New Delhi: Popular Prakashan, 1996.

Gardner 2007
: Daniel K. Gardner, trans. *The Four Books, The Basic Teachings of the Later Confucian Tradition*. Indianapolis/Cambridge: Hackett Publishing Company, 2007.

Gessel 1994
: Van D. Gessel, trans. *Deep River*, by Endō Shūsaku. New York: New Directions, 1994.

Grapard 1986
: Allan G. Grapard. "Lotus in the Mountain, Mountain in the Lotus: Rokugo Kaizan Nimmon Daibosatsu Hongi." *Monumenta Nipponica* 41:1 (Spring 1986), pp. 21–50.

Grapard 1992
: Allan G. Grapard. "*Yuiitsu shintō myōbō yōshū*." *Monumenta Nipponica* 47:2 (Summer 1992), pp. 137–161.

Grapard 2016
: Allan G. Grapard. *Mountain Mandalas, Shugendō in Kyushu*. London: Bloomsbury, 2016.

Groner 1984
: Paul Groner. *Saichō: The Establishment of the Japanese Tendai School*. Berkeley: Berkeley Buddhist Studies Series, 1984.

Grootenhuis 1998
Elizabeth Ten Grootenhuis. *Japanese Mandalas: Representations of Sacred Geography.* Honolulu: University of Hawai'i Press, 1998.
Hakeda 1972
Yoshito S. Hakeda. *Kūkai, Major Works.* New York: Columbia University Press: 1972.
Hardacre 1986
Helen Hardacre. *Kurozumikyō and the New Religions of Japan.* Princeton: Princeton University Press, 1986.
Hardacre 1989
Helen Hardacre. *Shintō and the State 1868–1988.* Princeton: Princeton University Press, 1989.
Hardacre 1998
Helen Hardacre. "Asano Wasaburō and Japanese Spiritualism in Early Twentieth Century Japan." In *Japan's Competing Modernities: Issues in Culture and Democracy, 1900–1930*, ed. Sharon Minichiello. Honolulu: University of Hawai'i Press, 1998.
Hardacre 2017
Helen Hardacre. *Shinto, A History.* Oxford: Oxford University Press, 2017.
Havens 1988
Norman Havens. "Matsuri in Japanese Religious Life." In *Matsuri, Festival and Rite in Japanese Life*, ed. Kenji Ueda, pp. 422–507. Tokyo: Institute for Japanese Culture and Classics, Kokugakuin University, 1988.
Havens 1998
Norman Havens. "Immanent Legitimation: Reflections on the 'Kami Concept.'" In Kami, ed. Inoue Nobutaka, pp. 227–46. Tokyo: Kokugakuin University, 1998.
Hearn 2009
Lafcadio Hearn. *Unfamiliar Glimpses of Japan.* Orig. pub. 1894. Tokyo: Tuttle Publishing, 2009.
Hōgen monogatari
Hōgen monogatari (The Tale of Hōgen). In *Hōgen monogatari, Heiji monogatari*, vol. 31 of *Nihon koten bungaku taikei*. Tokyo: Iwanami Shoten, 1961.
Hori 1980
Hori Ichiro. "Mysterious Visitors from the Harvest to the New Year." In *Studies in Japanese Folklore*, ed. Richard M. Dorson, pp. 76–106. New York: Arno Press, 1980.
Inoue 1998
Inoue Nobutaka, ed. *Kami.* Tokyo: Kokugakuin University, 1998.

Inoue ed. 2003
: Inoue Nobutaka, ed. *Shinto, A Short History*, trans. and adapted by Mark Teeuwen and John Breen. London: RoutledgeCurzon, 2003.

Inoura and Kawatake 1981
: Yoshinobu Inoura and Toshio Kawatake. *The Traditional Theater of Japan*. New York and Tokyo: Weatherhill, 1981.

Kamata 1999
: Kamata Tōji. *Reisei no nettowāku* (Spirituality Network). Tokyo: Seikyūsha, 1999.

Kamata 2000a
: Kamata Tōji. *Kami to hotoke no seishinshi, shinshin shūgōron josetsu* (The Spiritual History of Kami and Buddhas: An Introduction to Kami-kami Combination). Tokyo: Shunjūsha, 2000.

Kamata 2000b
: Kamata Tōji. "The Disfiguring of Nativism: Hirata Atsutane and Orikuchi Shinobu." In John Breen and Mark Teeuwen, eds., *Shinto in History: Ways of the Kami*, pp. 295–317. Richmond, Surrey: Curzon, 2000.

Kamata 2002a
: Kamata Tōji. *Hirata Atsutane no shinkai fīrudowāku* (Hirata Atsutane, Fieldwork in the Spiritual Realm). Tokyo: Sakuhinsha, 2002.

Kamata 2002b
: Kamata Tōji. *Hirayama Seisai to Meiji no Shintō* (Hirayama Seisai and Meiji Shinto). Tokyo: Shunjusha, 2002.

Kamata 2003
: Kamata Tōji. *Shintō no supirichuaritei* (Shinto Spirituality). Tokyo: Shinkusha, 2003.

Kato and Hoshino 1926
: Genchi Kato and Hikoshiro Hoshino, trans. *Kogoshūi: Gleanings from Ancient Stories*. New York: Barnes and Noble, 1926.

Kitagawa 1990
: Joseph M. Kitagawa. "Emperor, Shaman, and Priest." In Kitagawa, *Religion in Japanese History*, pp. 3–45. Columbia University Press, 1990.

Kohn 1993, 1995
: Livia Kohn. "Kōshin: A Taoist Cult in Japan." Parts 1, 2 and 3. *Japanese Religions* 18.2: 113-39; 20.1:34-55; 20.2: 123-42.

Kojiki
: *Kojiki*. Vol. 1 of *Nihon koten bungaku taikei*. Iwanami Shoten, 1958

Kojiki (Philippi)
: *Kojiki*. Trans. Donald L. Philippi. University of Tokyo Press, 1968.

Kojikiden
   Kurano Kenji. *Kojikiden*. Iwanami Shoten, 1940–44.
Lafleur 2003
   William R. Lafleur. *Awesome Nightfall. The Life, Times and Poetry of Saigyō*. Boston: Wisdom Publications, 2003.
Liden 2002
   Olof G. Lidin. *Tanegashima: The Arrival of Europe in Japan*. Copenhagen: Nordic Institute of Asian Studies, 2002.
Liman 2005
   A. V. Liman. "A Modern Text as Shamanistic Performance: Orikuchi's *shisha no sho*." In Intercultural Explorations, ed. Eugene Eoyang, pp. 183–91. Amsterdam: Rodopi, 2005.
Man'yōshū
   Man'yōshū. Vols 4, 5, 6, 7 in *Nihon koten bungaku taikei*. Iwanami Shoten, 1965.
Man'yōshū (Levy)
   Man'yōshū. Trans. Ian Hideo Levy. 4 vols. Princeton, N.J.: Princeton University Press, 1981.
Man'yōshū (Nippon Gakujutsu Shinkōkai)
   Man'yōshū. Trans. Nippon Gakujutsu Shinkōkai. New York: Columbia University Press, 1969.
Mason 1933
   J. W. T. Mason. *Kannagara no michi. Nihonjin no aidenteitei to sōzōsei no saihakken* (The Way of the Gods: A Rediscovery of Japanese Identity and Imagination). Translated by Imaoka Shin'ichirō. Tokyo: Fuzanbō, 1933.
Mason 1935
   J. W. T. Mason. *The Meaning of Shinto*. New York: E. P. Dutton and Co., 1935.
Masuda 1968
   Masuda Katsumi. *Kazan rettō no shisō* (Intellectual Culture of the Volcanic Archipelago). Tokyo: Chikuma Shobō, 1968.
Matsuo 1997
   Kenji Matsuo. "What is Kamakura New Buddhism? Official Monks and Reclusive Monks." JJRS 24:1–2 (1997), pp. 179–189.
Mayer and Ishiwara 1970
   Fanny Hagin Mayer and Ishiwara Yasuyo (trans.). *About Our Ancestors: The Japanese Family System*, by Yanagita Kunio. Tokyo: Japanese Society for the Promotion of Science, 1970.

McBride 2008
: McBride, Richard D. *Domesticating the Dharma: Buddhist Cults and the Hwaŏm Synthesis in Silla Korea*. Honolulu: Hawai'i University Press, 2008.

McCullough 1985
: Helen Craig McCullough, trans. *Kokin wakashū, The First Imperial Anthology of Japanese Poetry*. Stanford, CA: Stanford University Press, 1985.

Mikake 2005
: Miyake Hitoshi. *The Mandala of the Mountain: Shugendō and Folk Religion*. Translated and edited by Gaynor Sekimori. Tokyo: Keiō Gijuku Daigaku Shuppankai, 2005.

Naff 1987
: William E. Naff (trans.). *Before the Dawn, Shimazaki Tōson*. Honolulu: University of Hawai'i Press, 1987.

Nihon rettō no shizenshi
: Kokuritsu Kagaku Hakubutsukan, ed. *Nihon rettō no shizenshi* (A Natural History of the Japanese Archipelago). Tōkyō Daigaku Shuppankai, 2006.

Nihon shoki
: *Nihon shoki I, II*. Vols. 67 and 68 of *Nihon koten bungaku taikai*. Iwanami Shoten, 1965.

Nihon shoki (Aston)
: *Nihongi*. 2 vols. Trans. W. G. Aston. Tokyo: Tuttle, 1972.

Nosco 1996
: Peter Nosco. "Keeping the Faith: *Bakuhan* Policy towards Religions in Sevententh-Century Japan." In *Religion in Japan, Arrows to Heaven and Earth*, edited by P. F. Kornicki and I. J. McMullen, 136–55. Cambridge: Cambridge University Press, 1996.

Ooms 2015
: Herman Ooms. "Framing Daoist Fragments in Japan." In *Daoism in Japan, Chinese traditions and Their Influence on Japanese Religious Culture*, ed. Jeffrey L. Richey, 37–59. Abington: Routledge, 2015.

Orikuchi 1955a
: Orikuchi Shinobu. *Kuchibue* (The Whistle). In vol. 24 of *Orikuchi Shinobu zenshū*, pp. 1–78. Tokyo: Chūō Kōron Sha, 1955.

Orikuchi 1955b
: Orikuchi Shinobu. *Kami no yome* (The Divine Bride). In vol. 24 of *Orikuchi Shinobu zenshū*. Tokyo: Chūō Kōron Sha, 1955.

Orikuchi 1955c
   Orikuchi Shinobu. *Ikiguchi o tou onna* (The Woman Who Conducted Living Seances). In vol. 24 of *Orikuchi Shinobu zenshū*. Tokyo: Chūō Kōron Sha, 1955.
Philippi 1968
   Donald L. Philippi, trans. *Kojiki*. University of Tokyo Press, 1968.
Piggott 1997
   Joan Piggott. *The Emergence of Japanese Kingship*. Stanford: Stanford University Press, 1997.
Plutschow 1990
   Herbert E. Plutschow. *Chaos and Cosmos: Ritual in Early and Medieval Japanese Literature*. Leiden: E. J. Brill, 1990.
Pregadio ed. 2008
   Fabrizio Pregadio, ed. *Encyclopedia of Taoism*. New York: Routledge, 2008.
Pūraḷāsa (Sundarika bhāradvāja) Sutta
   Pūraḷāsa (Sundarika bhāradvāja) Sutta, Suttanipāta 3.4. Oxford: PTS 2001.
Rodd and Henkenius 1984
   Laura Rasplica Rodd and Mary Catherine Henkenius, trans. *Kokinshū, A Collection of Poems Ancient and Modern*. Princeton, N.J.: Princeton University Press, 1984.
Rodd 2015
   Laurel Rasplica Rodd, translated and introduced. *Shinkokinshu: New Collection of Poems Ancient and Modern*. Leiden: Brill, 2015.
Saddhatissa 2013
   H. Saddhatissa. *The Sutta-Nipāta: A New Translation from the Pali Canon*. London and New York: RoutledgeCurzon, 2013.
Sakamoto 1991
   Sakamoto Tarō. *The Six National Histories of Japan*. Trans. John S. Brownlee, Vanouver: UBC Press/Tokyo: University of Tokyo Press, 1991.
Sammaparibbajaniya Sutta
   Sammaparibbajaniya Sutta, Suttanipāta 2.13. See Saddhatissa 2013.
Sange gakushō shiki
   Saichō. *Sange gakushō shiki* (Regulations for Students of the Mountain School). In *Dengyō Daishi zenshū* vol. 1. T 74: 2377.
Sawada 2004
   Janine Anderson Sawada. *Practical Pursuits: Religion, Politics, and Personal Cultivation in Nineteenth-Century Japan*. Honolulu: University of Hawai'i Press, 2004.

Sekimori 2011
Gaynor Sekimori. "The Akinomine of Haguro Shugendo: A Historical Perspective," (revised and expanded). In *Japanese Religions*, vol. 4, Lucia Dolce ed. London: Sage, 2011.

Shimazono and Graf 2012
Shimazono Susumu and Tim Graf. "The Rise of the New Spirituality." In *Handbook of Contemporary Japanese Religions*, ed. Inken Prohl and John Nelson, 459–86. Leiden: Brill, 2012.

Shirakawa 1972
Shirakawa Shizuka. *Kōshiden* (Biography of Confucius). Tokyo: Chūō kōronsha, 1972.

Shirane ed. 2002
Shirane Haruo, edited with an introduction and commentary. *Early Modern Japanese Literature, An Anthology, 1600–1900*. New York: Columbia University Press, 2002.

Shōji jissōgi
Shōji jissōgi. In *Kūkai, Major Works*, trans. Yoshito S. Hakeda. Columbia University Press, 1972.

Shugen sanjūsan tsūki
Shugen sanjūsan tsūki. Shugendō shōso II. Tokyo: Kokusho Tankōkai, 2000.

Snellen 1934
J. B. Snellen, trans. *Shoku Nihongi*. TASJ Second Series Vol. IX (December 1934): 169–239.

Staemmler 2009
Birgit Staemmler. *Chinkon Kishin: Mediated Spirit Possession in Japanese New Religions*. Munster: LIT Verlag, 2009.

Stalker 2008
Nancy K. Stalker. *Prophet Motive: Deguchi Onisaburō, Oomoto, and the Rise of New Religions in Imperial Japan*. Honolulu: University of Hawai'i Press, 2008.

Stone 2009
Jacqueline I. Stone, "Realizing this World as the Buddha Land," in *Readings of the Lotus Sutra*, eds. Stephen S. Teiser and Jacqueline I. Stone, New York: Columbia University Press, 2009.

Suzuki 1968
Suzuki Daisetsu. *Nihonteki reisei* (Japanese Spirituality). *Daisetsu Suzuki zenshū*, Vol. 8: 3–223. Tokyo: Iwanami Shoten, 1968.

Suzuki 1972
D. T. (Daisetz) Suzuki. *Japanese Spirituality*, trans. Norman Waddell. Tokyo: Japan Ministry of Education, 1972.

Takagami 1942
Takagami Kakushō. *Hannya shingyō kōgi* (Lectures on the Heart Sutra). Tokyo: Kadokawa Bunkō, 1942.

Takagami 1989 (1937)
Takagami Kakushō. *Mikkyō gairon* (Outline of Esoteric Buddhism). Rev. ed. Tokyo: Daihōrinkaku, 1989.

Teeuwen and Rambelli 2003.
Mark Teeuwen and Fabio Rambelli. "Introduction, Combinatory Religion and the *Honji Suijaku* Paradigm in Pre-modern Japan." In Teeuwen and Rambelli, eds, *Buddhas and Kami in Japan*. London and New York: Routledge/Curzon, 2003.

The Larger Sutra on Amitāyus
The Larger Sutra on Amitāyus (Taishō 12: 360) translated from the Chinese by Hisao Inagaki in collaboration with Harold Stewart. Numata Center for Buddhist Translation and Research, 2003.

Threefold Lotus Sutra
The Threefold Lotus Sutra, translated by Bunnō Katō, Yoshirō Tamura and Kōjiro Miyasaka with revisions by W. E. Soothill, Wilhelm Schiffer and Pier P. del Campana. New York and Tokyo: Weatherhill/Kosei, 1975.

Tuvataka Sutta
Tuvataka Sutta, *Suttanipāta* 4.14. Oxford, UK: Pali Text Society, 2001.

Tyler 2003
Royall Tyler, trans. *The Tale of Genji*. New York/London: Penguin, 2003.

Ueda ed. 1988
Kenji Ueda, ed. *Matsuri, Festival and Rite in Japanese Life*. Tokyo: Institute for Japanese Culture and Classics, Kokugakuin University, 1988.

Vesala Sutta
Vesala Sutta, *Suttanipāta* 1.7. Oxford: PTS, 2001.

Watson 2013
Burton Watson, trans. *Record of Miraculous Events in Japan. The Nihon ryōiki*. New York: Columbia University Press, 2013.

Wigen 1996
Kären Wigen. "Politics and Piety in Japanese Native-place Studies: The Rhetoric of Solidarity in Shinano." *Positions, East Asia Cultures Critique* 4:3 (1996), pp. 491–517.

Wilson 1971
William R. Wilson, trans. *Hōgen monogatari, Tale of the Disorder in Hōgen*. Sophia University, 1971.

Wilson 2013
: Wilson, William Scott (trans.). *The Spirit of Noh: A New Translation of the Classic Noh Treatise the Fushikaden* by Zeami. Boulder, CO: Shambhala Publications, 2013.

Yamanouchi and Quinn 2000
: Midori Yamanouchi and Joseph L. Quinn, trans. *Listen to the Voices from the Sea: Writings of the Fallen Japanese Students*. Scranton: University of Scranton Press, 2000.

Yanagita 1989–2015
: Yanagita Kunio. *Yanagita Kunio zenshū* (Collected Works of Yanagita Kunio). 35 vols. Tokyo: Chikuma Shobō, 1989–2015.

Zhong 2016
: Yijiang Zhong. *The Origin of Modern Shinto in Japan: The Vanquished Gods of Izumo*. London: Bloomsbury, 2016.

Index

Abe no Seimei 89
Amaterasu ōmikami 24, 27, 101, 108, 128, 129
   at the Ise Shrines 55, 102–104, 105, 160, 190n
   in Tōshōgū network 116
   Kitabatake Chikafusa 111
   story of the cave 14, 47–48, 49, 50
   theological elements 22, 24
amatsukami (kami of heaven) 51
Ame no Uzume no mikoto (Uzume) 13, 46–47
ancestors 33, 164
   veneration of 87
   Yanagita Kunio 136, 141, 171–174
animism 27, 30, 39
Asuka 53, 91, 143
   Orikuchi Shinobu 139, 144

Benzaiten 43, 61, 62
Brahmanism 38, 39, 41, 43
Buddhism
   coming to Japan 53–57
   ethics 76, 157
   monastic faith 154
   protection of state 63–66
   sectarian 154, 155, 156, 158
Buddhist Dharma (*buppō; hōriki*) 16–18, 38, 55, 74–76, 83–84
Buddhist divinities 7

bunmei kaika ("civilization and enlightenment") 118, 125, 131, 170

cap-rank system 58, 74
chihayaburu (powerful kami) 26, 32, 51, 54, 60, 63
Christianity 27, 32, 34–37, 180–181
   ban lifted 125, 127, 131, 170
   edicts banning 115, 119, 125, 152
   medieval (Europe) 112
   Nobunaga encouragement of 110, 114–115
conch 2–5
Confucianism 56–57, 75, 86–88
   classics of 57, 71, 87–88
   ethical concepts 56
   male supremacy 45
   Wangren 87

Daigongen 116–117
danka (parishioner) system 115
Daoism 61, 71, 75, 88–90
Dharma (*see* Buddhist Dharma)
Dōgen 68, 71, 97, 99, 100, 113, 177

education 133, 162
   Daigakuryō 70–71, 74–75
   Fundamental Law of Education 167–169
   Imperial Rescript 131, 153, 159

INDEX

of Shinto priests 129
Tokugawa period 88, 118
Emperor Meiji 86, 126, 134
spirit of Sutoku Tennō 84
emperor system 130, 153, 155, 160
Engishiki (Procedures of the Engi Era) 15, 90
En no Gyōja (En no Ozuno, En no Ubasoku) 29, 58–63
and Kūkai 71, 72, 76
as founder of Shugendō 125
exile 98
Enryakuji Temple 67, 78, 94, 114
esoteric Buddhism 43, 68, 69, 72, 74–75, 160
esoteric rituals 79, 80
ethics 34, 57, 76, 86, 157, 159, 177, 191n
exorcists 80, 81, 121

freedom and popular rights movement 131, 170
fudoki (almanacs) 25–26, 31, 35
Fujiwara clan 70, 72, 82, 95–96, 107, 108, 153, 194n
Fujiwara no Fuhito 64–65, 146
Fujiwara-kyō (palace) 59, 63, 89
Fujiwara no Michinaga 79, 97, 173
Fujiwara no Nakamaro 64
Fujiwara no Tadamichi 12
Fujiwara no Tadazane 83
Fujiwara no Yorimichi 97–98
Fujiwara Seika 88
in *Kami no yome* story 142
Kasuga Onmatsuri 12–13
political power 64–66, 95, 150, 153
succession disputes 82–83, 95, 194n
funeral rites 87, 129, 155, 160
Fūshikaden (Book of the Transmission of the Flower) 13

gagaku (court) music 12

Gautama Siddhartha 37, 38
government 68
and *matsuri* (rites) 36
and Manchuria 157
Buddhism and 154
forcible separation of kami and buddhas 175
in *Nihon shoki* 22
insei (regency) 95
Iraq war and 162
Kūkai and 74
land 31, 96
local 132
Meiji 123–130, 133, 149, 152–153, 155, 175
Ōmotokyō 176
ritsuryō system 31, 63, 86, 88
suppression 176
tennō in 122
warrior-led 86, 96–97, 115, 151
Yanagita Kunio 137
Gukanshō 82, 83, 170, 194n

haibutsu kishaku (eradicate Buddhism) 124, 154
Hayashi Razan 88
Hearn, Lafcadio 33–35
Heiji disturbance 82, 95, 96, 162, 170, 194n
Hinduism 41, 43
Hirata Atsutane 118–122, 135–136, 141, 159, 178, 191n
Hirata school 128, 130–153
Hōgen disturbance 82–83, 84, 85, 95–96
Hōnen 71, 98, 99, 100
honji suijaku (original forms and local traces) 8, 183n
hwarang (military bands of Silla) 44, 186n

Ise Shinto 97, 100–105

210

Ise Shrines 15, 31
　Outer Shrine 102, 104, 105, 107, 108, 160, 190n
Islam 27, 34, 35, 36, 176
Isora deity 13
Izanagi no mikoto 10, 45–47
Izanami no mikoto 10, 45–47
Izumo Ōyashirokyō 133, 176
Izumo Taisha shrine 15, 33, 51–52, 129, 133, 176, 191n
　excavations 52
　faction 128–129

Jien 82, 170, 194n
Jingikan 100, 101, 102, 123, 124, 126, 133, 135
Jinmu Tennō 52–53, 60, 111, 123
　Kigensetsu 128
Jinshin disturbance 31
jinushi no kami (local tutelary deities) 77
jōmin ("abiding folk") 135–137, 141, 171, 173
Jōmon period 5

kagura (shrine) dance 12, 13, 14, 47
kaji kitō (prayer rituals) 84, 121, 106
Kakinomoto no Hitomaro 18–19
kami and buddhas: fundamental differences 14–16
kami
　categories of 10
　etymology with *kamo* 60
　in ancient records 23
　meaning of word 8–9, 25–27
　relationship to buddhas 8, 29, 56, 183n
　relationship to human beings 33
kami-buddha combination (*shinbutsu shūgō*) 5, 6, 7, 16, 43, 140, 145, 149, 180

kamigakari (*see also* possession) 47–48, 135, 142
Kamiyama site (Niigata prefecture) 5
kamiyo (age of kami) 21–22
kamunagara (*kannagara*; "as a kami") 17–19, 20, 27, 37, 178
Kanmu Tennō 67, 72
Kasuga Taisha Onmatsuri 11–15
Kitabatake Chikafusa 111
kitōsō (magico-religious ritualists) 79
Kojiki 9, 21–27
Kojikiden (Motoori Norinaga) 26, 186n
Kokugaku (*see* Nativist Studies)
kokutai (national polity) 131, 135, 159
Kōtoku Tennō 17, 55–56
Kūkai 43, 67, 68, 69, 70–78
　at Daigakuryō 70–71, 74–75
kunibiki (land-pulling) myth 25
Kunitokotachi no mikoto 24
kunitsukami (kami of earth) 51, 61
kuniumi (creation of the land) 45
kuniyuzuri (transfer of the land) 51

land
　creation of 25, 47
　"land-pulling" 25
　myths of 44
　ownership of 31
　system 95
Lotus Sutra 1–5, 35, 67, 69, 100, 113, 134, 183n

magic 33–34, 37, 38, 41, 42, 59, 64, 67, 75, 88, 90
　ban on magic healing 128
　practices 39
magico-religious practices 58, 71, 74, 79, 81, 84, 121, 184n
　Buddhism 74
Man'yōshū 18, 26, 31, 119, 139–140, 147

mappō 97–99
marebito (outsider/visitor) 140, 141, 172, 174, 192n
marōdo-gami ("guest kami") 92, 93
Matsuo Bashō 143
matsuri (rites, festivals) 15, 19, 32, 33, 35, 47
  Kasuga Onmatsuri 11–13, 15, 95
  Nanomatsuri 90
  wazaogi (act of invitation) 15
  word 36
Meiji Restoration 110, 118, 122–123
  Hirata Atsutane and 122, 135
  Nativists in 130, 155–156, 158–159
  shrine priests 130, 133
Minakata Kumagusu 132, 142
Minamoto 82, 95–96, 141, 162, 164, 194n
Minamoto no Yoritomo 96, 164
minzokugaku (folklore studies) 135, 171, 175, 192n
  Orikuchi Shinobu 138–142, 172, 175
  Yanagita Kunio 136–137, 173
mito no maguwahi (sexual contact) 45
miyaza (village shrine groups) 16
mono no aware (pathos of things) 79, 119–121, 159
mononoke (possessing spirits) 79–81, 121, 143, 159
Motoori Norinaga 9, 22, 26, 79, 118, 119–121, 159, 186n
Mt. Hiei 67–68, 71, 78–79, 94, 99
  set ablaze 152
  sōhei of 110, 114
Mt. Kōya 70–71, 77, 115, 188n
Murasaki Shikibu 79–81, 121
mythology 33, 51, 150
  early modern 116, 122
  exoteric 102
  Hirata Atsutane 119
  medieval Shinto 101

ritsuryō state 44, 99
  state 30, 44–53, 101
  unifying 123, 130, 150–154

Nachi Taisha 61
national isolation (*sakoku*) 115, 119, 152
national polity (*kokutai*) 131, 135, 159
Nativist Studies (Kokugaku) 117–118, 136, 154, 155, 158–160
  and *minzokugaku* 171
  Hirata Atsutane 120, 122–123, 125, 130, 135, 153
  Motoori Norinaga 9, 79, 119
  Suzuki Daisetsu and 177–178
nenbutsu 94, 98–100, 113
new Nativism 135, 140, 166, 171, 175
Nichiren 2, 68, 71, 98, 99, 100, 113, 128, 134, 152, 193n
Nihon ryōiki 58, 91, 93
Nihon shoki 16, 17, 18, 21–25, 31, 37
  and Prince Shōtoku 56–57
  beginning of *kagura* 48
  cited by Yoshida Kanetomo 107
  Daoist terms in 89–90
  description of kami 49, 50
  introduction of Buddhism to Japan 43, 53
  myths in 35, 44–45, 52, 101
  regarding Shinto and Buddhism 55–56
  story of miraculous floating log 91
Ninigi 48, 51–52, 131
Nirvana 15
noh 13

Oda Nobunaga
  and Mt. Hiei 110, 113–114, 152
  encouragement of Christianity 114, 115
Okinawa 164
  and kami 9

Kina Shōkichi 195n
onari-ukeri system 36
Ōkuninushi 10, 25, 50–52, 129, 133
Ōkunitama 10
Ōmi 31
Ōmononushi 10
Ōnin War 97, 105
onmyōji (yin-yang master) 79, 81, 89, 90, 121
Onmyōryō 89–90
oral traditions 36, 37, 44–45
Orikuchi Shinobu 138–148, 172, 174–175, 192n
   on nature of kami 51, 123

Paekche 53, 88, 186n
"Parable of the Magic City" 1
performing arts 13, 141
   ritual and 47–48
   marebito (outsider/visitor) 174–175
possession 135
   divine 48
   religious 39
   spirit 142, 145, 192n
   yorikitō (prayer performers) 127
precepts 41, 157
   and Zen 68
   Mahāyāna 67–68, 70
precepts platform 67, 70, 72
Pure Land 140, 147
   faith 98–100, 113
   movement 98
   of Sukhāvatī 15
   Shin Pure Land 110, 114, 125
Pure Land school 68

ritsuryō
   codes 25
   state 31, 131
   system 63, 86, 88, 131
ritualist 39, 42
   and *wazaogi* 47–48

magico-religious 79
Takakamo family 60

Saichō 67–73
Saigyō 12, 85, 184n
sakaki tree 11
sarugaku (performing art) 13–14
Sarutahiko ōkami 25, 48–49, 50
seinō dance 13–14
Seventeen Article Constitution (604) 57, 169
shaman 3, 39, 127, 185n
   and Gautama Buddha 39
   Kami no yome story 142
   Uzume 53
shamanism 27, 39
   and Buddhism 41, 42, 187n
   and Shinto 42, 55, 176
   Meiji ban 127
   Prince Shōtoku 56–57
   Tōshōgū network and 117
   Uzume's possession 47
shinbutsu bunri (Shinto-Buddhism separation) edicts 124–125, 131, 134, 149, 153, 170, 175–176, 180
Shinran 68, 99
Shinto 20
   apocryphal literary works 151
   as religion 35–37, 151
   commentaries 100, 101, 106
   Confucian-Shinto synthesis 88
   discourse on 135, 179
   for protection of the state 63–66
   Hirata Atsutane 120, 121
   in state policy 124, 126–129
   Kamakura period movements 97
   medieval Shinto 88, 101, 104
   Motoori Norinaga 120, 121
   new sects 123, 134
   Restoration Shinto 117, 121, 122, 135, 159
   secularized 116–117, 151

State Shinto 136, 153, 155
  thirteen sects 133, 152
  usages of word 16–17, 100, 108
Shinto mandala 43
Shinto priests 124, 126, 128, 129, 130
Shoku Nihongi 59, 64
Shōtoku, Prince 14, 29, 56–58, 65, 74, 111, 187n
  Shōtoku Taishi 110
  Seventeen Article Constitution 169
Shōtoku Tennō 64–65
shrines 27, 35, 93
  and land 96
  sacerdotal lineages 55, 102, 104, 105, 107, 127
  shrine merger policy 132–134
  Tōshōgū 116–117
  under *ritsuryō* system 101, 103
  weakening of 102
Shugendō 2, 5, 29, 43, 58, 61, 63, 186n
  and En no Gyōja 58
  Meiji ban 125, 127
  Ōmine 61
  Tokugawa codes for 115
  Zaō Gongen 63
shugenja (mountain ascetic) 81, 82, 121, 127
Soga clan 31, 53–54, 55, 58, 91
sōhei (monk warriors) 68, 110, 114
sokushin jōbutsu (attaining buddhahood in this body) 69, 77
sonnō joi (revere the emperor, expel the barbarian) 122
spirit pacification (*chinkon*) 84, 140, 147, 175
spirituality 177, 179–182
  Hirata Atsutane 123, 136, 159
  Motoori Norinaga 120
  of Japanese 135
  Suzuki Daisetsu 104, 177–179
  Yanagita Kunio 173

state protection (*chingo kokka*) 63, 77, 188n
Sun Goddess 111 (*see also* Amaterasu ōmikami)
Susanoo no mikoto 46–47, 50–51
  as *marebito* 141
Sutoku Tennō 83, 84, 85, 96, 101, 188n, 194n
Suzuki Daisetsu 99, 104, 136, 177–179, 189n–190n

Taika reforms 31, 55–56, 64, 66
Taira 82, 85, 95–96, 162, 164, 194n
Takamanohara 22, 24, 44
Tale of Genji 79, 119, 120, 121
tamafuri (spirit reinvigoration) 48, 174, 192n
tantric tradition 68, 73, 94
Tendai Buddhism 32, 35, 67–69, 82, 84, 99–100
  Enryakuji complex 78, 94
  Kantō region 115
Tendai Sannō Ichijitsu Shinto 116–117
Tenji Tennō 31
Tenmu Tennō 31, 89, 146–147
tennō (sovereign) 44, 52, 57, 63, 64, 65
  discourse on 135, 193n
  family disputes 95
  in Seventeen Article Code 57
  Motoori Norinaga treatise 159
  restoration of 122, 134
  ritsuryō state 30–31, 150–151
  two-tiered system 86, 96–97, 99, 151
  word 89
theology
  Buddhist 34
  Hirata Atsutane 122
  Kunitokotachi 24
  political 22, 30, 44, 104, 116, 122
  Shinto 34, 103, 105
  Takamanohara 22

Yanagita Kunio 173, 175
Tōdaiji Temple 64, 72, 78, 188n
Tokugawa Ieyasu 113–116
  as cultural deity 26, 191n
tonseisō (reclusive priests) 98, 189n
Tōshōgū network 116–117
Toyotomi Hideyoshi 110, 113, 114
  and Christiantiy 115
  and Mt. Hiei 152
  Yoshida Shinto 116
Toyouke no ōkami 102–104, 160
Tsukiyomi 27, 46

unifying figure (*issha*) 149–150
Uzume (*see* Ame no Uzume no mikoto)

veneration
  of ancestors 87, 141, 172–173
  of Buddha relics 55
  of kami 124, 175
vengeful spirits 81, 83–86

Waterai sacerdotal lineage 102–105
wazaogi (act of invitation) 15, 47–48
Wei zhi Chronicles of Wei) 36

Yamata no orochi 50, 51
Yamato 19, 22, 31, 63
  court 25, 44, 88
Yamatogokoro (Japanese spirit) 22, 119
Yamato Takeru no mikoto 21, 26, 50
Yanagita Kunio 123, 130, 135–137, 139, 141, 171–174, 175
  and Minakata Kumagusu 132
  influence of Hirata Atsutane 135
yaoyorozu (countless deities) 9, 27, 179
Yasukuni Shrine 126, 128, 157
yatagarasu (legendary crow ancestor) 60–61
Yayoi period 30
yōkai (monsters) 120, 135
Yōmei *tennō* 16, 55–56, 93
Yomi (Otherworld) 46
yonaoshi (world-renewal) 134, 176, 193n
Yoshida Kanetomo 100, 101, 105–112, 177–178
Yoshida Shinto (Urabe Shinto, Yuitsu Shinto) 101, 105–112

Zaō Gongen 61–63
zazen (meditation) 100
Zen 68, 105
  Dōgen 97, 99, 113, 177
  priests 88
  Yōsai 99
  zazen 100

About the Author

Born in Tokushima prefecture in 1951. After graduating from Kokugakuin University, majoring in philosophy, Kamata pursued doctoral research in Shinto theology at the same university. He is currently professor emeritus, Kyoto University, and guest professor at the Sophia University Institute of Grief Care. His research interests range widely over religion, folklore studies, Japanese intellectual history, comparative civilizations, and other fields. He holds a doctoral degree in literature. He is qualified to hold Shinto rituals and is a Shinto songwriter. He performs on the stone flute (*iwabue*), horizontal flute, and conch shell (*horagai*). A devotee of pilgrimages to holy sites since the age of seventeen, he has visited many sacred sites in Japan and abroad over the last forty years. Among his published works are *Shinkai no fīrudowāku* [Fieldwork in the World of the Gods], *Okina-warabe ron* [Thoughts on Age and Youth], 4 volumes; *Shūkyō to reisei* [Religion and Spirituality], *Reiteki ningen* [Spiritual Humans], and *Seichi kankaku* [The Sense of Holy Ground].

(英文版) 神と仏の出逢う国
Myth and Deity in Japan: The Interplay of Kami and Buddhas

2019年1月27日 第1刷発行

著　者　鎌田 東二
訳　者　ゲイノー・セキモリ
発行所　一般財団法人出版文化産業振興財団
　　　　〒101-0051 東京都千代田区神田神保町3-12-3
　　　　　　　電話 03-5211-7282(代)
　　　　　　　ホームページ http://www.jpic.or.jp/

印刷・製本所　株式会社ウイル・コーポレーション

定価はカバーに表示してあります。
本書の無断複写 (コピー)、転載は著作権法の例外を除き、禁じられています。

© 2009 by Tōji Kamata
Printed in Japan
ISBN 978-4-86658-052-4